TRADITIONAL
Arabic
COOKING

TRADITIONAL
Arabic
COOKING

Miriam Al Hashimi

PHOTOGRAPHS BY GLORIA DARINA KIFAYEH

GARNET PUBLISHING

DEDICATION

One thousand and one thanks to the family and friends whose assistance made this book possible. My family inspired and helped with the research, testing and tasting of each and every recipe - except for the camel dish. My friends aided with the gathering of recipes, compiling the manuscript and editing. Also many thanks to those who lent a helping hand with the photography and props. In writing a book such as this, one learns to appreciate the meaning of true friendship.

© 1993 Miriam Jo'el Givens Al Hashimi
© original photographs Miriam Jo'el Givens Al Hashimi and Gloria Darina Kifayeh

Published by Garnet Publishing Limited
8 Southern Court, South Street, Reading RG1 4QS, UK

Food preparation for photography: Leo Kennedy Martins
Project management and editing: Jackie Jones
Design: Christine Wood
Diagrams: Rob Shone
Index: Hilary Bird
Reprographics: MacImage
Printed in Lebanon

The Islamic motif is reproduced from Eva Wilson's *Islamic Design* (British Museum Publications), by kind permission of the author.

Photograph on pages 39 and 127 Michelle Garrett/INSIGHT. Pages 105 and 109 by Christine Osborne

ISBN 1 873938 03 9

A catalogue record for this book is available from the British Library

CONTENTS

INTRODUCTION

Along the Caravan Trail

Arabian cooking reflects a lifestyle that crept from the East towards the West, by slow-moving camel caravans and by *dhows*, the vessels that used to criss-cross the Arabian Gulf and the Indian Ocean. Looking at the historic trade along the Frankincense Trail, the Spice Routes and the Silk Road, one reaches the conclusion that the customs, culture, climatic and geographical differences along those routes have all played a key role in the development of Arabic cooking.

The recipes within this book incorporate some of the culinary influences of the ancient trading routes in the countries which now make up the Arab World: the Levant areas of Lebanon, Syria, Jordan and Palestine; the Gulf states of Saudi Arabia, Oman, Bahrain, Qatar, Kuwait and the United Arab Emirates; the North African 'Maghreb' countries of Libya, Algeria, Tunisia and Morocco; and others, including Egypt, Yemen and Iraq.

Food and eating habits differ from region to region, depending partly on the availability of ingredients. For example, locust fruit were once abundant in the Arabian Peninsula, whereas today they are rarer and considered a delicacy.

Regional differences aside, all nations of the

Arab World are united by one distinctive bond, Islam. This influences many practices, from the butchering of animals by the *halal* method, when the name of God is spoken in reverence before the animal's throat is slashed, to the everyday event of making homemade yoghurt.

The prescribed five-times-a-day prayers are often followed by meals. During *Ramadan*, the holy month of fasting from dawn until dusk, elaborate meals are prepared for consumption after prayers at sundown. However, more traditionally, the fast is broken with dates, yoghurt and juice before prayers, followed by the extravagant meal of the day and plenty of sweets afterwards.

During E*id Al Fitr*, the holiday which marks the passing of the month-long fast of *Ramadan*, the celebration begins with prayer. Specially designed outdoor prayer grounds are filled to capacity at the break of dawn on the first day of E*id*. Often families visit the graves of departed loved ones before returning home to greet visitors with a variety of sweets, coffee and tea. Children are given monetary gifts called *eidiya* as a reward for good behaviour throughout the year.

E*id Al Adha* is a holiday commemorating the end of the pilgrimage, *Haj*, to Mecca, a trip every

Muslim should take at least once in his lifetime. The event is marked by the roasting of lambs, a portion of which is donated to the poor and sick.

Even at deaths strict, yet simple, customs are followed. Before burial, the body is washed and anointed with a strongly-scented oil, *zait al kafour*, and wrapped in a shroud. Once the burial has taken place, the family receives condolences in their home, offering guests strong black, unsweetened coffee and tea. During the official mourning period for dignitaries (when regular television and radio transmission is replaced by Koran reading and no special events are held) the mood of the country is solemn. One week after the death, and again 40 days after the burial, the Koran is read in the home, followed by feeding of guests in massive proportions.

Feasts, which sometimes contain hundreds of dishes, are prepared to mark new beginnings as well as sad endings. Whole roast lambs, mounds of colourful rice, stacks of sweets, jugs of water, and fragrant coffee and tea are the markers of almost any important Arab event: religious days, births, weddings and circumcisions.

Some remnants of the ancient agrarian society have survived in the Arab world. Food gathering is still a family affair even in modern society. Men undertake the primary responsibility for shopping in the *souk*, open market places, while the women prepare the food. At large gatherings, men and women are usually seated separately in the *majlis* (gathering place) and the elders are respectfully served by the younger family members.

Perhaps traditionally because of the high noon heat in the desert countries, Arabs prefer to have their main meal mid-afternoon, followed by a nap before returning to work in the cooler evening hours. Even the shops shut for the afternoon siesta. Breakfast usually consists of cheese, bread, spicy *zaatar* and a cup of strong tea, except on Fridays (normally a day off work) when more complicated dishes are prepared. Dinner is often light and late, a simple snack before prayers and bedtime.

The very act of eating a traditional Arab meal imparts a vision of days gone by, a simple pleasure uncomplicated by knifes and forks.

Routinely, the entire face, behind the ears and the arms, at least up to the elbows, are washed before and after meals. Traditionally, with the diners seated on the floor, food is eaten with the right hand only and cutlery seldom used, except for the occasional large spoon for inexperienced eaters of rice. Large metal trays of rice and meat or fish form the centre-piece, with all the space in between filled by many small bowls and plates of salads, pickles, fresh herbs, yoghurt, vegetable dishes and piled-high Arabic bread.

After the meal is even more elaborate. Trays of assorted fruit, the colours of an artist's palette, are served, followed by tiny cups of sweet dark tea and dainty pastries along with espresso-type thick black coffee. Once all food has been consumed, the aroma of the room changes with the burning of fragrant incenses - frankincense or *bahour* - and the hands and clothing are sprinkled with rose water. Gentle tugs from the hose of an ornate water pipe are interspersed with conversation and story-telling.

Methods of food preparation vary from place to place, as do the cooking utensils themselves - most of which are hewn of metal, wood, or clay. Terracotta jugs keep precious water cool by the basic process of evaporation. Moulds and spoons were, and still are, carved from hardwood. Today, the tools of cooking are designed for special chores: a slender, pencil-long *mawara* is used to scoop out the centres of squash to be stuffed, and the crescent-shaped, two-handled *makhrata* is ideal for fine chopping. Arab cooks labour over food preparation, some even spread newspaper or a grass-woven mat on the floor before sitting down to begin the long process involved in peeling, chopping, grinding and stuffing.

IN THE BEGINNING

The first known civilisations of Mesopotamia, the Indus Valley and the Nile transported timber, copper, ivory, textiles, cane and reed mats, shoe leather, bricks, quarried stone and asphalt, along with cattle and small livestock, hay, grain, flour, bread, dates, milk products, onions, herbs, fish and vegetable oil.

Mesopotamia - the seat of early civilisation

between the Tigris and Euphrates Rivers - was known for its grains, sesame seed oil and woollen goods. The first signs of civilisation in southern Arabia - grave mounds built just over 5,000 years ago - contained pottery from Mesopotamia, an area often referred to as Sumeria. The great Sumerian civilisation, close to the head of the Arabian Gulf, burgeoned in importance and its trading vessels plied the seas. Even as early as 3,000 BC, Mesopotamian merchants seem to have established trading outposts in towns along the Silk Route, where they collected the produce of local herders, miners and farmers and transported the goods down into Western Asia for trade among the great cities of Egypt and the Levant.

Egyptians from the Nile civilisation conducted expeditions to the land of Punt, probably the coast of Somalia today, to fetch frankincense, while the civilisation of the Indus Valley (also called Melluha) traded with the other civilisations.

Archaeologists continue to uncover evidence of trade between the first great civilisations, but that also the great river valleys - which surrounded the Arabian Peninsula - may have conducted trade with a fourth civilisation: Megan was probably located in the Arabian Peninsula near Sohar, which lies on the mouth of a once major river - an area which now encompasses Oman and the United Arab Emirates. Neolithic pottery from Mesopotamia dating back to 4,000 BC has also been found in Southern Arabia and lends some credence to the theory that yet a fifth civilisation, seldom discussed in history, existed in present-day Yemen.

The community would have been an important half-way trading post linking the river valley civilisations. Further discoveries suggest that copper mined from the hills of the area may have been transported down to the shores of the Gulf before being shipped via Dilmun (present day Bahrain) onwards. Ancient copper mines discovered in the rugged Hajar mountains indicate that the area mined copper as far back as the 3rd millenium BC, where perhaps some of the first hard metal cooking utensils were made. Copper would have been traded for spices, garden produce and exotic fruit from the Indus Valley and Mesopotamia.

THE SPICE ROUTES

Arabia was the spice emporium of the ancient world. Its trade was immense, lucrative and well organised. The Arabs were astute and competent in keeping a hold on the origins of the spice trade.

The first long voyages to the East were probably undertaken by the Arabs of Oman and the Persian Gulf Area, where sea-borne routes had undoubtedly been known from ancient times. Southern Arabian traders and sailors were certainly the founders of trade with the Eastern spice lands which later entailed risky voyages across the Indian Ocean. Sailing from the Persian Gulf, the Arabs pushed trade eastward along the coasts of what is now Iran and Baluchistan, to the mouth of the Indus, and then worked their way southward along the Indian coast until they reached the ports of Malabar.

From the East African region of Ethiopia, a mixed Arab and African people from an area then called Axum, came to supply the Mediterranean lands with all of the goods of the Spice Route. Alexandria, in modern Egypt, was still the main trading port that connected the Spice Route with Europe.

With the domestication of the Arabian camel around 1,800 BC, caravans began to cross the searing desert of Southern Arabia. Groups of travellers and merchants banded together for the sake of helping and defending one another while crossing unsettled and hostile country. The caravans - some known to reach massive proportions, forming trains of 2,000 camels and 500 men - would wind their way along the northerly Frankincense Trail toward the Red Sea.

Camels were used to transport goods, but also in battle and as currency, as well as for their wool, leather, milk and meat. Camel herdsmen of southern Arabia amassed fortunes by transporting goods that originated in India and Africa from southern ports such as Aden, to Egypt and the Mediterranean world of the North. Basically three caravan trails were used to ferry desirable goods northwards: one up the eastern coast, one along the western coast, and a third tracking from west to east through central Arabia. From southern Arabia to Aleppo and Antioch, the Incense Road finally linked with the Silk Road somewhere in the Fertile Crescent. The great caravan cities of Syria, including Damascus in particular, truly came into their own, receiving goods from the Silk Road as well as spices and perfumes from Arabia's Frankincense Road and other luxuries brought by sea on the Spice Routes from India.

The Silk Road lay between China in the East and Rome in the West - the overland route which for at least 4,000 years was the main avenue of communication between the Mediterranean and the Orient. East to west along the Road oranges, peaches and pears were routed and west to east grapes, alfalfa, cucumbers, figs, pomegranates, sesame, chives, coriander and safflower were routed along a major highway some 5,000 miles long. The first parcels of cassia and cinnamon may have made their way across Asia by slow-moving neighbour-to-neighbour trade routes offering the least resistance to travel. A possible route from China could have wound its way west between the mountain ranges through the valley of the Tarin River, and then southwards to the ancient port of Hormozia on the Persian Gulf or to Bassorah (Basra) at the head of the Arabian Gulf. Another route from China could have led similarly to Bukhara, continuing westward through the ancient provinces of Parthia and Media to the Tigris and Euphrates Rivers. A route from Northern India could have led from the Indus through ancient provinces to Persia.

But the ancient Spice Routes are certainly the greatest influence on Arabian cooking today: in Mesopotamia, the Sumerians built large barges and ships and used them to transport goods on the Tigris and Euphrates Rivers and across the Persian Gulf. Along these trading routes, spices from India were brought to the Middle East more than 3,500 years ago.

The western part of the Spice Route started with the Red Sea and the Persian Gulf, on both sides of the Arabian Peninsula. The eastern part of the Spice Route was China and the Spice Islands, and to the south was the east coast of Africa, spanning as far south as the island of Madagascar. All or the routes came together at the tip of the Sub-continent, between India and the island of Ceylon (Sri Lanka).

For years, the Arabians controlled the spice trade and acted as middlemen, receiving spices from the East and transporting them onward to the markets of Egypt and Mediterranean Europe. The Portuguese soon took over the routes and managed to avoid the Arabs of the Middle East by diverting their vessels around the Cape of Good Hope in Africa, sailing directly to European markets. However, even at the time of Columbus, from approximately the 8th to the 12th centuries, Arabic was considered to be the language of traders. It is interesting to note that when Columbus attempted to sail to India, he even took an Arabic-speaking interpreter with him in the belief that Arabic was 'the mother of all languages'.

Much later, in 1501, Vasco da Gama returned to Lisbon with costly supplies of pepper, ginger, cinnamon, nutmeg, mace and cloves. In 1522, Ferdinand Magellan picked up a precious cargo of spices, the sale of which more than paid for the entire cost of the expedition.

During the Middle Ages, spices were extremely expensive and were in great demand by those who could afford them. Peppercorns were used as currency to pay taxes, tools, rents and dowries.

THE FUTURE OF ARABIC COOKING

Remnants of the Spice Routes, Caravan Trails and Frankincense Road can still be found in the modern Arabian marketplace. Souks teem with stalls of colourful fruits and vegetables grown locally, as well as world-wide imports, once brought in by caravan or ocean-going dhow, but now in modern times brought in refrigerated containers by truck, sea or air. The aroma of a variety of spices still lingers in the market.

Modern-day cooking practices have in some cases the old traditional methods. The pounding of the pestle and mortar which could once be heard in every Arab household, has been exchanged in many instances for the more convenient whir of a food processor or an electric grinder.

Although times have changed, Arab cooks are still extremely protective of their food preparation customs and place great emphasis on passing along these traditions to their children - the future cooks of the Middle East. This book strives to chronicle the influences of ancient trading routes and promote traditional cooking in the Arab World.

Mezza

HORS D'OEUVRE

FEAST BEFORE THE MEAL

The very core of Arabian hospitality is exemplified by the *mezza*. Deeply-rooted in Arab culture is the belief that a host must always offer his invited or even unexpected guest his best, whether great or meagre. The presentation of *mezza* is varied ranging from the simply sufficient to the bountifully arabesque hors d'oeuvre - before-the-meal feast.

Anything from four to forty dishes can be served in the *mezza*: hot and cold, spanning the array of countless colours, tastes, textures and aromas. *Mezza*, which is commonly eaten with the fingers, should be prepared in small, bite-sized portions. The various dips are scooped up in torn-off pieces of Arabic bread, and some of the salads with lettuce leaves.

Preparation of this diverse display of tasty samples and then pleasing each guest with an abundant flow of food and drink can keep even the most diligent hostess on her toes. So here, while preserving the Arab tradition of the *mezza*, I have offered some hints on saving time by using the food processor and freezer. Mixing up dishes quickly, preparing food in advance and preserving food such as dips and savoury pastries, can make it easier to present 'one's best' to a guest.

The mezza

AUBERGINE DIP

Baba ghannouj, or Mutabbal

The term baba ghannouj, which literally translated means 'my father is spoiled like a child by my mother,' would never be uttered at a Lebanese family gathering. The father would be insulted and the mother and children shamed.

The more honourable name badenjan mutabbal (aubergine dip) is a tahina sauce mixed with garlic and lemon juice. Breaking the norm of how aubergine is usually prepared, this smoke-flavoured dip is an amalgamation of Arabic cooking - extraordinarily tasty!

The key to the recipe lies in the searing of the aubergine. The skins can be blackened over a gas flame or roasted in the oven. Prepare an imaginative starter for a barbecue by adding a couple to the flaming grill. The charred outside skins are discarded and the smooth inner pulp is puréed with strong garlic and mild tahina. If the smoke-flavour is too harsh, add a heaped tablespoonful of yoghurt to the dip to produce a milder version.

Roasting aubergine for badenjan mutabbal

2 large aubergines/eggplant
4 tbsp tahina
2-4 tbsp lemon juice
3 cloves garlic
1/2 tsp salt
1 tbsp yoghurt (opt)

GARNISH
1 black olive
1 tbsp parsley, chopped
1 tomato, finely chopped
1 tbsp olive oil
paprika

1 Cook the aubergine over charcoal, a gas flame or in a hot oven until the skins are crackling black and the flesh is soft. Leave to cool.

2 Peel off the skin of the aubergine, removing all the charred pieces. Mash the flesh with a wooden spoon or blend to a purée.

3 Crush the garlic with the salt and add to the aubergines. Beat to a smooth pulp. Alternately add the tahina and the lemon juice to the aubergines, mixing thoroughly between each addition.

4 Garnish with chopped tomatoes, parsley, paprika and a black olive in the centre. Serve the dip drizzled with olive oil. Scoop the mutabbal from the serving dish with pieces of Arabic bread.

VARIATION
● Another version of baba ghannouj is to slightly mash the aubergines with a little garlic, lemon juice and salt and pepper. Then stir in a finely chopped tomato and onion. This version has no tahina.

Hummos bil tahina

CHICKPEA DIP

Hummos bil tahina

Chickpeas, indigenous to the Levant, were once used to feed the Arab armies in their conquests of North Africa and Spain.

Hummos is the Arab world's answer to healthy fast food. Restaurants and cafés regularly offer free of charge a small dish of this nutty-flavoured dip with many meals, especially roasted chicken. Small pieces of Arabic bread are torn off and plunged into the creamy puréed chickpeas topped with a swirl of olive oil.

To prepare hummos bil tahina at home, freshly boiled chickpeas are recommended for a fuller flavoured dish; however, the canned variety may be used.

An essential ingredient in the dip is tahina, a thin paste made of ground sesame seeds, which is available in most speciality shops and good supermarkets.

8 oz (225g) dried chickpeas
5 tbsp *tahina*
2 cloves garlic, crushed
3 tbsp lemon juice
I tsp salt
GARNISH
olive oil
I black olive
paprika

1   Soak the chickpeas overnight and drain.

2   Cover with cold water and simmer until the chickpeas are tender, removing the surface scum when necessary. (A pressure cooker will reduce the cooking time to 40 minutes.)

3   Drain the chickpeas, reserving a cup of the liquid and a few chickpeas for garnishing.

4   Remove the skins of the remaining chickpeas by rubbing or pressing with a rolling pin.

5   Purée the chickpeas and the garlic. Allow to cool. Alternately, add the *tahina* and lemon juice. The purée should have a creamy consistency. If too thick, add a little of the reserved liquid. Add salt and adjust seasoning to taste.

6   Serve in individual bowls or a large flat serving dish. Smooth the dip with the back of a spoon, leaving a very slight hollow in the centre. To garnish, drizzle with a little olive oil. Add a few whole cooked chickpeas, a sprinkling of paprika and a black olive in the centre

VARIATION

● *Hummos bil laham* can be made by garnishing the dish with small pieces of meat or minced meat nuts, and a little lemon juice.

FENUGREEK DIP

Hilbeh

Fenugreek - seeds from the pods of a flowering plant - combined with hot chillies are the essence of hilbeh. Native to the southern Arabian Gulf, the spicy dip often has a bitter taste which can be lessened by soaking the seeds before use. This dip can also be used as a relish with the main meal. The Yemeni version is a fiery paste which is spread on bread prior to baking.

Hilbeh

2 tbsp fenugreek seeds
2 tbsp fresh coriander, chopped
3-4 tomatoes, quartered
4-8 cloves garlic, crushed
1 large onion, chopped
2-3 chilli peppers, chopped
3 tbsp lemon juice
1 tsp *baharat*
salt and pepper
oil for sautéing

1   Soak the fenugreek seeds for about 12 hours, allowing the seeds to swell and soften, and attain a jelly-like coating.

2   Sauté the onions and the garlic. Strain the fenugreek seeds and fry for about 3 minutes. Stir in the *baharat* and coriander, and cook for a further 3 minutes. Leave to cool.

3   Blend to a thick purée, adding the tomatoes, chillies and lemon juice.

LENTIL AND RICE DIP

Majroush

An unlikely combination, rice and lentils, becomes a savoury dip garnished with crispy fried onions. Yellow or brown tender lentils are occasionally puréed with the rice after cooking, sometimes mashed before being added to the rice, but more frequently simply cooked until very tender before adding to the rice.

2 cups lentils
1/2 cup short-grain rice
4 large onions, chopped
1/4 tsp cumin, ground
1/2 tsp butter or *samn*
oil for shallow frying and sautéing
1 tsp salt

Majroush

YOGHURT DIP

Labnah

1pt (575ml) yoghurt
2 tbsp dried mint, or fresh dill
1 clove garlic, crushed
lemon juice

1   Mix all ingredients together, adjusting the lemon juice to taste.

2   Serve as a dip for vegetable strips or to accompany *foul medames* (see p. 131).

Labnah

1   Wash and cook the lentils until very tender. Add the cumin and salt and cook for a further 5 minutes. Strain the lentils, reserving $1/2$ cup of the cooking liquid.

2   Sauté two of the onions until lightly browned.

3   In a large pot, layer the sautéed onions, lentils, the washed rice and the butter. Add $1/2$ cup of the cooking water. Stir and simmer covered on a medium heat for 15-20 minutes or until the rice is tender, adding water as required.

4   Stir-fry the remaining onions in very hot oil until well browned and crispy.

5   Garnish with the crispy onions. Serve the rice and lentil dip to be scooped up with torn-off pieces of Arabic bread.

STUFFED VINE LEAVES

Waraq ainab

Two bites and these neatly packed and rolled parcels are devoured. Vine leaves can be served hot with a meat filling as a main dish or cold with a rice and herb stuffing as a snack for parties. The secret to preparing vine leaves is in the rolling up. Most Arab cooks describe the shape and size as, 'thin as a pencil and as long as the little finger'.

Young fresh leaves are bright green and the tastiest, though vine leaves packed in brine are frequently used and work very well. A little extra lemon can be squeezed over the vines for anyone who prefers a more tart flavour.

WARM VERSION

8 oz (225g) vine leaves

8 oz (225g) minced meat

1/2 cup short-grain rice

1 onion, finely chopped (opt)

3 tbsp parsley, finely chopped

2 tbsp lemon juice

1-2 cloves garlic, crushed

2 tbsp olive oil

oil for sautéing

salt and pepper

5 lamb chops, or

4 tomatoes, sliced (opt)

COLD VERSION

8 oz (225g) vine leaves

1 cup short-grain rice

1 onion, finely chopped (opt)

2 tbsp parsley, chopped

2 tbsp mint, chopped

5 tbsp olive oil

2 tbsp lemon juice

1/4 tsp cinnamon, ground (opt)

1/4 tsp allspice, ground (opt)

1-2 cloves garlic, crushed

salt and pepper

2 onions, sliced or

2 potatoes, sliced (opt)

1 Clean and cut stems off the vine leaves. Blanch fresh leaves until softened and pliable, or rinse the leaves packed in brine in warm water.

2 To make the filling, wash the rice, soak for 20 minutes and finally drain. For the warm version, sauté the onions and meat. Add the rice, parsley and salt and pepper. For the cold version, mix the rice, onion, parsley, mint, 3 tbsp olive oil, spices and salt and pepper.

3 Place one vine leaf on a plate, vein side up (see pics *i* and *ii*, facing page). If the leaves are too large for making small parcels, cut in half.

4 Place a scant teaspoon of the filling mixture onto the leaf near the stalk end (*iii*). Fold the stem end over the filling, tuck in both sides and roll tightly (*iv*). Lightly squeeze each parcel to make it firm (*v*).

5 To prevent the stuffed leaves from sticking to the pan, layer the bottom of a large saucepan with the potato and onion slices for the cold version. For the warm version layer with the lamb chops and/or tomato slices. Pack the stuffed vine leaves in tight layers, changing the direction of each layer.

6 Mix the lemon juice, 2 tbsp olive oil, garlic and salt and pepper. Add with enough water to half cover the vine leaves.

7 Place a inverted plate over the leaves to prevent movement. Cover with a tight-fitting lid.

8 Simmer gently over low heat for 30 minutes or until the rice is tender.

9 Garnish with lemon and sprigs of mint or parsley. The cold version is served as an appetizer. The warm version, which includes meat, can be served as an appetizer or as a main course.

VARIATIONS

● One peeled and chopped tomato may be added to the meat filling.

● For the Lebanese version, add 4 cloves of

crushed garlic and ¹/₄ teaspoon cinnamon to the meat filling.

● Rice may be replaced with *farika*, unripened *burgul*.

i

iv

ii

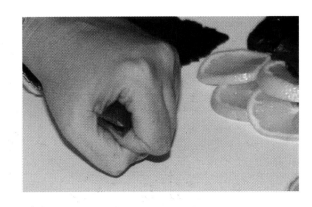

v

iii

vi

FRIED BEAN CROQUETTES

Falafel

Walking hungrily along the street in Arab countries, you turn the corner to almost certainly find a street-side stall with tasty, dark brown, crispy falafel. Your attention is immediately drawn to hands manipulating at lightning speed a shiny brass tool that identically shapes each mound of puréed beans. The mixture is spooned into the top of the tool, smoothed over, and then pushed out to deep-fry in a big black wok called a hala or saj. Buy some to appease the appetite, as the snack is only a few pence for a full bag. Before carrying them far you will be tempted to sneak a taste of these irresistibly warm and crumbly croquettes.

The more patient (and less hungry) may wait for a rolled sandwich of Arabic bread, stuffed with broken falafel, tahina, mint, parsley, lettuce, and sometimes tomatoes.

Egyptian tamia is similar in shape to falafel, but is made from different ingredients including ground bread.

8 oz (225g) dried chickpeas
8 oz (225g) fresh or dried broad beans
4 cloves garlic, crushed
4 onions, finely chopped or
6 tbsp spring onions, finely chopped
4 tbsp parsley, chopped
2 tbsp fresh coriander, chopped
1-2 tsp coriander, ground
1 tsp cumin, ground
2-3 tbsp flour or $\frac{1}{2}$ tsp baking powder, if required
salt and pepper
oil for deep-frying

1 Soak the dried chickpeas and broad beans overnight, then drain and wash. Wash the fresh or frozen green broad beans. Grind the chickpeas and beans to a paste. Add all the remaining ingredients except the oil.

2 Mix thoroughly and let stand for 30 minutes. If the paste does not hold together add 2-3 tbsp flour or ¹/₂ tsp baking powder.

3 Form into small flat balls and deep fry until brown and the crust is crisp. Drain on absorbent paper.

VARIATION

● 1 lb (500g) chickpeas or broad beans can be used rather than the combination of the two.

Frying the *falafel*

MIXED NUTS

Makhlouta

Nuts are a social part of Arabian life, when at almost every gathering conversation is punctuated by the gentle picking of nuts and seeds. The cashew, one favourite, has a long history: taken from Brazil by the Portuguese, the nuts probably came to Arabia on their way to Goa in India where they were planted in the 16th century.

A typical Arabian roaster is filled with bins of warm nuts, the mouth-watering aroma often wafting out of the door and into the streets, luring in customers for a bag of makhlouta. Almonds, walnuts, pistachios, hazelnuts, cashews and seeds of watermelon, sunflower or pumpkin are salted, roasted and served in bowls.

BEAN SNACK

Leblabi, or Balila

In many Middle Eastern cities, the cry of the bean seller can still be heard. Huge pots, containing one of several varieties of simply boiled beans, are perched on wagons toiling through the streets. Buyers rush with their dishes to purchase a bowl or two to be eaten plain or further spiced up as a dinner dish.

Dried chickpeas or broad beans are boiled until tender before spices are added. Then the pulses are drained and eaten as a snack, as one would serve nuts in a bowl. For further details on preparing bean snacks see Foul nabet *or* bagella, *on p.132.*

For snacking, large beans are best given a very full soaking in the refrigerator so they look thoroughly plump, not wrinkled, before being cooked.

FRIED SARDINES

Sardine makli

The Mediterranean has been fished for delicate, transparent sardines since ancient times. Sardines, sprats and wee anchovies, deep-fried whole in a batter, become an Arabian speciality when plunged into tahina. *These crispy snacks are eaten whole including the bones and tails, and sometimes even the heads.*

2 lb (1 kg) fish, cleaned
2 tbsp lemon juice
3 cloves garlic, crushed
2 onions, finely chopped
salt and pepper
oil for deep-frying
tahina sauce (p. 46)

1   Clean the sardines and rub with the lemon juice, garlic and salt. Add the chopped onion and allow to stand for 30 minutes.

2   To keep the fish crisp, only fry a few at one time.

3   Serve the *tahina* sauce as a dip.

Sardine makli

● A delicious but more Western version is sardines fried in a batter. Dip the sardines into an egg and milk mixture, then coat in flour (drop the sardines into a bag of seasoned flour and shake gently).

LAMBS' TONGUES

Lisanat mutabbleh

5 lambs' or 2 calves' tongues
4 cloves garlic, crushed
2 tbsp lemon juice
4 tbsp olive oil
2 tsp salt

GARNISH
2 tbsp parsley, finely chopped

1   Wash the tongue and simmer in water, salt and 1 clove garlic for 1-2 hours or until tender. Leave to cool.

2   Drain the tongue, remove the skin and gristle. Then cube or slice the meat.

3   Mix with lemon juice, oil, remaining garlic and salt to taste. Allow to stand for 1 hour.

4   Serve garnished with finely chopped parsley.

VARIATION
● The prepared tongue can be added to a lettuce and tomato salad.

BRAINS

Nukhaat, or Mokh

To many, the thought of eating brains is unappetizing. However, if all preconceived notions are ignored, the adventurous will find that mokh has a uniquely delicate and savoury flavour.
   Always use fresh brains, which are pale pink and have a clear transparent membrane.

4 lambs' or 2 calves' brains
1 onion or 3 spring onions, chopped
4 lemon slices
2 tbsp lemon juice
5 tbsp olive oil
salt and pepper

GARNISH
2 tbsp parsley, finely chopped
lettuce
lemon wedges

1   Remove the surrounding thin membrane and any large veins from the brains. Rinse well.

2   Simmer in enough water to cover, with the lemon slices and salt, for 10-15 minutes or until tender.

3   Drain the brains until dry. Then slice the brains when cooled, as the fine texture crumbles easily when warm.

4   To prepare the dressing, mix the onions, lemon juice and oil. Season to taste.

5   Serve on a bed of lettuce with wedges of lemon. Sprinkle the dressing over the brains and garnish with chopped parsley.

VARIATIONS
● After the brains are boiled, they can be baked for 10-15 minutes with a mixture slices of boiled potato, chopped onions, tomatoes and topped with butter.

● The prepared brains can also be sliced and used as a sandwich filling.

PASTRAMI

Bastirma

One of the oldest methods of preserving meats is by drying. The most primitive method of drying is to hang out strips in the sun to harden. Salt and pepper offer preservative qualities.

Arabic pastrami is rarely prepared at home because of the long drying time involved. However, if unavailable in the market, pastrami can be home-made with little effort. Sometimes the spicy, dried meat is used as an ingredient in pastries, but most typically, fried in paper-thin slices, is served for breakfast with eggs. When frying, make sure to put bastirma *into cold oil, and cook only enough to heat through, as over-cooking produces a bitter taste.*

Commercially produced bastirma *has a dark brown outer rind and is deep red when sliced. The shape varies on the cut of meat and the mould used.*

2 lb (1 kg) lean fillet or premium cut of beef
6 oz (175g) salt
6 oz (175g) fenugreek seeds, ground
2 tbsp chilli pepper, ground
6-7 heads garlic, crushed

1   Trim the meat, removing all the fat. Dry well, then score lightly in 3-4 places. Roll the meat in 4 tbsp salt or enough to coat.

2   Place the slab of salted meat on a wire rack. To help drain the moisture put a heavy weight on the meat. After 3 days, remove the weight from the meat. Thread and knot a string through one end of the meat for hanging. (It may be wrapped loosely in muslin.)

3   Purée the garlic, fenugreek seeds, pepper and remaining 4oz (100g) salt. Completely coat the meat and hang for 3-4 days, allowing to dry sufficiently.

4   Slice paper-thin pieces, as required, and remove the rind.

5   Place the slices in cold oil and fry lightly for several minutes.

6   Serve with fried eggs, for breakfast.

LAMB SAUSAGE

Mumbar, Krush, or Farareg

The Phoenicians, the great sea traders of the Mediterranean, probably introduced the concept of spicy sun-dried sausage. Sailors preserved meats which could be used a little at a time.

Today it is more practical to make a large quantity of sausage to be frozen for later use. Casings of fresh lamb intestine can be used, however these require an intense cleansing process. Some butchers supply artificial casings.

A common sausage in the Arab world is the purplish-reddish type with only minced meat and spices. As with all types of sausage, this version with rice can be served as an appetizer in the mezza, *a main course for breakfast or added to other dishes such as beans.*

FILLING
1 1/2 lb (675g) lamb, coarsely minced
6-8 cloves garlic, crushed
1 onion, chopped
1 tsp *baharat*
6 tbsp olive oil
2 tbsp parsley, chopped

Mumbar

1 cup short-grain rice
salt and pepper

FINISH
2 tsp salt
6 ft (2m) thick sausage casing
1 *loomi* (opt)
1 tsp pepper

1　Mix all the filling ingredients together.

2　To fill the sausage, use a large funnel, a piping bag with a large nozzle, or a mincer adaptable for sausage. Feed the dampened sausage casing completely over the end of the nozzle. Tie a knot in the end of the casing. Push the sausage filling into the casing, twisting the sausage into small lengths. Fill as evenly as possible, running hands along the sausage to distribute the filling evenly. Knot the other end.

3　Cover the sausage with water. Add the *loomi*, pierced or slightly crushed, and the pepper. Invert a heavy plate over the sausage to keep it in place. Cover and simmer on a low heat, for 1 hour or until the rice is tender. Adjust water as required.

4　Serve whole lengths or cut into slices.

SAUTÉED LIVER

Kibdah makliya

Sheep, goat, lamb and chicken liver are served in the mezza, but surprisingly enough are more popular as a breakfast food. Strips or cubes (and in the case of chicken whole) livers, are mixed with spices and fried. In Morocco, paprika, cumin and coriander are added to the frying oil. In Qatar, an abundance of garlic is added to yield kibdah bil toum, *and in Egypt a variation is prepared with goose liver. Libyans roll liver in partially crushed cumin seeds. In the Levant, freshly chopped tomatoes are added to the frying pan. Above all, the spice of this dish varies from mere salt and pepper to fiery hot in Tunisia and Yemen. The Iraqi recipe listed is more mildly spiced.*

Kibdah makliya

8 oz (225g) liver
2 cloves garlic, crushed
1 tsp *baharat*
9 tbsp plain flour
salt and pepper
oil for shallow-frying

GARNISH
2 tbsp fresh coriander, chopped
lemon wedges
1 onion, sliced

1　Wash the liver and remove any large veins. Cut into small strips and mix with the garlic.

2　Mix the flour, *baharat* and salt and pepper. Coat the liver.

3　Stir-fry a few pieces in hot oil until evenly browned. Over-cooking the liver will make it tough.

4　Serve hot with lemon wedges and garnish with slices of onion and the coriander.

VARIATION

● Many Arab cooks omit the flour when they prepare this dish.

Jibnah makliya

STUFFED MEAT

Kibbah, or Koubba

The art of shaping and sometimes stuffing spicy minced meat, kibbah, has been long been practised in the Levant countries of Syria, Jordan, Lebanon and Palestine, while Iraqi versions are called koubba.

The meticulous motion of shaping and filling the meat is like the action of a potter delicately moulding clay. Some women seem to have 'kibbah fingers' in the way that some gardeners have 'green fingers' and are often called upon to prepare the delicacies for weddings and other special occasions.

Patience and stamina are the main qualifications for making the long, American football-shaped, stuffed balls. In just a couple of bites the meatball is gone, not nearly long enough to gain an appreciation for the craft of making kibbah. With the advent of the food processor, the process of grinding, mincing and mixing is minimized and the ordeal of balling and stuffing seems less strenuous. But encasing the spiced meat in a shell of burgul or of rice and meat minced to a paste still takes considerable practice.

In the Arab world, lamb is used, but beef can be substituted. Ideally, the pink flesh of yearling mutton should be used to make kibbah.

FRIED CHEESE WITH OLIVES

Jibnah makliya

The best cheeses for frying are the firm blocks of white cheese similar to the Greek fetta: salted nabulsia, *soaked overnight, or unsalted* haloum.

8 oz (225g) firm white cheese
olive oil for frying
black olives

1　Cut the cheese into ¹/₂ in (1.3 cm) cubes.

2　Heat the olive oil and add the cheese. Gently fry until crispy brown.

3　Serve immediately, garnished with black olives and accompanied by Arabic bread.

RAW KIBBAH

Kibbah niyah

Oddly enough this spicy raw meat dish is appetizing and delicious. Kibbah niyah, prepared with very fresh, lean, choice cuts of meat tastes anything but raw. Fresh lamb shoulder will provide the softest meat for mincing.

The dish should be prepared and served immediately to preserve the freshness of the meat. We were shown the 'old way' of mincing the meat by finely crushing it on a stone or slab of marble, and removing the veins and fat.

1 lb (500g) lean lamb, finely minced
2 large onions, quartered
4 oz (100g) *burgul*
salt and pepper

GARNISH
3 tbsp parsley, chopped
1 tbsp pine nuts
spring onions
olive oil

1   Soak the *burgul* in water for 30 minutes. Squeeze out the excess liquid and purée.

2   Mince the meat to a very fine paste and add the *burgul*.

3   Blend the onions until liquidised. Add the meat paste and salt and pepper. Purée the mixture until smooth, adding an ice cube or two to achieve the desired texture.

4   Spread the raw *kibbah* on a flat serving dish. Top with parsley, roasted or parched pine nuts and drizzle with olive oil. Serve immediately, accompanied with stalks of spring onions. Arabic bread can be used as a scoop.

VARIATIONS
●   Proportions of meat and *burgul* can be varied.

●   Adjust the seasonings by adding a pinch of cumin, allspice, and cayenne pepper.

KIBBAH IN A PAN

Kibbah bil saniyah

Simply three layers of spicy meat, this dish is the least complicated of all the cooked kibbah *dishes to prepare. The outside, paste-like layer uses virtually the same ingredients as the raw version, while the inside is stuffed with a coarsely ground, nutty meat filling. For a crusty bottom and a kibbah that stays intact, use a thin metal baking pan when layering, baking and later serving.*

1 lb (500g) lean lamb, finely minced
4 oz (100g) *burgul*
2 large onions, chopped
FILLING
8 oz (225g) minced lamb
2 onions, finely chopped
1/2 tsp cinnamon, ground
1/2 tsp allspice, ground
4 tbsp pine nuts
oil for sautéing
salt and pepper

1   Soak the *burgul* for 30 minutes. Squeeze out the excess moisture and purée. Blend the onions until liquidised. Blend the finely minced meat, *burgul*, onions and salt and pepper. Add a spoonful of iced water or an ice cube to make a smooth paste.

2   To make the filling, sauté the onions, and add the meat and pine nuts. Partially cook the meat, but do not brown. Add a tablespoon of water or enough to soften the meat. Add the cinnamon, allspice and salt and pepper, and sauté for a further 2 minutes.

3   Smooth half the *kibbah* mixture onto an oiled baking pan. Layer with the filling. Flatten the remaining half of the *kibbah* mixture. Transfer to the pan to form the top layer.

4   Slightly cut the surface with diagonal lines crisscrossing in opposite directions. Place a pine nut in the centre of each square.

5   Bake at 300°F (150°C) gas 3 for 1 hour or until brown and crisp.

6   Serve hot or cold with yoghurt.

STUFFED MEAT BALLS

Kibbah makliya

At first glance, these small American football-shaped meat balls seem quite ordinary, but a bite reveals a hidden prize, a crumbly meat and nut stuffing.

The key to making this kibbah is to keep the thin outer shell consistently even and each ball the same size. The deep-fried crust and succulent filling have the same ingredients as kibbah bil saniyah, but are shaped differently.

1 lb (500g) lean lamb, finely minced
8 oz (225g) *burgul*
1 large onion, chopped
oil for deep-frying

FILLING
8 oz (225g) minced lamb
1 onion, finely chopped
4 tbsp parsley, chopped (opt)
$^1/_2$ tsp cinnamon, ground
$^1/_2$ tsp allspice, ground
4 tbsp pine nuts
salt and pepper

1   Soak the *burgul* for 30 minutes. Squeeze out the excess moisture and purée. Blend the onions until liquidised. Blend the finely minced meat, *burgul*, onions and salt and pepper. Refrigerate until chilled.

2   To make the filling, sauté the onions and garlic. Add the meat and pine nuts. Partially cook the meat, but do not brown. Add a tablespoon of water or enough to soften the meat. Add the cinnamon, allspice, parsley and salt and pepper to sauté for a further 2 minutes.

3   With damp hands divide the chilled *kibbah* mixture into twelve equal balls, smoothing each with a little water.

4   To hollow the inside, put a thumb into the centre of the ball. Pinch the sides while rolling the ball around the hand. This potter's action is continued until an 'oh so thin' round shell is formed.

5   Put 1 tbsp of the filling into each hollowed ball. Pinch closed with wet fingers and again, shape into a ball.

6   Deep-fry, for 6-8 minutes or until golden brown. Drain on absorbent paper.

VARIATIONS

● *Kibbah* can be prepared ahead of time and frozen before frying.

● An Iraqi version is a flat disc shape filled with finely chopped almonds and raisins instead of pine nuts. The crust of meat is mixed with *jaresh*, a cracked wheat finer than *burgul*.

POTATO AND MEAT PATTIES

Batata chap

Though potatoes are newcomers to the desert regions of Arabia, these cakes are eaten throughout the Eastern world. The potato belongs to the nightshade family and is a native of the Andes, and was an important staple for the Incas of South America before making its way to the Middle East.

The uniqueness of this Iraqi version lies in the addition of an Arabian spice blend called baharat. *Boiled and mashed, potatoes are used to encase a spicy meat filling. This recipe makes small patties which are great for the mezza. Larger patties are served with the main course.*

2 lb (1 kg) potatoes
1 egg, beaten
4 tbsp plain flour
flour for coating
oil for shallow-frying
salt and pepper

FILLING

8 oz (225g) minced lamb
1 onion, finely chopped
2 cloves garlic, crushed
1 tsp *baharat*
1 tbsp parsley, finely chopped
oil for sautéing
salt and pepper

GARNISH

parsley
lemon wedges

1   Peel, quarter and boil the potatoes. Drain and mash to a purée. Leave to cool. Blend the egg, 4 tbsp flour, and salt and pepper with the potatoes.

2   To make the filling, sauté the onions, garlic and meat, until crumbly and lightly browned. Add the *baharat*, parsley and salt and pepper to taste for a further 2 minutes.

3   With damp hands, flatten about a tablespoon of the cooled potato mixture. Put a teaspoon of the filling in the centre and close the potatoes around it. Roll into a ball.

4   Roll each ball in flour and flatten to make a patty.

5   Shallow fry, until golden brown on each side.

6   Drain on absorbent paper and serve garnished with parsley and lemon wedges.

Presenting the *kibbah*

Shorbat
SOUP

During Ramadan, the month-long period of fasting from dawn to dusk, soups are served with regularity. The moment the cannon sounds, or the call to prayer is heard from the neighbourhood mosque, the self-disciplining fast is broken, usually with a smooth, light soup. However, soups are not commonly served as a starter in Middle Eastern households, probably because the main course is often a stew with a rich, meaty sauce made from stock.

All good soups start with a stock, which can be made ahead of time and frozen, to be enriched later with vegetables, grains, or pulses (see recipe for basic stock, p. 47). Today, many Arabs add a stock cube to enhance the flavour and reduce the need for salt. The spices used in soup are usually mild, but the adventurous cook can try adding allspice, cumin, coriander, ginger, cinnamon, pepper, paprika or cayenne. For colour and flavour tomatoes or saffron threads are occasionally added to the soup. Most soups are served (meat bones removed) with Arabic bread and a variety of relishes adorning the table.

Preparing *shorbat*

LENTIL SOUP

Shorbat adas

Lentil soup is abundantly popular and usually served free of charge in even the tiniest of Arab restaurants. The soup is admired for its tangy flavour - a perfect balance between the savoury lentils and the sour lemon juice. A thicker tex-tured, spicy Moroccan version is prepared with red lentils and cubes of lamb.

1 lb (500g) yellow lentils
2 onions, quartered
1/4 tsp cumin, ground
2 tbsp lemon juice
oil for sautéing
salt and pepper

GARNISH
2 onions, sliced
oil for shallow-frying
lemon wedges

1 Wash and drain the lentils.

2 Sauté the onions. Simmer the lentils, onion, cumin, salt and pepper and 7 cups stock or water for 30-45 minutes or until the lentils are tender. The soup can be puréed, if preferred.

3 Add the lemon juice and adjust the seasoning to taste.

4 Serve garnished with crispy fried onions. Accompany with lemon wedges and Arabic bread.

VARIATION
● For a thicker soup add 1 cup rice to boil with the lentils.

MEAT SOUP

Shorbat bil laham

The possibilities for this hearty soup are endless. Rich in ingredients, it is almost a meal in itself. Various meat cuts as well as an assortment of vegetables can be used to create this substantially filling and nutritious soup, which tastes almost like a Hungarian goulash.

Cubed lamb or beef, or meaty bones, will make a good pot of soup. Vegetables are chosen for their individual flavours and should be added to the simmering stock according to their required cooking time. Onions, tomatoes, celery, turnips, pulses, potatoes and carrots are added at the beginning. Squash/courgettes, cabbage, cauliflower and spinach require only about 10 minutes of cooking, so are added near the end of the cooking process.

1 lb (500g) stewing meat
1 large onion, chopped
2 squash/courgettes, sliced
2 potatoes, chopped
2 carrots, chopped
2 tbsp parsley, finely chopped
1 cardamom, cracked
1/2 tsp cinnamon, ground
1/2 tsp cloves, ground
1 tbsp lemon juice
salt and pepper

GARNISH
parsley

1 To make a stock, simmer the meat or bones and the onion in 9 cups water for 1 hour. Skim the froth as it rises. Remove the bones.

2 Add the spices. According to cooking times, add the vegetables. Simmer until tender. Adjust the seasoning by adding the lemon juice, pepper and salt to taste.

3 Serve garnished with chopped parsley.

FISH SOUP

Shorbat bil samak

From the southernmost tip of Yemen to Morocco in the West, fish from the Mediterranean, Red Sea and the Gulf are used to prepare soups with a range of flavours. The taste of the soup is dictated by the type and quantity of fish and by the spices. However, most are coloured with saffron threads and flavoured with vinegar or lemon juice and mint or cinnamon.

2 lb (1 kg) fish including bones, heads and tails
2 large onions, chopped
4 tbsp spring onions, chopped
2 tomatoes, skinned and chopped
2 tbsp lemon juice
$1/2$ tsp cinnamon, ground
$1/4$ tsp cloves, ground
1-2 cloves garlic, crushed
4-5 saffron threads or
$1/4$ tsp turmeric
salt and pepper

1 Clean and wash the fish, saving the heads, bones and tails.

2 To make a stock, simmer the fish heads, bones and tails in 10 cups water, with the onions, spring onions, garlic, lemon juice, spices and salt and pepper. The saffron or turmeric are added for colour. Simmer slowly for about 20 minutes. Do not boil. Skim the froth as it rises. Strain to remove all bones.

3 Drop the boneless fish pieces into the stock. Simmer for a further 5 minutes or until the fish is tender.

VARIATION
● A spicy Libyan fish soup, uses tomatoes along with *chermoula*, a hot-chilli paste.

CHICKEN SOUP

Shorbat dajaj

Almost each time a chicken is boiled, Arabs make a stock or soup which is adapted to make use of any available vegetables. Classically, squash or courgettes are used, though carrots, leeks, celery, green beans and the like can be substituted in their place. However, vegetables can be omitted altogether.

Unlike ordinary chicken soup, the Middle Eastern style strikes a sour, aromatic balance between the spices and lemon juice. The proportions used vary from house to house, and are a constant subject for debate!

1 chicken or several carcasses and giblets
2 onions, chopped
3-5 cardamom, cracked
$1/2$ tsp cloves, ground
2-3 squash/courgettes or other vegetables (opt)
salt and pepper

GARNISH
lemon wedges
parsley

1 To make a stock, simmer the chicken or carcasses and giblets with the onion in 10 cups water for 1 hour. Skim the froth as it rises. Remove the bones.

2 Add the cardamom and cloves to the stock. Season to taste with salt and pepper.

3 According to cooking time, add the squash or other vegetables and simmer until tender. Remove the cardamom and cloves.

4 The soup can be served on a bowl of rice and garnished with finely chopped parsley. Accompany with lemon wedges.

GREEN LEAF SOUP

Shorbat melokhiya

No English translation could be found for melokhiya, which is made from the green, oval-shaped leaves of a plant that thrives in the Middle East and is very popular throughout Egypt. Akin to spinach in colour and texture, the cooked leaves can take on the sticky and syrupy properties associated with okra. However, sautéing the leaves reduces their glutinous properties.

Normally melokhiya is chopped in a rocking motion with a makhrata, a crescent-shaped, two-handled blade. However, the leaves can be cooked whole.

The leaves are available frozen or dried all year round from specialist shops, and in the Middle East fresh from May to September (1 1/2 cups dried replaces 1 lb (500g) fresh or frozen leaves).

1 lb (500g) fresh or frozen melokhiya leaves
2 onions, finely chopped
3 cloves garlic, crushed
1 tbsp coriander, ground
5 cups stock or water
oil for sautéing
salt and pepper

1 Sauté the onions and garlic.

2 Only for the fresh melokhiya leaves, wash and finely chop. Sauté for 2 minutes, to prevent the fresh melokhiya leaves from becoming sticky.

3 Mix and simmer the melokhiya, onions and garlic, salt and pepper and 5 cups stock or water for 15 minutes.

4 Add the coriander and sauté for a further 2-3 minutes.

STUFFED MEATBALL SOUP

Koubba hammouth

Italians associate meatballs with spaghetti, but Iraqis drop their koubba into soup. Koubba, a meat filling encased in a shell of rice flour mixed with finely minced meat, is added to a soup of leafy saleq, similar to French sorrel.

A thinner meatball 'feast-day' soup without the saleq is eaten in Jordan on special occasions. This process of making the filling and dough, and of stuffing each meatball is time-consuming, yet the end result is rewarding. Koubba can be prepared in large quantities and frozen. The following recipe yields about 25 meatballs, enough for 8-12 servings of soup, as each bowlful usually has two or three.

FILLING
1 lb (500g) minced lamb
2 large onions, finely chopped
1/4 tsp cumin, ground
3 tbsp parsley, finely chopped
1/2 tsp cinnamon, ground
1/4 tsp loomi, ground
oil for sautéing
salt and pepper

DOUGH
1 cup short-grain rice or ground rice
1 lb (500g) lean lamb, finely minced

1 To make the filling, lightly sauté the onions, meat, parsley and spices. Do not brown. Season with salt and pepper. Leave to cool.

2 To make the dough, wash and then soak the rice for 15 minutes. Spread and leave to dry. Grind the rice to a fine powder, if not using ready-ground rice. Thoroughly mix the ground rice and the uncooked lean meat. With damp hands, roll the dough mixture into golf ball size. To hollow the inside of the ball for stuffing, put a thumb into the centre. Pinch the sides while rolling the ball around the hand. This potter's action is continued until an 'oh so thin' casing is formed.

3 Place a teaspoon of the filling into each hollowed ball. Pinch closed with wet fingers.

SOUP
20 *saleq* leaves
2 large onions, chopped
8 oz (225g) chickpeas or rice (opt)
2-3 turnips, chopped (opt)
oil for sautéing
1/4 tsp turmeric
1 tbsp lemon juice
salt and pepper

1 Sauté the onions. Add the turnips and *saleq*, and cook for a further 2 minutes.

2 Boil the chickpeas and/or rice in 4 cups chicken stock until tender. Add the fried onions, turnips, *saleq*, lemon juice, turmeric, and salt and pepper. Bring to the boil.

3 Carefully drop each meatball into the soup, as they will break easily. Turn occasionally with a spoon.

4 Simmer slowly for about 30 minutes or until the meatballs float.

Koubba hammouth

Salatat

SALAD

Salads are generally simple - usually a tray piled high with green leaves and vegetables which have been left whole or sometimes quartered. However, mixed Arabian salads can be slightly more complex with toasted bread, finely chopped herbs, yoghurt, or tangy *sumac* providing a special Middle Eastern flavour.

Most Arabian salads traditionally contain olive oil and freshly squeezed lemon juice. Virgin olive oil - from the first pressing - was one of the first types of oil used and is still recommended in Arab kitchens for salads (see the glossary entry 'olive oil' for more details). The word 'oil' comes from the root word 'olive'. The Spanish word for oil, 'aceite' comes from the Arab word *az zait*, meaning fruit of the olive.

Each recipe in the salad section can be served as *mezza* or as an accompaniment to the main course.

Virgin oil, for salad

TIPS FOR GOOD SALADS

1 Always choose vegetables and herbs that are fresh and crisp.

2 Vegetables and herbs should be kept cool and dry. After washing, shake off excess water and wrap in a dry cloth; refrigerate until ready to chop.

3 Vegetables, except those to be mashed, should be steamed lightly so they remain firm. Use as little water as possible, to avoid the loss of nutrients into the cooking liquid.

4 Lemon juice used in dressing should always be freshly squeezed.

5 Olive oil for the dressing should ideally be of the best quality, from the first pressing. Some fresh oils from the Fertile Crescent have a particular sweetness that is very tasty in salads.

6 The proportion of olive oil to lemon juice or olive oil to wine vinegar is debatable. Salads using lemon juice are normally more tart than in most western countries.

7 The tossed salad with the dressing should be left for a few minutes to absorb the flavour before adjusting the seasoning. Cooked vegetables and pulses absorb the dressing better when hot.

8 Keep salads refrigerated until serving.

Tabouleh (opposite)

CHOPPED HERB SALAD

Tabouleh

Parsley, of Mediterranean origin, is the flavourful component of this minutely chopped herb salad. Most admired by the Lebanese, tabouleh has won widespread admiration in the rest of the Arab World and beyond. Mixed with fine grains of burgul, the tart salad is encircled with cos lettuce leaves. The tiny tender leaves are used to scoop up each succulent bite.

Always available, burgul was the staple grain in the past and the ratio to herbs used in tabouleh was large. The proportions are still debated. Some Arabs favour an almost white, totally burgul salad, with green and red highlights of herbs and tomatoes, while others argue for a green herb salad with only a few speckles of grain. For a crunchy salad, decrease the soaking time for the burgul or mix the soaked grains with the herbs just before serving.

1-3 oz (25-75g) fine *burgul*
4 oz (100g) parsley, finely chopped
5 tbsp mint, finely chopped
5 tbsp spring onions, finely chopped
3 tomatoes, seeded and finely chopped
4 tbsp olive oil
3 tbsp fresh lemon juice
1 tsp salt
GARNISH
sprig of mint
8 cos/romaine lettuce leaves

1 Soak the *burgul* in water for 15-20 minutes or until softened but a little resistant to the bite. Drain and squeeze out excess moisture.

2 Add the *burgul* to the onions, parsley and mint.

3 Mix the salt, lemon juice and olive oil. Toss into the salad and leave to stand for 15 minutes, allowing the flavours to absorb. Peel, seed and finely chop the tomatoes. Adjust the seasoning to taste by adding more salt, olive oil or lemon juice. Toss the salad.

4 To serve, encircle the salad with small lettuce leaves and garnish with a sprig of mint.

SALAD WITH TOASTED BREAD

Fattoush

Fattoush, *which literally means 'wet bread', is a tangy mixed salad with about 12 other ingredients. The red specks of sumac give the salad a distinct tartness.*

Purslane, which is a popular addition to Levantine salads, grows wild over most of southern Europe and Asia and in the United States is considered a common weed. Although said to have originated in India - where it is known as 'kulfa' - the leaves are popular in the Arab countries as bagli. *The tender shoots, which can be gritty, should be washed thoroughly before being added to a salad.*

The toasted bread can be mixed with almost any herbs or vegetables. In the Arab world, the salad differs in each region according to the availability of ingredients. In Egypt, for example, dark green leaves of melokhiya *are tossed with the salad. Others use spinach, which is thought to be of Persian origin, but was probably introduced to Europe by the Arabs.*

Spring onions and green chilli peppers are sometimes left whole to rim the bowl. Although carrots and radishes are rare in Arabic fattoush, *almost any favourite vegetable can be chopped and added to the colourful and tangy combination.*

1 Separate the two layers of the Arabic bread. Toast in the oven until crispy. Break into small pieces.

2 Wash and chop or pinch the herbs and vegetables.

3 To make the dressing, mix the garlic with the lemon juice and olive oil.

4 Toss the toasted bread, the *sumac,* and the dressing into the salad. The dressing will soften the bread, which most Arabs prefer. (For the bread to remain crispy, add just before serving.) Leave to stand for a few minutes and adjust the seasoning by adding salt or lemon juice.

¹/2 large loaf of Arabic bread, toasted
6 lettuce leaves
5 spinach leaves (opt)
4 tbsp spring onions, chopped
4 tbsp parsley, chopped
2 tbsp mint, chopped
2 tomatoes, cubed
1 capsicum pepper, chopped (opt)
1 large or 2 small cucumber, cubed

DRESSING
2-3 tbsp fresh lemon juice
4-6 tbsp olive oil
1 clove garlic, crushed (opt)
3 tsp *sumac*
salt

Fattoush

HERB AND VEGETABLE PLATTER

Saniyat khodara

A tray piled high with herbs and vegetables serves as a decorative centre-piece and is nibbled from at intervals during
the meal. Stalks of spring onions, sprigs of parsley and
mint and tender leaves of lettuce and spinach lie beside
whole or quartered cucumbers, tomatoes and radishes.
White radishes were a favourite in ancient Egypt and have
been cultivated for so long that the wild ancestor is
unknown. Today white as well as the red variety of radish
are found whole on the salad tray - the tops are eaten as
well as the roots.

In the Arab world, some unlikely raw herbs adorn the
table, including exotic leaves of saleq, jirjear (watercress)
and kuzbara (coriander), as well as beetroot tops, sorrel,
purslane, fresh chicory, endive, chives, dill, mustard, basil,
fennel and tarragon (see the glossary for further details).

Listed below is a sample combination, which may be
adjusted according to availability. These herbs are usually
served freshly washed and cleaned on a tray.

1 head cos/romaine lettuce
2-3 spinach leaves
4-5 spring onions
3-4 beetroot tops
3-4 carrots
2-3 tomatoes
4-5 red or white radishes
5-6 small cucumbers
4-5 chilli peppers
2 lemons
sprigs of herbs:
parsley, chives, dill, basil, watercress,
mint and coriander

1 Wash and shake the herbs dry. Remove any
coarse stalks and discoloured pieces.

2 Arrange whole on a tray.

3 To retain crispness, cover and place in the
refrigerator for about 2 hours or until chilled.

TOMATO SALAD

Salatat bandoura

5 firm tomatoes, cubed
1/2 onion or 1 spring onion, chopped
1/2 pt (275ml) yoghurt
1 tbsp mint or parsley, finely chopped
1/2 tsp salt

GARNISH
sprigs of parsley or mint

1 Mix the cubed tomatoes and onion. Mix the
yoghurt with the chopped parsley or mint and
pour over the salad. Salt to taste. Chill for 45 minutes in the refrigerator.

2 Garnish with a few sprigs of parsley or mint.

BEETROOT AND YOGHURT

Shamandar bil laban

Beets have been selected for their roots for over 1,000 years,
but it is only in the last century that horticulturists have
perfected the knobbly roots into symmetrically uniform tender bulbs.

Beetroot are usually boiled and served simply in the Arab
world. This less common version serves as a slightly tart,
slightly sweet combination. The vinegar helps the root
retain its deep red colour.

4 beetroots
1 tsp vinegar
1/2 pt (275ml) yoghurt
1 tbsp fresh lemon juice
salt

1 Do not peel the beetroot. Simply twist or cut

off the tops, leaving a little stalk. Wash and boil in water with the vinegar added for about 1 hour or until tender. Test for tenderness by rubbing the skins for easy removal. Drain, cool, peel and dice, slice or cube.

2 Beat the yoghurt and lemon juice together and mix with the beets. Add salt to taste. Serve chilled.

YOGHURT AND CUCUMBER SALAD

Khiyar bil laban

Cucumbers, one of the oldest cultivated vegetables, have been grown for some 4,000 years. They may have originated from southern India.

1 large or 2 medium cucumbers
1/2 pt (275ml) yoghurt
2 tbsp dried mint, crushed
salt and pepper

GARNISH
sprigs of mint

1 Peel and cube the cucumber.

2 To prepare the dressing, beat the yoghurt and salt and pepper.

3 Mix the dressing with the cucumber cubes. Sprinkle with the dried mint. Serve chilled and garnished with sprigs of fresh mint.

Mukhalalat

PICKLES AND SAUCES

For thousands of years, Arab homes have been decorated with earthenware jugs filled with pickles made from almost any root or vegetable. Prior to the invention of glass jars, which are now stacked in colourful arrays in Arabian kitchens, the jugs were sealed with sun-dried clay. Pickles were made to be eaten outside the growing season and gave variety to a diet which had once consisted mainly of dates, wheat or rice, and goat or camel meat and milk.

Today, pickles are served in small bowls to accompany almost every Arabic dinner: turnip, aubergine/eggplant, carrot, green tomato, garlic, chilli, beetroot, and onion just to name a few. Fruit pickles, such as orange and lemon rind, apricot and mango are typical condiments.

Pickling is an old method of preserving food by immersing it in salt water or vinegar. A 10 per cent solution of brine, as suggested in most of the following recipes, discourages unwanted bacteria and stabilises vegetables for the pickling process. Vinegar tends to harden vegetables, and will delay softening.

Arabic sauces, another food complement, range from mild stock (an essential ingredient in most stews and soups) to explosive ones laced with garlic or pepper. Sauces can be made ahead of time and stored in the refrigerator for later use. Some can be frozen, such as garlic and tomato sauces. *Tahina* sauce can be kept unrefrigerated, as can the onion and vinegar sauce.

TIPS FOR PICKLE-MAKING

1 Select only the freshest of vegetables. Clean, trim, core, remove seeds or otherwise pre-process when required. Put vegetables in clean jars with lids that seal tight.

2 Arabs use primarily the open-kettle canning method of filling jars without further heat treatment. Most open kettle pickles keep well for 6-8 weeks (Arabs prepare them in large quantities because pickles are eaten at almost every meal). When vegetables are pre-cooked, the pickles will keep for longer.

3 Pack the jars snugly, whether the vegetables are quartered, sliced or left whole. Mix the pickling salt and vinegar, pouring it over the vegetables in the jars (some people also cover them with oil). Then cover the pickles, jiggling the jars to burst any air bubbles, and seal tightly.

4 The proportions of the brine solution should take into account the storage temperature. For example, a brine strong enough to preserve in cool conditions may not work in warmer climates. Old recipes call for brine strong enough to 'float an egg'. In a 25 per cent salt solution, bacteria cease to exist. Brine for holding vegetables should be about 15 per cent brine, made from 8pt (5 litre) water to 1 3/4 lb (750 g) sea salt or cooking salt and 1/2 pt (0.3 litre) vinegar. Roughly 14 oz (400 g) of salt per 4 1/2 lb (2 kg) of vegetables. Brine for fermented vegetable pickles should be 5 per cent brine, 8 pt (5 litre) water, 1/2 lb (250 g) salt and 1/2 pt (0.3 litre) vinegar.

5 Any white scum that forms on top of the pickles should be removed daily.

MIXED PICKLES

Mukhalal

A woman in the United Arab Emirates offered me a recipe for making pickles which has been used by her family for generations. First, vegetables are partially boiled in salt water until slightly softened and then placed outdoors in a cloth-covered basket to dry for a couple of days. Then, layered in jars with salt, garlic, dried red chilli peppers and ground coriander seeds and peppercorns, the vegetables are covered with brown vinegar. The pickles are kept in a cool, dark place for at least two months before opening.

A good combination for mixed pickles can include aubergine/eggplant, carrots, and sometimes cabbage. But other vegetables can be used, including cucumbers, cauliflower, turnips and green beans. The seasonings used can be adjusted to taste. Iraqis are known for using date vinegar which gives a distinctive flavour.

2 lb (1 kg) mixed vegetables

SEASONING (opt)
4 cloves garlic
2 or 3 dried red chilli peppers
2 tsp ground coriander seeds
1 tsp ground peppercorns

PICKLING BRINE
brown vinegar
salt

1 Clean and cut the vegetables into strips, quarters, or cubes.

2 Boil the vegetables in salted water until slightly tenderised, but still firm. Strain to remove the water.

3 Place in a basket or other porous container which has first been covered with a cotton cloth.

4 Place in a shaded area to dry for a couple of days.

5 Tightly pack each jar, alternating vegetables and the ground seasoning with salt and peeled garlic.

6 Fill the jar with brown vinegar.

7 Allow the pickles to stand in a cool, dark place for a couple of months before opening.

PICKLED TURNIPS

Mukhalal left

Turnip pickles are the most popular as they have a distinctive taste and colour. The appearance can be deceptive, as the turnips are coloured pink by the addition of beetroot, sometimes as richly coloured as the purple and red dyes of ancient Phoenicia. These pickles are often eaten as part of the mezza, with drinks, and can be seen in shops everywhere from Lebanon to the southern tip of the Arabian Peninsula.

Many turnip pickles in the Middle East are made in a salt solution. However, the following recipe uses a salt and vinegar solution, allowing the pickles to be stored for several months.

2 lb (1 kg) white turnips
1 beetroot, peeled and sliced
3 cloves garlic (opt)
2 pt (1 litre) water
$^1/_2$ pt (275ml) vinegar
4 tbsp salt

1 Peel and wash the turnips. Cut into quarters and pack into jars, adding pieces of the beetroot.

2 Add the garlic, if desired.

3 Dissolve the salt into the vinegar and water. Fill each jar until the turnips are covered. Seal tightly.

4 The pickles will be ready in about 5 days.

PICKLED TOMATOES

Bandoura kudar

2 lb (1 kg) firm green tomatoes
5 fl oz (150ml) vinegar
2 pt (1 litre) water
3 tsp pepper
6 cloves garlic
3 tsp paprika (opt)
2 tsp coriander, ground
3 tbsp salt

1 Wash the tomatoes.

2 Mix the vinegar, salt and water.

3 Pack the tomatoes into sterilised jars alternating with layers of garlic and other spices. Cover with the vinegar, salt and water solution and seal.

4 Remove the scum as it rises.

5 Leave for about 1 month, checking weekly.

Mukhalal

PICKLED GARLIC

Mukhalal toum

Considered to have originated from Central Asia, the builders of the pyramids were reputed to have gained part of their sustenance from garlic, which is often stored for long periods to improve in flavour and texture. One Arab woman told me of a jar of pickled garlic she has stored for 20 years. (In that recipe the peel is left on the garlic, and the jar should not be opened for at least two years.) This recipe for garlic pickles does not last for so many years, but is prepared more easily. Garlic preserved with vinegar is the perfect condiment for any main course.

10-15 cloves garlic
vinegar
salt (opt)

Peel the garlic and crush with salt or leave whole. Place in a jar and cover with vinegar. Leave crushed garlic for at least 24 hours and whole garlic for one week before use.

AUBERGINE/EGGPLANT PICKLE

Macdus

A nutty relish, pickled aubergine is extremely easy to prepare. Although they do not look particularly pleasing, the oblong stuffed vegetables are very agreeable to the palate.

8-10 very small aubergines/eggplant
8 cloves garlic, crushed
8 oz (225g) walnuts, chopped
3-4 chilli peppers, finely chopped or
1 tbsp chilli paste/*shatta* (p. 44)
olive oil
2 tsp salt

1 Wash the aubergines and boil in lightly salted water for 15 minutes, holding them down with a inverted plate. Remove; leave to dry overnight.

2 Trim off the stalks and make a slit down the centre of each aubergine. Remove the seeds.

3 To make the stuffing, mix the walnuts, chilli peppers, garlic and 2 tsp salt.

4 Stuff each aubergine.

5 Pack the stuffed aubergines into a sterile wide-mouthed jar. Cover with olive oil and seal with an airtight lid.

6 Leave to stand at room temperature for 2 weeks. The pickles can be stored for months if the vegetables remain covered with oil.

7 To serve, slice the aubergines into small portions and garnish with a sprig of parsley.

PICKLED ONIONS

Mukhalal basal

Evidence of onion pickling, one of the most ancient forms of pickling, was found in the ruins of Pompeii. Today Arabs serve them alongside meat, chicken or fish dishes. Onions can also be chopped and soaked with vinegar to add as a relish when served layered in Melokhiya (see p. 77).

8 oz (225g) small onions
1/2 pt (275ml) vinegar
1 tsp salt
1 chilli pepper

1 Peel the onions.

2 To make the pickling solution, mix the vinegar, salt, and chilli pepper.

3 Boil the onions in the solution for about 3 minutes or until the onions have softened slightly.

4 Pack the onions into sterilised jars and top up with the solution. Seal tightly and leave to pickle for about 10 days.

PICKLED CHILLI PEPPERS

Mukhalal filfil

Pickled in a vinegar and salt solution or topped with oil, chilli peppers are popular condiments for an Arabic meal. The green chilli is said to be milder than the red, although the red is simply the ripened green pepper. Removing the seeds will calm both. Larger red and green hot peppers are found in the Arab world and are used especially in Yemen and the Maghreb countries.

1 lb (500g) green or red chilli peppers
1 pt (575ml) vinegar
1/2 tsp salt

1 Wash and dry the chilli peppers. Pack into a jar.

2 Mix the salt and vinegar and pour over the chilli peppers. Jiggle the jar to remove air pockets before sealing.

3 After 3-4 days cover with more vinegar and leave to pickle for a further 4 weeks. Use the vinegar and serve the peppers.

PICKLED OLIVES

Zaytun

Olives are an integral part of the mezza table and can easily be bought pickled in brine or vinegar. However, the adventurous may like to try this spiced up recipe. In the Arab world, Palestine was historically known for its great abundance of olives, and today the best olives and olive oils come from this region. A typically Palestinian olive condiment can be made by adding finely chopped fresh chilli peppers or one teaspoon harissa, a red chilli paste (see p. 44).

The Middle East produces a bewildering number of varieties: green olives with their stones; green stuffed with pieces of sweet red pepper, anchovies, almonds or hot green chillies, or black olives. A taste test can tell more about the type and quality than the eye alone. Arab merchants expect shoppers to ask for a sample!

1 lb (500g) fresh ripe olives
3 chilli peppers
2 lemons, sliced
water
salt
olive oil
carob leaves (opt)

1 Discard any damaged olives. Soak in several changes of water for 24 hours to remove bitterness. Rinse them and place with the lemon slices and chilli peppers into glass or earthenware jars.

2 Make the pickling solution by adding around 3 tbsp salt to every pint (575ml) water.

3 Pour the pickling solution over the olives, then cover with a layer of olive oil and a layer of carob leaves. Cover tightly.

4 Leave for about five months in a cool, dark place before trying them.

LEMON OR ORANGE RIND PRESERVES

Muraba lemon wa Portucal

The first citrus fruit to reach Europe probably was the 'citron' and is thought to have come from India. The Greeks discovered the fruit in the land of the Medes and the Persians, but it was also grown in the hanging gardens of Babylon.

The ancient fruit - large, warty and lemon-like - was used to perfume toilet water, but citron is beloved today for its fruit and thick rind. The peel is either pickled in vinegar and salt or made into sweet preserves.

The ugli fruit, a cross between a grapefruit and a tangerine, is also pickled or preserved, but lemons and oranges can also be used.

This sweet rind preserve - similar to jam or marmalade - is thought to be an Iraqi speciality.

6 oranges or lemons
2 tbsp lemon juice
1 lb (500g) sugar
2-3 tbsp rose water (opt)
2 cardamom, cracked

1 Peel the lemons and/or the oranges into small wedges. Remove the white pith from inside the rind, as this is bitter.

2 Soak the rinds in cold water for 12 hours.

3 Simmer for 1 hour, adding water as needed. Drain the rinds.

4 Mix the sugar, lemon juice and cracked cardamom pods with 3 cups water. Bring to the boil and add the rinds. Simmer for 30 minutes. Allow to cool and add the rose water, if preferred.

5 Fill and seal the sterilised jars.

HOT CHILLI SAUCE

Harissa, Shatta, or Bisbas

Fiery-hot deep-red paste is used in Yemen and the Maghreb countries of North Africa - Libya, Algeria, Tunisia and Morocco. It is served in small bowls, as a condiment, but can be added to meats, stews, and soups. In other regions of the Arab world shatta, a similar condiment, is stored in jars with a thin layer of oil to seal it from the air. The Yemenis use large red chilli peppers plus garlic and salt to make yet another similar relish called bisbas. Harissa is a very hot chilli-based mixture from North Africa, which may contain up to 20 spices.

These hot chilli sauces can be bought in specialist shops - the precise combination of ingredients is usually a secret. If you are unable to obtain them, and only a small quantity is required for a recipe, a pinch of cayenne or some chilli can be substituted - though it will not render quite the same flavour.

However, you can make your own. In this recipe, the chilli and capsicum peppers combined together offer a milder version than the chilli peppers alone. The quantity of chilli powder and peppers added to the recipe determines the amount of 'fire'. The recipe can also be made without the oil and frozen in small containers.

10-20 red chilli peppers
2 red capsicum peppers
1 tsp cumin, ground
1 tsp coriander, ground
4 small tomatoes
1-4 tsp chilli powder
olive oil

1 Slit and seed the tomatoes, chilli peppers and/or capsicum peppers.

2 Blend all the ingredients except the oil until smooth. Fill sterilised jars and cover with 2 inches of oil.

GARLIC MAYONNAISE AND SAUCE

Toum

Garlic was one of the predominant flavours in Middle Eastern cooking even in the earliest recorded history. It was eaten in the Euphrates and Nile Valleys about 5,000 years ago, and it is said that the workers who built the pyramids gained their strength from garlic. The powerful root was used for barter in the Pharaonic era. This book alone records over 200 uses of the strong-smelling bulb. According to Arab writers, garlic gives strength, cures diseases and revitalizes the complexion.

When uncooked, garlic has a unique pungency. Combined, as here, with mayonnaise, garlic seasoning becomes milder, smoother, softer and an unparalleled accompaniment for grilled chicken.

This recipe makes a small quantity of garlic sauce for addition to mayonnaise. A large portion, for freezing in small containers, may be made with 40 cloves of garlic, 6 tbsp lemon juice, 8 tbsp olive oil and salt. Seal tightly when freezing to avoid the aroma seeping into other foods.

GARLIC SAUCE
6 cloves garlic, crushed
1 tbsp lemon juice (opt)
2 tbsp olive oil
1 tsp salt

HOME-MADE GARLIC MAYONNAISE
1 egg yolk, beaten
1 egg yolk, hard boiled
20 fl oz (575ml) olive oil
1 tbsp lemon juice
2-4 tbsp garlic sauce

SAUCE

1 Blend all the ingredients into a purée or until well combined. Add a little water when necessary.

MAYONNAISE

1 To make the mayonnaise, mash the hard-boiled egg yolk and add the beaten raw egg yolk. Beat continually while adding the olive oil, drop by drop. When beating, make sure not to change direction as the mayonnaise will curdle. While continually stirring add the lemon juice to taste, drop by drop.

2 For a strong flavour, add 4 tbsp garlic sauce and blend well.

VARIATION

● The garlic sauce can be added to a commercially produced mayonnaise.

YOGHURT SAUCE

Labnah

To be served with added dill and mint as a dip for vegetable crudités or plain to mix with vegetables and salad, this sauce can also be stabilised and added to stews or casseroles. For the procedure to stabilise yoghurt see p. 52.

1 pt (575ml) yoghurt
2 tbsp dill or mint, finely chopped (opt)
1 tsp lemon juice (opt)

Mix all ingredients together and adjust the lemon juice to taste.

TOMATO PURÉE

Nasfa bandoura

Home-made tomato purée has an enhanced flavour, making it well worth the effort. In the Arab world, tomato sauce has been - and in some regions still is - sun-dried to a paste. Alternative preservation methods include storing in the freezer or in jars topped with an oil seal. Kuwait is known for its daqous, which is made by boiling 5 peeled tomatoes in a little water until a sauce is formed. Add a clove of crushed garlic, a dash of chilli powder, 1 tsp lemon juice, 1 tbsp oil and salt and pepper to simmer for a further 10 minutes. Daqous is served with fish, shrimp or a bean rice (see p. 124).

Some recipes for tomato purée include celery seed, cloves, cinnamon, bruised ginger, allspice berries, and peppercorns to be boiled with vinegar and cooled before adding the strained tomato purée, garlic and olive oil. Add vinegar and salt to taste as the ingredients simmer.

2 lb (1kg) tomatoes
1 large onion, finely chopped
4 cloves garlic, crushed
2 tbsp parsley, finely chopped
2 tsp fresh basil, finely chopped
2 tsp fresh thyme, finely chopped
1 tsp sugar
olive oil
salt and pepper

1 Loosen the skin of fresh tomatoes by dropping into boiling water. Remove skin and cut into quarters. Simmer for 30 minutes, adding water only if required. Purée the tomatoes. The tomatoes can be pressed through a funnel-shaped sieve to remove the seeds and pulp.

2 Sauté the onions and the garlic until tender. Add the tomato purée, parsley, basil, thyme, sugar and salt and pepper.

3 Cover and slowly simmer for 20 minutes.

4 Pour the sauce into sterilised jars and cover with a thin layer of olive oil. Seal tightly and store in a cool place. Alternatively freeze, omitting the olive oil.

SESAME SEED PASTE SAUCE

Tahina

No Arabic home would be without tahina, an oily paste made from crushed sesame seeds. Historically, simsim (sesame) has held a cherished position in Arab cooking. The legends of 1,001 Arabian Nights notes that when Ali Baba and his 40 thieves were hiding their valued possessions, he respectfully addressed the stone covering the entrance to the cave, saying 'iftah ya simsim' or 'open sesame!' Sesame seeds were treasured and a sign of wealth!

Tahina, which is similar in taste and appearance to a thin peanut butter, is used in many Arabic dishes, most notably in a chickpea purée, hummos (see p. 9). The thinned sauce is used as an accompaniment to crispy fried sardines (see p. 16) and a thickened sauce is used over baked fish (see p. 85). The quantity of water is determined by the consistency needed for each recipe.

To make this sauce and the subsequent recipes tahina paste is needed. Tahina tends to separate and needs to be stirred well before use. Storing jars or cans upside down can help.

The recipe below is for a relatively thin sauce, for serving with fish. The desired tartness determines the amount of lemon juice used.

4 fl oz (100ml) *tahina*
3 tbsp lemon juice
6 tbsp water
3 cloves garlic, crushed (opt)
4 tbsp parsley, finely chopped (opt)
1 tsp salt

1 Alternately add water and lemon juice, one spoon at a time, to the *tahina* until a creamy sauce forms. The water thins and the lemon juice stiffens it.

2 Add the garlic and parsley to the *tahina*, if required. Mix well and adjust seasoning to taste.

ONIONS AND VINEGAR

Basal bil khal

Sharply flavoured onion and vinegar sauce is most often used to top melokhiya *(see p. 77), but can be used as a relish on almost any vegetable or salad. Cover one finely chopped onion with vinegar. Red or white wine vinegar or home-made herbal vinegars may be used for a more savoury taste. A pinch of chilli powder or* sumac *can be added.*

STOCK

Maraq

All good stews, soups or sauces begin with a rich stock of meat, bones, fish, fowl, game or vegetables, made by simmering the selected ingredients for a long time to extract their essence.

TIPS FOR A GOOD STOCK

1 When preparing a stock, use only fresh vegetables. If bruises are not removed, the stock will have an unpleasant flavour and will sour quickly.

2 Remove the scum as it rises to avoid spoiling the colour and flavour.

3 Do not add salt to the stock while cooking. Fish stock should be simmered for 20 minutes only.

5 Cool the stock and skim off the fat to avoid greasiness.

6 Strain and remove any bones before use.

BASIC STOCK
4 pt (2 litre) water
2 lb (1 kg) poultry, meat or fish bones
4 onions
other vegetables, as available

Cover the bones with water and add the chopped vegetables. Gently simmer for 2-3 hours, or 20 minutes for fish. Skim the froth as it rises. Strain and allow to settle. Remove any fat from the surface.

Mushtakat al laban wa al baid

MILK PRODUCTS AND EGGS

Since early herdsmen first learned to extract nutritional strength from their animals, milk has been a staple food. Oxen, sheep, asses, goats and horses were long milked by tribesmen before domestication of the dairy cow. Camel milk provided vitality for nomadic Bedouin and is still consumed today - although more rarely - in the desert regions. Though nourishing, the milk from the 'Ship of the Desert' is purgative. Nowadays, fresh cows' milk is produced at dairies throughout the Arab world, and processed yoghurt, cheese and *samn* are consumed regularly.

Arab legend has it that yoghurt developed at a time when bags made of goat and camel stomachs were used for storage of fresh milk. The milk would warm and the natural bacilli present in the containers multiplied, forming yoghurt. Yoghurt is still frequently home-made, often daily, and is the most essential milk product in the Middle Eastern diet.

Milk products and eggs form an essential part of breakfast. In some parts of Arabia they may be served any time of day, including as a starter in the *mezza*, as a snack or simply a side dish to accompany main-course stews, roast meats and poultry.

Salt-preserved white cheese stored in vats of salt water is a typical sight in shops throughout the Arab world. Usually served uncooked in the *mezza* or for breakfast, cheese is sold in many varieties.

THE EXTRAORDINARY EGG

In 106 BC, the Chinese wrote of finding giant 'camel birds' (ostriches) on the plains of the Iranian Plateau - they had probably been imported from the deserts of south-west Asia. Two decades later a traveller along the Silk Road spoke of Persian birds in the same area 'whose eggs are like urns'. The domestication of the hen, probably a descendant of a species of Indian or Indonesian jungle fowl, took place quite early in human history.

Even ordinary hens' eggs are turned into something special when they are cooked Middle Eastern style. On special occasions and feast days, coloured eggs are served alongside other exotic dishes as a symbol of the potential and mystery of life. A traditional method of dying the shells involves boiling the eggs with natural dyestuffs: with the skins of purple onion skins for purple, turmeric or saffron for yellow, and a pinch or two of Arabic coffee for brown.

Ordinarily, eggs are served for breakfast, but in the Arab world are often spiced strongly - with up to two cloves of garlic to each egg - and eaten almost any time of the day. Hard-boiled eggs are dipped or rolled in blended spices. Also, the yolks are scooped out of boiled halves, mixed with yoghurt and spices and re-stuffed. Eggs are also fried and scrambled with onion and tomato, or the hard-boiled variety dropped into or served on top of stews. The unique *ujjah*, which is often compared with omelette, is actually loads of vegetables, meat, herbs and spices held together with just a little egg.

YOGHURT

Laban

Leben in Egypt and the rest of North Africa, and laban in Syria and Lebanon, yoghurt plays an important role in the Middle Eastern diet.

More rapidly digested than raw milk, yoghurt is easy on the stomach and most Arab cooks testify that the home-made version - sometimes made with sheeps' or goats' milk - is even more wholesome. The tartness can be adjusted to taste and the consistency altered to fit each recipe.

Arabs eat yoghurt in a variety of ways. Natural yoghurt, never sweetened, is added to the main-course dish or used as a sauce. It is thinned and spiced for drinks, spread over lamb or chicken to marinade before grilling, or eaten as a snack scooped up with pieces of Arabic bread.

Any milk or combination of milks can be used to prepare yoghurt - from full fat to skim - and either powdered, UHT (ultra-high temperature) long-life or fresh. Choice of milk should be determined by availability and by the individual's or family's nutritional requirements.

Some people warn against the use of reconstituted powdered milk in the yoghurt-making process, but I have had very good results by adding a little powdered milk to some whole milk - it thickens the yoghurt and gives it a creamier taste.

Actual preparation of yoghurt is extremely easy, but the right conditions are needed to guarantee success. Follow these five tips to a fail-free yoghurt:

1 A glass or earthenware bowl and jars, and a warm place for fermentation, are required to make yoghurt.

2 Boiling the milk kills all bacteria in it, allowing the new culture to grow freely. To ensure that the heat does not kill the new culture, let the boiled milk cool to about body temperature, 105°F (40°C). To check the temperature without a thermometer, put the little finger into the milk and count to 10. It should feel neither hot nor cold.

3 A live bacterial culture - either the Bulgaris culture or a lactic acid culture - is required. The culture normally comes from the stomach of the unweaned calf, and is purchased as rennet tablets. Alternatively a few spoons of either

commercially produced or home-made yoghurt can be used to transfer the culture to a new batch. (After 4-5 batches a new culture must be used as the bacteria will die.)

4 A warm, draught-free place allows the culture to grow. The warm top of a hot-water heater or warm oven can be as effective as a thermostatically controlled yoghurt maker. Fermentation time ranges from 6-12 hours, depending on the desired consistency and tartness.

5 Refrigerating the yoghurt halts fermentation and prevents the yoghurt from souring.

2 pts (1 litre) milk
3 tbsp dry milk (opt)
2 tbsp commercial yoghurt; or
2 tbsp Bulgaris culture; or
1 tablet rennet enzyme or
2 tbsp liquid essence of rennet

1 Bring the milk to the boil. Add the powdered milk.

2 Remove from the heat and allow to cool to about body temperature [105°F (40°C)].

3 Blend in the culture.

4 Pour into 6 clean jars and keep in a warm place for 6-12 hours, depending on desired tartness.

5 Refrigerate for at least 1 hour before most uses.

An array of yoghurt dishes

DRAINED YOGHURT

Labnah

Soft, slightly sour cream cheese can be made from home-made or bought yoghurt. Arabs eat this cheese spread on bread at breakfast with a little honey or jam. Labnah is a standard dip in the mezza, thinly spread around a bowl, drizzled with a little olive oil, sprinkled with crushed mint and garnished with a few whole olives or fresh mint leaves. For a party, try forming the labnah into a 'tennis ball' and rolling in zaatar to make shankalis, an attractive cheese ball.

The consistency and tartness of the cheese depends on the amount of time the yoghurt is drained. The amount of salt added is determined by the intended use.

Sweet labnah, which is only slightly sour, should be firm enough to cut with a spoon. The smooth texture should never be grainy, and only a little whey should trickle from the edges. To serve as a dip, drizzle with a little olive oil and garnish with a black olive.

1 pt (575ml) yoghurt
¹/₂-1 tsp salt

1 Mix the salt into the yoghurt.

2 Place the salted yoghurt in a piece of damp cheese-cloth, muslin or a loosely woven cotton cloth. Gather up the corners of the cloth and tie securely. Suspend the bundle from a fixed object over a dish to catch the whey.

3 Leave to drain for about 10 hours. The whey will drain, leaving a creamy-white yoghurt cheese.

4 Refrigerate for up to 3-4 days.

YOGHURT CHEESE BALLS

Labnah mackbouseh, or Jameed

In the old marketplaces of the Middle East, sun-dried yoghurt balls, jameed, made from goats' or sheeps' milk are still sold from baskets. The dried cheese can be eaten as a snack or crumbled and used for cooking.

Marble-sized labnah balls can also be found bathing in bottles of pure, sweet olive oil with a chilli pepper. The cheese balls can be made at home from firm drained yoghurt and are a frequent addition to the mezza. Yoghurt cheese is formed into larger balls and rolled in zaatar to make shankalis.

1 Take one tablespoon at a time of refrigerated drained yoghurt and roll into smooth marble-size balls. (To facilitate the shaping, moisten the hands with olive oil.)

2 Place the balls side by side on an oiled tray. Refrigerate for several hours or until firm.

3 Pack the balls into sterilised jars. Fill the jars with the olive oil mixed with a pinch of chilli powder, and dried herbs such as dill, mint, or basil.

4 Seal and store at room temperature for up to 10 weeks, or in the refrigerator for several months. Alternatively, the labnah balls can be dried in the sun to make jameed.

STABILISED YOGHURT

Yoghurt is added to the sauces of several Arabic dishes, including meaty mansaf (see p. 62). Because yoghurt, like milk, curdles in the cooking process, it should be first stabilised. Adding a little cornflour or egg, or a combination of both, will keep the yoghurt from separating. Once stabilised, the yoghurt may be brought to the boil and simmered as a cooking liquid in the intended recipe.

2 pt (1 litre) yoghurt
1 tbsp cornflour/cornstarch
1 egg white, beaten

1 Beat all ingredients for 5 minutes.

2 Slowly bring the yoghurt mixture to the boil, stirring continually.

3 Lower the heat and simmer uncovered for about 10 minutes or until the sauce thickens. Do not cover, as the yoghurt may separate.

Varieties of *jibnah*

CHEESE

Jibnah

Herdsmen in Mesopotamia, along the Tigris and Euphrates Rivers - the first to domesticate sheep and goats about 10,000 years ago, and wild cattle 2,000 years later - certainly made cheese. Sumerians were known to have made cheese some 6,000 years ago, and these ancient Middle Easterners were known to use the milk of asses and mares in the process.

Today, sliced white cheeses are drizzled with olive oil and garnished with fresh mint leaves. Customarily, Arabs keep a supply of dried mint on hand, which can be crushed between the palms, and sprinkled over the cheese and olive oil. A Bedouin igt cheese is made by boiling down sour curd until it is almost dry, smoothing it into a paste and adding desert herbs for flavour.

Nabulsia, which originated in the town of Nablis, is a very salty cheese and should be soaked in several changes of water overnight, then served fresh or fried. Unsalted haloum is much like mozzarella in texture and is excellent for frying.

Yellow cheeses are used less sparingly. Roomi, Roman cheese, is a delicately mild crumbly variety which is dotted with coarsely ground black peppercorns. This spotted variety is mixed with tomatoes or cucumbers and wrapped in Arabic bread. Kaskawan, a much sharper yellowish cheese, is eaten in small triangular wedges in the mezza.

Some Arabic cheeses are plaited in braids, such as the Egyptian aged dumiyati, which hails from an area in Cairo and mujadallah, a white cheese which is often described to look like 'a young girl's plaits'.

Each type of cheese - whether hard or soft - should be considered for its purpose. Very hard cheeses can be cut into wedges to eat in the mezza or grated for use as an ingredient in Arabic sweets (see chapter on sweets). Soft cheeses can be simply spread on bread, made into a dip or rolled into yoghurt balls (see facing page).

CLARIFIED BUTTER, OR GHEE

Samn

Ancient herders invented butter, one of the earliest methods of preserving milk. With most mammals, except that of the camel, milk can be made into butter by agitating it until the fat globules come together. The Bedouin 'mirjahah' and other nomadic tribes in the Middle East were known to use skins filled with milk in the butter-making process. Syria is known for its bright yellow butter made from ewe's milk.

Long ago, cooking oil was considered a delicacy in some regions of the Arab world. At one time, highly valued samn was purchased by the spoonful in the Gulf countries. This clarified or drawn butter, which will keep for many months, imparts a distinctive flavour when used in cooking or as a sauce for foods already prepared. Use sparingly, as butter is high in saturated fats. Advantageously, samn can withstand higher temperatures for frying than normal butter which burns at a fairly low temperature. Samn can also be stored unrefrigerated.

The process of clarifying, so the solid impurities can be taken off, is simply to simmer the butter for a half hour. The water will have evaporated, and the salts and sediments settled. Strain and store.

Clarified butter can be used for frying, sautéing or as a sauce to top cooked food. Regular butter can be used instead in many recipes, but the butter taste seems to be more enhanced after the clarifying process.

HARD-BOILED EGGS

Baid maslouk

Throughout the Arab world, ordinary hard-boiled eggs are flavoured and coloured, especially on special occasions such as the birthday of the prophet Mohammed, the pilgrimage to the sacred well or Eid which follows the month-long fast of Ramadan. Halved hard-boiled eggs adorn the bed of rice which surrounds festive qouzi, a whole roast lamb.

In the Arab world, special attention is devoted to the boiled egg, which is sometimes cooked slowly overnight. Add a drop or two of cooking oil to protect and coat the delicate shells. The whites are tanned and easily separated from the shell. On ordinary days, with the shells gently scrubbed,

eggs are added to stews and beans. Over the long, slow cooking time, the yolks are transformed so they have an almost creamy texture.

Commonly, plain boiled eggs are dipped into zaatar - a blend of thyme, sesame seed and tangy red sumac - or simply sprinkled with a mixture of salt and cumin.

Coloured eggs are served in the Levant on festive occasions. The addition of turmeric or saffron colours the eggs yellow, while a pinch of Arabic coffee is added for brown and purple onion skins for a soft lilac.

FRIED HARD-BOILED EGGS

Baid mutajjan

Tiny packages of blended spices wrapped up in cones of newspaper are sold in the streets of Cairo to flavour hard-boiled eggs. A selection of spices - zaatar, a thyme, sumac and sesame seed blend; duqqa, a ground chickpea and peanut blend or simply cumin and salt - are sprinkled on top of boiled eggs. (See spice blend recipes at the end of this book.)

To fry boiled eggs, first shell the egg and then prick with a fork or toothpick. Turn the eggs in hot oil until browned. The eggs can then be rolled in spices.

EGGS FRIED WITH GARLIC

Baid bil toum

Powerfully flavoured eggs, even for breakfast, exemplify the use of garlic in Arabic cooking. Tart lemon juice or sumac can be added to the sautéed garlic or sprinkled over once the eggs are fried. Crushed, green, refreshing mint enhances the colour and flavour when sprinkled over the top of fried eggs.

A Lebanese friend mentioned a special breakfast prepared by his grandmother when eggs were fried in qawwrama, mutton preserved in its own fat. Kisk, a soured mixture of wheat and milk which has been dried and powdered for *storage, is mixed with water, onions and garlic and finally fried with* qawwrama *for an old-fashioned egg and meat breakfast.*

4 eggs
2 cloves garlic, crushed
l tbsp lemon juice; or
1 tsp *sumac*
oil for shallow-frying
salt and pepper

GARNISH
dried mint, crushed

1 Sauté the garlic.

2 Add the eggs and fry gently until the eggs begin to set.

3 Sprinkle with the crushed mint, salt and pepper and lemon juice or *sumac*.

FRIED EGGS WITH LIVER

Kibbah wa baid

At the first sign of feeling weak, Arabs are known to breakfast on liver, considered to be a food of strength. Whole fried or scrambled eggs can be added to small cubes of fresh lambs' liver or whole chicken livers which have been sautéed in cinnamon and then topped with parsley.

4 oz (100g) lambs', calves' or chicken liver
4 eggs
2 cloves garlic, crushed
l tsp lemon juice
1/2 tsp cinnamon, ground
l tsp parsley, finely chopped
oil for shallow-frying
salt and pepper

1 Lightly sauté the liver with the garlic. Add the cinnamon, lemon juice and salt and pepper.

2 Add the eggs, lightly season with parsley and more salt and pepper. Fry until set.

EGGS WITH TOMATOES

Shakshouka

Arabs give scrambled eggs a new dimension. Sometimes a special sauce is prepared - stewed tomatoes, onions, salt and pepper - and mixed in with scrambled eggs or used to top eggs which have first been boiled and then finely chopped.

The simplest version is eggs fried with tomato slices, halves or quarters.

1 onion, chopped
1/2 capsicum pepper, chopped (opt)
4 small tomatoes, chopped
4 eggs, beaten
oil for sautéing
salt and pepper

1 Sauté the onion and capsicum peppers. Add the tomatoes and gently simmer until soft. Add the beaten eggs and salt and pepper to taste.

2 Simmer until the eggs are set.

3 Serve hot with Arabic bread.

VARIATION
● 5-6 heaped tablespoons of minced meat can be browned and added before serving.

THICK OMELETTE CAKES

Ujjah

Though translated as 'omelette', ujjah bears little resemblance to the texture, colour or flavour of omelette. The only similarity is that the eggs are beaten and combined with flavoursome ingredients.

Generally, ujjah consists of considerably less egg than omelette - just a little is used simply to hold together all the ingredients. The ratio of other ingredients to eggs is estimated at two-to-one. Firm through to the centre, ujjah hardly has the flavour of eggs at all, but is overpowered by the herbs, vegetables, potatoes, meat, fish or chicken.

The key to a successful ujjah is retention of moisture through slow, even cooking in a heavy frying pan with a tight-fitting lid. A heat diffuser is useful, especially with cooking rings that do not distribute heat evenly on low heat (a simple diffuser can be a metal plate of the same circumference slid underneath the pan). However, the mixture can also be slowly baked.

Turned out, the firm round cake is cut into wedges, and served hot or cold for breakfast, as a snack or in the mezza. Larger quiche-like wedges, usually with a meaty base, are part of a main course.

BASIC INGREDIENTS AND METHODS

12 oz (350g) main ingredients (see individual recipes)
4 eggs
oil for sautéing
salt and pepper

1 Wash and chop the herbs and vegetables or prepare the meats or nuts. Sauté in stages, according to cooking times.

2 Beat the eggs. Add all ingredients.

3 Pour the egg mixture into the hot, oiled heavy frying pan. Cover tightly and cook slowly for about 15 minutes or until the underside is brown and dry (use a heat diffuser if available - see above).

4 Carefully turn the *ujjah* to brown the other side by sliding it onto a plate, then putting it back into the pan upside down. Cover and cook slowly for a further 10-15 minutes or until the crust is brown and dry.

5 Serve cut into wedges accompanied with pickles, yoghurt and a salad.

● Vegetable *ujjah*: Any vegetable can be used alone or in combination with others, a total quantity of at least 12 oz (350g). Arabs usually select the fresh vegetables of the season. Thinly sliced or grated squash, cubed tomatoes or potatoes, chopped onions or spinach are but a few suggestions. Aubergines are sliced, salted and drained of their bitter juices (see p. 112). A few herbs and/or garlic can also be added.

A *suggested recipe*: Sauté 1 chopped onion, 2 cloves crushed garlic and 2 tbsp chopped parsley with 12 oz (350g) of vegetables, according to cooking time. Follow the method for preparing the basic *ujjah*.

Another variation is to add 5-6 tbsp minced meat with the vegetables.

● Herb *ujjah*: To the basic *ujjah* add the preferred herbs, finely chopped: 4 oz (110g) spinach, 6 tbsp spring onions, 4 tbsp parsley, mint, and chives and 2 tbsp chervil, watercress, basil and/or dill. Sauté the herbs with 1/2 tsp turmeric. Add 5 saffron threads crushed with 1 tsp sugar. Follow the method for preparing the basic *ujjah*.

● Garlic *ujjah*: In many areas of the Arab world, garlic is believed to have curative medical properties. This particular *ujjah*, believed to purify the blood and speed up recovery, is offered to women following childbirth.

One Arab recommended eight cloves of crushed garlic to four eggs - a recipe he said was designed to cure or kill!

● Chicken or meat *ujjah*: The spices vary to complement the choice of meat, chicken or fish. For example, minced meat may be seasoned with onion, cumin and parsley; chicken with ground cardamom, turmeric and parsley, and fish with paprika, lemon juice, and mint or coriander. Tender lamb or calf brains are poached in lemon juice (see p. 17). The membrane is removed, and the brains are chopped, salted and peppered.

Vegetables, such as potatoes, can be substituted for equal portions of meat, poultry or fish. Follow the method for preparing basic *ujjah*.

Ujjah

Kharouf

MEAT

THE SHIP AND THE SHEPHERD

Some 10,000 to 12,000 years ago, in one of the earliest stages of civilisation, the domestication of animals began. As nomadic herdsmen roamed from place to place in order to provide food and water for their animals, a tradition of herding was born that still characterises some aspects of Arabian life.

A special relationship, that between mankind and the camel, began four or five thousand years ago in southern Arabia. 'The Ship of the Desert' is thought originally to have been used as a beast of burden, but in addition camels were - and still are - prized for their meat.

Generally though, camels, sheep and goats would provide milk and wool for clothing, while their valued meat was reserved for special events, such as sacrifices or festivals. (The shepherds would eat game as their source of protein.) Even today important occasions - such as the birth of a child, circumcisions, or weddings - are marked by the slaughter of a lamb. Some Arabs plan well in advance of a special event, actually buying a live lamb or two to bring home and fatten in anticipation of the occasion. A speciality in the Arab World is milk-fed baby lamb, usually three or four weeks old and weighing 9-11 lbs (4-5 kilos).

The status symbol of slaughtering a lamb - a ceremony akin to 'the killing of the fatted calf' - also goes hand-in-hand with the charitable tradition of giving half to the poor or less fortunate. Islamic countries are known for their orange-spotted sheep, their wool has been dyed with henna to mark them for a forthcoming feast.

In the Middle East it can be difficult to distinguish sheep from goats - they have both been crossbred and, like the camel, can survive in arid conditions. One distinctive type of sheep typical of the region is the fat-tailed variety, adapted by

nature so that the animal is able to store nutrients in the tail, much as camels can in their humps. A trip to the animal market, *souk*, will reveal stall after stall of bleating sheep that will later be slaughtered according to the strict religious guidelines of the *halal* method. Before proceeding with their slaughter, the Moslem butcher must first proclaim '*bismillah*', 'in the name of God'.

Most meats are sold both from traditional outdoor *souks* and indoor modern supermarkets, and while beef can be used in most of the meat-based recipes, lamb is by far the most favoured meat in the Middle East.

CAMEL

Jamal

First domesticated in the depths of south-eastern Arabia around 1300 BC, camels for centuries were used only for transport. More precious than jewels to the nomads, who depended on the humped beasts for their very survival, as food the beloved camel was usually passed over in favour of sheep or goats. These days, in the Gulf States, the camel is rarely eaten and is more often used as a source of milk - or seen on the race track! One camel dish, though, a tribal recipe similar to the qouzi (recipe follows), is served only in the Gulf. It is regarded as a rare delicacy, and is held in high esteem. However, camel meat is quite commonly eaten in some other regions of the Arab world during the winter, when sheep are considered too lean for butchering.

In preparation for a wedding or other feast in the Gulf countries a jointed camel may occasionally be found simmering slowly in a huge aluminium pot over an open fire. Chopped onions, saffron threads, cardamom pods, cinnamon bark, cloves, pierced loomi and peppercorns are added to the pot, which is occasionally stirred with a long-handled, oversized ladle.

We have heard of a whole young camel being stuffed with a whole roasted lamb, which had been filled with a whole chicken. The empty cavities were filled with rice, nuts, raisins and spices.

WHOLE ROAST LAMB

Qouzi

On special occasions a whole lamb or goat - either grilled, or stuffed and roasted - is laid on a huge tray, encircled with rice and rounds of Arabic bread. The celebration is typically held on the floor of a majlis (meeting place) or tent, to commemorate a wedding, birth, circumcision, religious event or even to inaugurate a new business or completion of a building. (For more details on cooking the lamb see pages 100-101.)

The qouzi, lamb, is usually marinated and then roasted on a turning spit over a trench of slow-burning coals. A huge arch-shaped oven called a tanour can also be used. A recipe steeped in tradition calls for stuffing the whole lamb or portions, along with spices, into an earthen jug, which is perched atop burning coals and subsequently buried in sand while gentle cooking continues from the retained heat. Often a portion of the qouzi is also allotted for the poor. Huge pots full of lamb quarters and heavy spices are a common sights at special events in the Gulf countries.

The ritual of the qouzi begins when the words 'bismillah' (in the name of God) are spoken as the animal is slain. The young lamb or goat can be prepared as qouzi mahshi, stuffed roast lamb (see below). In Saudi Arabia and some of the other Gulf countries the lamb is stuffed with spiced rice, a whole chicken and eggs.

STUFFED ROAST LAMB

Qouzi mahshi

SERVES 25
20-25 lb (10-12 kg) lamb
8 tbsp lemon juice
8 cloves garlic, crushed
10 cups long-grain rice
4 large onions, finely chopped
1 cup almonds or cashews
1/2 cup pistachios
1/2 cup pine nuts
4 tbsp *baharat*
2 tsp turmeric

1 tsp saffron threads
1/2 cup rose water (opt)
81/2 cups water
1/2 cup oil
salt

1 Rub the cleaned lamb with 3 tbsp *baharat*, 2 tsp turmeric, garlic, lemon juice, salt and 1/2 cup oil. Cover and leave overnight to marinate.

2 Soak the saffron in rose water for 10 minutes.

3 Wash and drain the rice.

4 To make the stuffing, sauté the onions in the remaining oil. Add 1 tbsp *baharat*, salt and the rice for a further 2 minutes. Add the water and bring to the boil, stirring occasionally. Cover and cook slowly for 10 minutes. Blanch the almonds to remove the skins. Add the nuts and the saffron rose water. Cover tightly and leave to stand until the liquid has been absorbed.

5 Stuff the cavity of the lamb with the rice filling. Sew up the opening with strong thread.

6 Grill over charcoal for 5-7 hours or bake at 250°F (175°C) until tender, basting occasionally with the marinade. The lamb may be covered to prevent dryness.

7 Serve the lamb on a large tray or platter, surrounded with the rice stuffing. (Traditionally the succulent meat is served by pulling off pieces, but it can equally well be carved.)

SHEEP'S HEAD

Ras kharouf

In the Roman period, Greek sailing ships would return from the ports of south India with their holds loaded with spices, of which pepper was a primary commodity. Although Arabian merchants usually acted as middlemen along the spice routes, they were less involved in the trading of pepper. Black peppercorns found their way to the Arab World, and they form an essential part of this traditional dish.

The auspicious status attached to lamb in the Arab world is demonstrated in the belief that almost every part of the lamb should be eaten, including the head. Sheep's head may sound a bit unpalatable, but can be eaten as a delicious spiced version of brawn, with the very tender meat held together by a jelly made from the stock. Alternatively, the head can be boiled with spices (including peppercorns), then the delicate meat removed and used as a topping for stock-soaked bread in the dish Fatta, *or* Thesrib (*see p. 78*).

1 sheep's head
1 large onion, chopped
2 cloves garlic, crushed
1 tbsp lemon juice
1 carrot, diced
4 celery stalks, chopped
4 cardamom, cracked
6 peppercorns
4 bay leaves
2 *loomi*, pierced twice
salt and pepper

1 Crack the skinned skull lengthwise with a cleaver (you can ask the butcher to do this) and soak in several changes of salted water.

2 Cover the head and the remaining ingredients with water and boil for 11/2-2 hours. Remove any scum as it forms.

3 Remove the head and reserve the strained stock. Remove the bones and slice the meat.

VARIATION
● To serve cold in a mould, boil some peas and carrots in salted water until tender. Drain and add chopped pickles. Layer the bottom of a cake mould with half the meat, vegetables and the remaining meat. Cover with stock from boiling the head. Refrigerate until the gel sets. Turn out onto a serving dish.

LAMB

Mansaf

Mansaf, *literally translated as the 'large tray' on which food is served, is actually a vast communal meal, consisting of layers of bread, rice and jointed lamb with a sauce poured over. The sauces range in flavour from a basic stock made from the juices of the boiled lamb to the more intense* jameed, *dried sheep's or goat's yoghurt, which has been crumbled and dissolved into the stock.*

Thickened cow's milk yoghurt sauce is more typical today and can be found in the dish known as laban ummo *in Syria and Lebanon, and as mansaf by Palestinians. In the dish* ummo (His Mother's Milk), *young tender lamb is stewed in ewe's milk - reflecting the limited cooking resources when the dish was developed. With or without yoghurt, whether sitting around the tray on the floor of a Bedouin tent, crossed-legged in a majlis (meeting place) or at a more urban Arab's dinner table, one thing is for certain: a tray of mansaf is a feast.*

SERVES 10

10-12 lb (5-6 kg) lamb, jointed
10 large onions, chopped
6 cloves garlic, crushed
2 tbsp lemon juice
6 oz (175g) dried yoghurt (*jameed*) or stabilised yoghurt (p. 52)
2 large Arabic bread
4 cups rice
2 cups mixed pine nuts and almonds
oil for sautéing

1 Sauté the onions and garlic. Add the lamb to sauté for a further 5-7 minutes or until slightly browned. Add water to cover and simmer for 1 hour or until tender. Remove the scum as it rises.

2 Separate the lamb from the stock. The stock is reduced with stabilised yoghurt or dried yoghurt (*jameed*). Stir in lemon juice.

3 Prepare rice with nuts (see p. 123)

4 To serve the *mansaf*, the Arabic bread is opened and placed on a tray. Rice is spooned onto the bread. The lamb pieces are then placed on the bed of nutty rice. The stock sauce is used to saturate the tray of *mansaf* and individual servings.

ROAST LEG OF LAMB

Fakhid kharouf

Leg of lamb should be roasted slowly for an evenly browned, tender and moist main-course dish that in the Arab world is consumed with heaps of bread, an occasional side bowl of smooth yoghurt and plenty of salad. In the once-vast terrains of the Empty Quarter of Arabia, the lack of water sources led the Bedouin tribes to substitute the milk of goats, sheep and camels in the cooking process. Today the meat is sometimes marinated and even cooked in a yoghurt stock.

4 lb (2 kg) leg of lamb
4 tbsp lemon juice
8 cloves garlic, crushed
2 tsp *baharat*
1/2 tsp turmeric or
1/4 tsp saffron threads
salt and pepper

GARNISH
sprigs of parsley or mint
lemon wedges

1 Mix the garlic, lemon juice, *baharat*, turmeric or saffron and salt and pepper.

2 Make 8 slits in the leg of lamb. Rub the meat, including inside the slits, with the mixture.

3 Marinate for 6 hours or overnight in the refrigerator.

4 Cover and bake at 250°F (120°C) gas 1/2 from 1-3 hours. Remove the cover and brown for a further 30 minutes.

5 Serve on a bed of rice, garnished with parsley or mint and lemon wedges.

Fakhid kharouf

LAMB STEWS

Murkat lahma

Known as yakhni to the Syrians and Lebanese, and tagine to the North Africans, meat stews are one of the most prominent features of Arabian cooking. In the past, meat was preserved in anticipation of winter, when sheep were considered too lean for slaughter. Sheep were fattened for butchering in late autumn, the fat cut from the carcass and rendered down in large brass pans. Mutton, preserved in its own fat, was placed in ceramic jugs and sealed with clay.

The preserved meat and fat, qawwrama, is occasionally used in lamb stew. Everyday dishes in the Arab world, stews are a breathtaking combination of flavours, textures and aromas which have been subtly blended and balanced. Sometimes, the stew is heavier on the vegetable side, with a little meat for flavouring, and accompanied by rice, wheat, pulses or bread. Any meat will suffice because stews are simmered slowly over a long period of time. Unlike chicken, the meat is commonly cubed and sautéed until brown before being added to the pot.

Herbs and spices selected for the stew can vary according to taste, but some of the most typical include onion, garlic, parsley and mild chilli peppers, as well as an array of vegetables. Pulses such as lentils and chickpeas are added to give bulk or to thicken a stew. A dash of wine vinegar or lemon juice and a few cloves of crushed garlic take away the strong flavour that can be found in mutton. The colour is adjusted by adding saffron for yellow, tomatoes for red and pomegranate juice for brown stews. Often nuts are added, including almonds, walnuts, pistachios or hazelnuts and occasionally raisins or fresh or dried fruits.

Although cooking times may differ with the contents, generally stews are covered and simmered gently over a low heat for several hours. However, reduce the liquid by half and stews can be covered and cooked in a moderate oven at 300°F (150°C) gas 2.

STEWED LAMB AND RICE

Qouzi laham al timman

Although this dish contains all the basic ingredients of qouzi mahshi *on p. 60, the scaled down Iraqi speciality of lamb and rice is served regularly with salad and Arabic bread. The delicately spiced lamb pieces are cooked to a glazed texture, served on a bed of fluffy rice and garnished with morsels of crusty rice.*

2 lb (1 kg) lamb, jointed
4 cloves garlic, crushed
2 large onions, chopped
4 tomatoes, peeled and chopped
1 tsp *baharat*
1 *loomi*, pierced twice
salt and pepper
crusty rice, *timman* (p. 120)

1 Sauté the onions and garlic. Add the lamb until browned.

2 Add the tomatoes, spices and enough water to cover the lamb. Cover and simmer for 2$^1/_2$ - 3 hours or until a thick sauce forms and the meat is tender.

3 Remove the *loomi* and the bones, if preferred. Serve on a bed of steaming hot *timman* rice, with Arabic bread and a green salad.

VARIATION
● *Habeet*, a similar dish is made in the same way by omitting the tomatoes and *loomi* and by adding malted vinegar to stew with the lamb.

MEATBALLS IN TOMATO SAUCE

Daoud basha

A dish with the look and flavour of Italian meatballs and spaghetti sauce, daoud basha *is eaten on a bed of rice or a combination of rice mixed with tiny vermicelli noodles.*

This dish is an amalgamation of ingredients which passed along major trading routes before finding a home where this dish is best-loved: Lebanon. Onions and garlic are combined with lamb. The cinnamon and nutmeg from the Spice Islands of the East blended perfectly with the allspice and tomatoes that Columbus brought from the New World. Pine nuts are native to the Mediterranean region.

2 lb (1 kg) finely minced lamb
1 onion, finely chopped
10 very small onions, peeled and whole
3 cloves garlic, crushed
8 tbsp pine nuts
3 tbsp tomato purée
$^1/_2$ tsp cinnamon, ground
$^1/_2$ tsp nutmeg, grated
$^1/_2$ tsp allspice, ground
oil for sautéing
salt and pepper

1 Add the finely chopped onion, garlic and salt and pepper to the meat. Shape into walnut-size balls.

2 Sauté the whole onions until golden.

3 Sauté the meatballs for about 10 minutes or until browned. Add the cinnamon, nutmeg, allspice and half the pine nuts for a further 2 minutes.

4 Mix the tomato purée with 3 cups water. Simmer for about 30 minutes or until the sauce has thickened.

5 Lightly fry the remaining pine nuts until golden. Press one nut into each meatball. Drop the meatballs into the tomato sauce and simmer for 5 minutes. Adjust the seasoning to taste with salt and pepper.

6 Serve hot with a separate platter of plain rice or rice mixed with vermicelli noodles (see p. 123). Serve each portion of *daoud basha* on a bed of rice or rice mixture.

OKRA/LADIES' FINGER STEW

Bamia

Cultivated around 575 AD, the rocket-shape pods of the okra plant (a relative of the cotton family) are native to Africa. The vegetable made its way to Mediterranean Europe via Egypt in the 13th century.

Although this okra dish is typically prepared using lamb, it can also be made with beef or veal. For a variation, the okra can be substituted with other vegetables: peas, aubergine, or a pulse such as chickpeas or lentils.

In Middle Eastern cooking, especially in the Levant countries where okra is abundant, attempts are made to reduce the gluey quality of the cooked vegetable. To prevent stickiness, they can be soaked for 30 minutes to an hour in vinegar, lemon juice or a mixture of vinegar and water before cooking. Alternatively, okra can be sprinkled with salt and left in the sun for an hour to dry, a common sight in the Mediterranean countries where tiny pods are threaded onto strings in open marketplaces alongside garlic. Great care is often taken to pare off the stalk, without cutting into the pod, or by simply frying first, both of which help reduce glutinosity. A little sugar cuts the acidity of the tomatoes and the lemon juice adjusts the tartness.

1 lb (500g) lamb, cubed
1 large onion, chopped
2 cloves garlic, crushed
8 oz (225g) fresh okra/ladies' fingers
4 tomatoes, peeled and chopped
2 tbsp tomatoes purée
2 tbsp lemon juice
1 tsp sugar
oil for sautéing
stock or water
salt and pepper

1 Sauté the meat with the onions and garlic.

2 Add the tomatoes, tomato purée, salt and pepper, and cover with stock or water. Cover and simmer for 30 minutes or until the sauce has thickened. Adjust the seasoning by adding lemon juice, sugar and more salt.

3 Remove the stems and sauté the okra for several minutes. Add to the tomato sauce and simmer for a further 10 minutes or until the okra is tender.

4 Serve with onion rice (p. 121) or burgul (p. 126).

Timman bagella

BROAD BEANS IN RICE

Timman bagella

Cultivated by the ancient Egyptians, broad or fava beans are green when fresh, frozen or tinned. The dried beige-brown variety, although not normally used in this Iraqi recipe, must be pre-soaked and cooked for 15 minutes before the rice is added. Pungent fresh dill lends aromatic properties to the dish. Palestinians add garlic and yoghurt for the dish called foul bil laban, *omitting the dill altogether.*

2 lb (1 kg) lamb, cubed
1 tsp *baharat*
1 large onion, chopped
1 cup green broad beans
2 cups long-grain rice, washed
1 cup fresh dill, finely chopped
oil for sautéing
salt

1 Sauté the meat and onions and add the *baharat*.

2 Place the broad beans in 2¹/₂ cups salted boiling water for 5 minutes. Add the rice.

3 Cover and simmer for 15-20 minutes or until the rice is tender. Add the dill and leave to stand for 10 minutes.

4 Serve the sautéed meat on a bed of rice. Accompany with yoghurt and pickles.

SPICED RICE WITH LAMB

Machbous

Machbous *has some similarities with* biryani, *which originated from India and was brought to the Gulf states during trade and cultural exchanges - the meat and rice are cooked together in one pot. Loomi, a small sour lime which has been dried, may have made its way to Europe when citrus fruit was introduced to Spain by the Arabs and later across the Atlantic to the Americas with Columbus.*

Cinnamon, one of the essential ingredients, was at one time the queen of all spices - the most expensive and sought-after seasoning of early time.

Richly spiced long-grain rice with lamb, chicken or fish is the essence of machbous, *which in the Gulf countries is sometimes a whole leg or shoulder, bone removed, and stuffed. Gigantic aluminium pots of* machbous *floating with whole spices are a common sight at celebrations in the Arabian Peninsula, especially at outdoor weddings. This recipe calls for the spices to be ground and mixed in* baharat. *However, the cardamom, cinnamon, cloves,* loomi *and peppercorns are more commonly left whole in the Gulf recipes. If left whole, rather than ground, a little more of each spice should be used as the whole version is less pungent.*

2 lb (1 kg) lamb, jointed
2 large onions, chopped
4 tomatoes, peeled and chopped
2 tbsp parsley, chopped
1 tbsp *baharat*
$^1/_2$ tsp *loomi*, ground
4-5 saffron threads or
$^1/_2$ tsp turmeric
2 cups long-grain rice, washed
$2^1/_2$ cups stock or water
oil for sautéing
salt and pepper

1 Sauté the onions with the lamb.

2 Add the *baharat*, saffron or turmeric, tomatoes, *loomi*, chopped parsley, salt and pepper and stock or water. Cover and simmer for 30 minutes.

3 Stir the rice into the boiling stock. Cover and simmer over a low heat for 20 minutes or until the rice is tender, dry and separate.

4 Serve with salad, Arabic bread and pickles.

LAMB AND APRICOTS

Mishmishiya

Apricots were originally grown in China and transported westwards. Coriander from the East must have been combined with the sweet fruit and lamb by Arab herdsmen somewhere along the Silk Road.

This dish can be prepared with other dried fruits, or a combination of fresh and dried. Moroccans use currants, prunes, quinces and apples, left whole or sliced.

2 lb (1 kg) lamb, cubed
8 oz (225g) dried apricots
2 onions, finely chopped
6 tbsp almonds, chopped
$^1/_4$ tsp ginger, ground
$^1/_4$ tsp cumin, ground
$^1/_2$ tsp coriander, ground
$^1/_4$ tsp cinnamon, ground
3-4 saffron threads
oil for sautéing
salt and pepper

1 Soak the dried apricots in water for several hours.

2 Sauté the onions and the lamb. Cover with water and simmer until tender. Remove any scum.

3 Simmer the apricots for 15-20 minutes. Drain and blend until puréed.

4 Add the apricots, almonds, saffron, ginger, coriander, cumin, cinnamon and salt and pepper to the simmering lamb.

5 Continue to simmer over a low diffused fire (or in a low oven) for $1^1/_2$ hours or until the sauce thickens.

6 Serve hot with plain or yellow rice (p.120).

COUSCOUS STEW

Couscous, or Maghrebiya

A *well of fine grain filled with savoury stew* is the celebrated dish of Morocco, Tunisia and Algeria. Although a similar maghrebiya *or* maftoul *is prepared in other parts of the Arab world without vegetables, the North African couscous is most distinctive - served in a tagine, a special red-clay cone-topped dish, and a typical adornment at any wedding feast. To the many subtle spices Tunisians add cayenne, chilli or* harissa - *a red pimento concentrate - for a fiery stew.*

The grain itself, couscous, *is a type of delicate semolina made from wheat, which is ground and rolled in fine flour (see pages 126-127). The dried grain cooks quickly, but needs to absorb a large amount of water to soften it, usually through steaming - it is usually prepared in a special steamer called a* couscousier. *Alternatively, the grains can be softened in a double steamer or in a sieve placed on top of the simmering stew.*

The combination of vegetables for the stew, which according to a Moroccan friend should include at least seven, varies from place to place and is left to the cook's own preference. Meat, chicken or fish can be cubed and added. The colour is determined by the addition of saffron or turmeric, tomato purée or parsley. Note that the stew can be prepared the day before serving, so that the meat marinades in the spices - see below.

1 lb (500g) *couscous*
6 tbsp oil or *samn*
salt
STEW
2 lb (1 kg) lamb, cubed
5 large onions, chopped
4 cloves garlic, crushed
4 large tomatoes, peeled and quartered
8 oz (225g) boiled chickpeas
3 carrots, sliced
4 oz (100g) green beans, squash/courgettes, turnips and/or aubergines, cubed
1 capsicum pepper, wedged
2 tbsp parsley, finely chopped
1 tbsp paprika

1/4 tsp cumin, ground
oil for sautéing
salt and pepper
COLOURING
3-4 saffron threads or
1/2 tsp turmeric or
2 tbsp tomato purée or
3 tbsp parsley, finely chopped

1 To prepare the stew, sauté the onions and garlic. Add the meat cubes and sauté until lightly browned.

2 Add vegetables in turn, depending on the cooking time they require, with sufficient water to cover, and the spices or herbs for colouring.

3 At this stage the mixture can be refrigerated overnight to allow the spices to marinate with the cooked meat and vegetables. In this case the cooking is continued the following day.

4 To prepare the *couscous*, moisten by gradually adding salted water, stirring gently to allow the grains to swell. Rub the grains of *couscous* between the fingers to remove any lumps. Allow to stand for 10 minutes. Coat evenly with the oil or *samn*.

5 Put the *couscous* in a sieve or double steamer and place on top of the simmering stew. Cover and steam for 30-45 minutes or until each grain softens, raking the grains occasionally to help them swell. Pre-cooked *couscous* is steamed for about 15 minutes. The stew will cook as the *couscous* steams.

6 Serve the meat and vegetables from the stew surrounded with *couscous*. Serve the sauce separately.

VARIATION
● Cayenne, chilli pepper or *harissa* (see p. 44) can be added to give the stew more 'bite'.

● *Maghrebiya* is commonly prepared in the same way as *couscous*, omitting the tomatoes and tomato purée.

Couscous stew

STEW OVER BREAD

Fatta hummos

Fatta, thesrib *or* thareed: *the dish is well loved throughout the region, though it goes by different names in Egyptian, Palestinian, Iraqi or the Gulf lands. A rich meat or chicken stock is poured over a dish of bread, and left to soak before being eaten. Any pieces of bread, sometimes toasted first, can be used to make the dish. The best bread to use is an almost paper-thin Arabic bread called* shraak. *Layered bread dishes enjoy immense popularity throughout the Arab world and may include a variety of ingredients, including one regal recipe which calls for the meat from a lamb's head. Fatta may also incorporate a layer of rice, puréed chickpeas or yoghurt atop the saturated bread. Thareed, a meat soup with potatoes and other vegetables, is poured directly over the bread.*

An Iraqi family-style recipe, thesrib *is generally made with lamb, but beef can be substituted. The meat is layered with saturated bread. The final layer of meat is topped with butter or* samn *and yoghurt, and sprinkled with crushed garlic. Other recipes of similar nature can be found in the chicken section on p. 78.*

1 lb (500g) lamb, cubed or minced
8 oz (225g) dried chickpeas
1 onion, chopped
3 cloves garlic, crushed
1 tsp *baharat*
1/4 tsp cumin, ground
3 tbsp lemon juice
1 green chilli pepper, chopped (opt)
3 fl oz (75ml) *tahina*
2 tbsp pine nuts
1 tsp *sumac* (opt)
salt
2 tbsp *samn* or butter
1 large Arabic bread, toasted

1 Soak the chickpeas overnight in water to cover.

2 Sauté the onion and the lamb in *samn* or butter. Add the *baharat*, pine nuts (reserve a few for garnish) and salt and pepper. Sauté until lightly browned.

3 Drain and wash the chickpeas. Boil in water to cover with the cumin until tender. Add a heaped tsp of salt and simmer for another 5 minutes. Drain, reserving 1 1/2 cups of the cooking liquid.

4 Blend the chickpeas with the *tahina*, lemon juice, chilli pepper, garlic and the reserved cooking liquid.

5 Toast the Arabic bread and break into small pieces.

6 Layer the bread, chickpeas and meat into a serving bowl. Top with remaining pine nuts and *sumac*.

VARIATION

● *Fatta* is also made by layering 1 1/2 cups cooked rice over the bread instead of the chickpeas. If rice is used, the stew needs to be more liquid, so another cup of water should be added to the cooked meat and pine nut mixture before the dish is compiled.

Toyour
FOWL
EASTERN FEASTS

In Arabian cooking, poultry is transformed into a royal feast, from the regal *fesanjune* (which was once prepared with peacock for the nobility) to *assafir*, tiny birds fried whole by the Lebanese. Duck, geese, quail, turkey and pigeon are still served on occasion.

Among the many breeds of ancient fowl was the enormous Cochin China fowl. Another, the peacock, of Indian origin, was brought westwards along the Frankincense and Spice Routes by East African traders. Turkey, originally from America, and pheasant, which was introduced to Europe several centuries ago from the East, are more modern festive fowl.

Chicken is popular throughout the Middle East, and is often seen at street-side cafés, with sometimes 20 or 30 turning on the rods of a glass-encased rôtisserie. A whole roasted chicken along with all the trimmings - garlic mayonnaise, *hummos*, pickles and salad - often costs just a couple of dollars.

Chicken is transformed into a gourmet's delight by the simple addition of spices and a few modified cooking methods. *Sumac*, a dark red spice, is a feature of *thesrib* and of *musakhan* ('She Has Fever') chicken - both of which are usually eaten with the hands. Chicken is often cooked with the Middle Eastern favourites of yoghurt or dates, and is also puréed to make *hariss*, which is sometimes eaten for breakfast like a porridge.

For the enterprising, a pigeon recipe is included. A version of this recipe is served at the numerous so-called 'casinos' (outdoor cafés) just outside the centre of Cairo, along the River Nile.

TART CHICKEN

Musakhan

A thick stock of chicken and nuts, heavy with onions, is almost a meal in itself. We were once told that the dish was given its name musakhan *(roughly translated as 'she has fever'), because of the sprinkling with the reddish, sour* sumac *spice that is essential to attain the unique taste.*

Generally thought to be of Palestinian origin, the spiced chicken was traditionally baked with the bread in a tabon, a clay oven. Only a few Arabs can still tell of the old custom of baking chicken in this special oven.

Musakhan *is served on a tray lined with paper-thin bread, and most easily eaten with the hands by pulling the saturated bread into pieces and picking the chicken off the bones.*

2 lb (1 kg) chicken
2 large loaves of thin Arabic bread
5 large onions, quartered
$^1/_4$ tsp cinnamon, ground
$^1/_4$ tsp nutmeg, grated
6 tbsp *sumac*
4 tbsp pine nuts
2 tbsp lemon juice
1 stock cube or stock (see p. 47)
8 tbsp olive oil
salt and pepper

1 Simmer the whole or jointed chicken in enough stock to cover (or in water with stock cube added) for 20 minutes or until almost tender. Remove the chicken and reserve the stock.

2 Rub the chicken with lemon juice, 1 tbsp *sumac*, pepper, cinnamon and nutmeg. Bake at 350°F (175°C) gas 4 for 20 minutes or until browned.

3 Meanwhile, sauté the onions in 4 tbsp olive oil with 2 tbsp *sumac*. Add the pine nuts and sauté until golden.

4 Mix 3 cups of reserved chicken stock with 4 tbsp olive oil (less if the stock is fatty).

5 When ready to serve, spread the bread onto a serving dish and sprinkle with the remaining *sumac*. Saturate the bread with the stock and oil mixture. Place the chicken pieces and the onion mixture on top of the bread. Pour over a little more stock to ensure saturation. Serve the remaining stock separately.

VARIATION

● The chicken and the bread dough can be baked together, using the dough recipe on p. 137. Shape the dough into 4 balls and place on an oiled pan. Brush the dough with 2 tbsp oil. Place the chicken and sautéed onions on top and bake for 45 minutes at 350°F (175°C) gas 4.

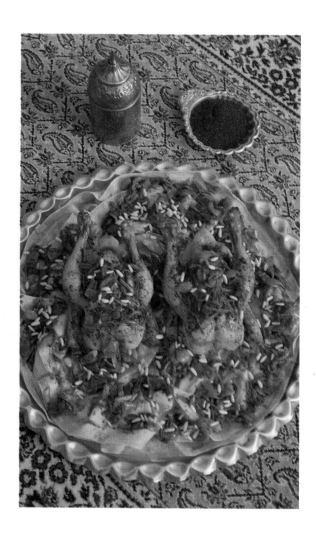

ROAST STUFFED CHICKEN

Dahah mahshi

At special Middle Eastern feasts, a lamb is often roasted and stuffed. However, chicken filled with nuts, rice or fruit, and sometimes perfumed with rose water, can also often be seen adorning huge platters at banquets.

Thought to be a speciality of the Assyrians, stuffed roast chicken has gained in prominence throughout the Arab world. A distinctive Gulf version, machbous al dajaj, features the additional ingredients of chickpeas, cardamom, blanched almonds, boiled eggs, cinnamon, saffron, rose water and dried lime. In Algeria the chicken is glazed with honey and stuffed with couscous and sultanas. Palestinians make a similar dish using farika, an unripened cracked wheat, instead of rice, and almonds rather than pine nuts. The stuffing can be varied to include the giblets or other meats and vegetables, but the nuts and rice in this dish exude the characteristic, exquisite flavour of Arabia.

3 lb (1 1/2 kg) chicken with giblets
1 cup long-grain rice, washed
5 tbsp pine nuts or almonds
2 cloves garlic, crushed
2 tbsp spring onions, finely chopped
2 tbsp parsley, finely chopped
2 tbsp honey (opt)
oil for sautéing
salt and pepper

1 Rub the cleaned chicken with the garlic, honey, salt and pepper.

2 To easily remove the thin skins from the almonds, pour boiling water over them and rinse in cold water. Lightly sauté the coarsely chopped giblets, parsley, spring onions and almonds or pine nuts. Stir in the rice for another 2-3 minutes.

3 Add salt to taste and 3/4 cup water. Simmer on a low heat for about 10 minutes or until the water has been absorbed.

4 Spoon the rice mixture into the cavity of the cleaned chicken. Secure the opening with a skewer or thread.

5 Bake at 350°F (175°C) gas 4 for 1 hour or until tender and browned.

6 Serve with Arabic bread and a mixed salad.

VARIATION

● The rice in the stuffing can be replaced with farika, an unripened cracked wheat.

UPSIDE DOWN

Makluba

Makluba *is a popular favourite, yet it can be tricky to prepare. The dish is made in a mould, and then turned out when firm, giving it a cake-like appearance. The key to maintaining the shape is to control the amount of liquid added to the rice, particularly by soaking the rice before cooking. There are two distinct versions of 'upside down' - one with tomatoes and one without - and Arabs swear by both. Some cooks add potatoes or cauliflower (which is recorded as having come from the Orient and been carried to the European Continent in the 12th century by Arabs) to the dish.*

Makluba *can also be prepared with lamb as well as with boneless chicken pieces.*

2 lb (1 kg) chicken
2 large onions, chopped
3 medium aubergines/eggplants, sliced
4 potatoes, peeled and sliced (opt)
6 tomatoes, peeled and sliced (opt)
$1/2$ tsp cinnamon, ground
$1/2$ tsp nutmeg, grated
2 cups long-grain rice
oil for sautéing
salt and pepper

GARNISH
3 tbsp pine nuts

1 Wash the rice and soak for 15 minutes.

2 Slice the aubergines. Sprinkle with salt and place in a colander. Place a heavy plate or weight on top and leave for an hour to drain the bitter juices. Wash and pat dry. Fry the aubergines until lightly browned on both sides.

3 Sauté the chicken and onions.

4 Layer the aubergines, tomatoes, potatoes, chicken and drained rice in a heavy pan or casserole.

5 To make the sauce, add salt to taste, cinnamon, nutmeg and cloves to 2 cups water or enough to cover the rice.

6 Cover and slowly simmer for about 35 minutes or until the rice is tender and the liquid absorbed. Add extra water only if it is needed to soften the rice.

7 Place the pot with the contents in cold water for a few minutes, which allows the *makluba* to pull away from the sides. Turn upside down, by placing a serving dish over the top. Turn the pot upside down onto the serving dish. Tap on the bottom so the contents are released undisturbed.

8 The result should be a cake-like mould of layered vegetables and rice. Garnish with a few sprigs of parsley and serve with yoghurt and a salad.

VARIATIONS

● *Capsa*, a Saudi Arabian speciality, is prepared with 7 fl oz (200ml) tomato purée, tomatoes and cubes of lamb.

● Like aubergine, $1/2$ head of cauliflower florets can be fried and used as a layer in the stew.

CHICKEN WITH WALNUTS AND POMEGRANATE

Fesanjune, or Yakhni baza

Fesanjune *is a sweet-and-sour dish fit for royalty. It was for generations served to the royal court and its guests. This recipe was once prepared with peacock. The original name for these proud birds is believed to come from a Southern Indian Tamil dialect. Peacocks were traded by East African Arabs along the Frankincense Trail and Spice Routes.*

Today fesanjune *is still prepared for some Iraqi weddings, other special celebrations or to honour dinner guests and is commonly prepared with game birds.*

Because of its ready availability, chicken is generally used now, and is boiled and boned instead of being used roasted whole, as in the traditional version.

In several regions of the Arab World, meats are combined with sweet fruit or juice, giving a sweet-and-sour flavour.

Makluba

Quince, a fruit related to the pear and apple, is used in some North African countries, especially in Moroccan lamb or chicken stews.

Pomegranate, originally from southern or western Asia, spread west along the Silk Route. Phoenicians popularised the fruit in the West and the Romans got theirs from Carthage.

The seeds of the fruit are often sprinkled on meat and chicken dishes in the Middle East as a garnish, but more importantly are used in main courses for their sweet-sour combination. If the opportunity arises, you might try making a separate rich sauce from fresh pomegranates to be ladled over wild duck, pheasant, turkey or quail.

2 lb (1 kg) chicken or game birds
8 oz (225g) walnuts, chopped or minced
1 large onion, chopped
5 tbsp pomegranate syrup or
juice of 4 pomegranates plus
2 tbsp lemon juice and
1 tbsp sugar
oil for sautéing
salt and pepper

GARNISH
5 tbsp walnuts, chopped
pomegranate seeds

1 Boil the poultry until tender.

2 Sauté the onion. Add the ground walnuts, poultry, pomegranate syrup or juice and water to cover. (If using fresh pomegranate seeds, boil in a little water for 5 minutes. Cool and strain the seeds. To get the juice, push the flesh through a sieve. The sugar and lemon juice must be added to the fresh pomegranate juice. The syrup can be used without the sugar and lemon juice addition.)

3 Simmer for about 15 minutes or until the sauce has thickened. Adjust seasoning and water as required.

4 Serve on a bed of plain rice. Garnish with fresh pomegranate seeds and chopped walnuts.

CHICKEN WITH VEGETABLES

Tagine dajaj

Tagine, a North African word for stew, is also the name of the dish in which the chicken is cooked. The tagine, a round wide earthenware dish with a sharply conical tight-fitting lid, usually sits on charcoal to cook slowly until the liquid has been reduced to a thick savoury sauce.

Dates, the most beloved fruit in the Arab world, can replace other vegetables. Moroccans stew their chicken with prunes or cooking apples and sauté quail with grapes. The ingredients used can vary with the meat, vegetables and spices of the cook's choice and the stew is commonly served upon a cone-shaped mound of couscous.

2 lb (1 kg) chicken, jointed
8 oz (225g) boiled chickpeas
4 onions, chopped
3 cloves garlic, crushed
1 capsicum pepper, wedged
3 tomatoes, peeled and chopped
2 carrots, sliced
4 oz (100g) squash/courgettes, green beans, or other vegetables, chopped or sliced
2 tbsp parsley, finely chopped
1 tsp paprika
1/4 tsp cumin, ground
2-3 bay leaves
4-5 saffron threads or
1/2 tsp turmeric
oil for sautéing
salt and pepper

1 Sauté the onion, garlic and chicken pieces.

2 Add the remaining ingredients with water to cover. Simmer for 30 minutes or until the chicken is tender, adding water as required. Adjust the seasoning to taste.

3 Serve over a bed of *couscous* or rice.

CHICKEN WITH YOGHURT

Dajaj souryani

In ancient times this dish was a favourite of the Assyrians - like the best of Arabian dishes it has been passed down through the generations, from mother to daughter, yet has seldom been recorded.

The special blend of yoghurt, almonds and sumac gives a hint of the richness and sophistication of that ancient culture. The dish can be made without sumac, if unavailable, however the flavour will be milder and less lemony.

Like many Arabic dishes, this dajaj souryani is typically eaten with the fingers. Newspaper is first spread on a carpeted floor, while guests sit cross-legged on cushions, each scooping, from a central platter, their share of the succulent chicken with rice.

2 lb (1 kg) chicken, jointed
2 cups long-grain rice, washed
2 onions, chopped
1 cup stabilised yoghurt (see p. 52)
3 tbsp almonds, whole or slivered
salt and pepper
GARNISH
1 tbsp *sumac*

1 Boil the chicken pieces and onions in enough water to cover for about 20 minutes. Strain, reserving the stock.

2 Combine the chicken, yoghurt, almonds, rice, 1 3/4 cups of the stock and salt and pepper.

3 Bake at 350°F (150°C) gas 4 for 45 minutes or until the rice is tender.

4 Garnish with *sumac*. Serve accompanied with pickles, Arabic bread and a salad.

MELOKHIYA

Melokhiya

There is no translation for the word melokhiya, *a stalky green vegetable of the mallow family, which is the base for stews used to top rice and usually meat. The oblong leaves are shaped like a cross between mint and spinach, but have the viscous property of okra, and are available from specialist shops fresh, frozen or dried.*

Chicken is conventionally either mixed with the green leaves or the stew is ladled over a roasted bird. Wild rabbit has been replaced with its domesticated counterpart and is still grilled and sometimes used in the place of lamb or chicken in melokhiya.

Fresh melokhiya *is prepared in traditional Arab fashion by pulling each individual leaf off its stalk, washing several times, drying and finally chopping with a* makhrata, *a crescent-shaped two-handled blade. The leaves, only 3 inches long (7.5 cm), can be left whole for beginners, but the best Arab cooks agree that, whether whole or chopped, the greens must be sautéed to prevent them becoming too glutinous.*

The best recipe I have ever sampled was prepared by a Lebanese businessman. The ingredients were layered: a bed of white rice mixed with golden fried vermicelli, sprinkled with toasted and broken Arabic bread, ladled atop with pieces of chicken and lamb mixed in with the melokhiya *and finally drizzled with chunky vinegary onions.*

2 lb (1 kg) chicken, lamb, or rabbit
2 lb (1 kg) fresh or frozen *melokhiya* or
6 oz (175g) dried *melokhiya*
2 onions, chopped
3 cloves garlic, crushed
1 tsp lemon juice
salt and pepper
TO SERVE
4 cups rice with vermicelli noodles (p. 123)
onions and vinegar (p. 47)
1 large loaf of Arabic bread

1 Boil and bone the chicken, lamb or rabbit. Reserve the stock.

2 Chop and sauté the *melokhiya*, if fresh.

3 Sauté the onions and garlic.

4 Boil the stock and add the meat, onions, garlic and *melokhiya* to simmer. If using fresh *melokhiya* simmer for 5-10 minutes. Dried *melokhiya* is simmered for 20-30 minutes. The *melokhiya* should remain suspended in the stock. Add the lemon juice according to taste. Season.

5 Toast and chip the opened Arabic bread.

6 Serve separately for each individual to layer their dish with rice, chipped Arabic bread, *melokhiya* stew, and a spoon of the vinegar and onions.

VARIATION

● If *melokhiya* is unavailable, spinach cooked with rabbit in this manner is lovely, though the other meats do not work well with spinach.

CHICKEN OVER BREAD

Thesrib, or Fatta

Curiously, stews and soups are poured over toasted pieces of bread and topped with strong garlic and smooth yoghurt, until the bread fuses with a rich spice blend called baharat. Saturated bread, although unfamiliar to Westerners, is common in the Arab world, going by the names fatta, thesrib *or* thareed, *depending on the country.*

The dish was probably at one time prepared with tripe and lambs' feet. Present-day variations call for broad beans or chickpeas. Chopped, tender lambs' tongue or meat from the head are also traditionally added to fatta *and* thesrib. *For the dish* fatta, *omit the yoghurt from the list of ingredients below, but add a layer of rice, chickpeas or broad beans. For* thareed, *the meat soup with potatoes is poured over the bread (see p. 69).*

The best bread to use for this exceptional dish is paperthin shraak, *slightly thicker* rukak *or any leftover pieces of almost stale Arabic bread.*

2 lb (1 kg) chicken
1 large onion, chopped
2 tsp *baharat*
oil for sautéing
salt and pepper

TO SERVE
1 1/2 large loaves of Arabic bread, toasted
1/2 pt (275ml) yoghurt
3 cloves garlic, crushed
1 tbsp *tahina* (opt)
2 tbsp pine nuts

1 Sauté the onion. Boil and bone the chicken. Return the chicken pieces to 2 cups of the stock, adding *baharat*, the sautéed onions and salt and pepper. Simmer for 15 minutes.

2 Toast and break the opened Arabic bread.

3 Layer the bread and the chicken sauce in a bowl, adjusting the liquid to saturate the bread. Top with the yoghurt and sprinkle with the garlic, *tahina* and lightly fried pine nuts.

VARIATION
● *Thareed* is made by adding 3 peeled and chopped potatoes and tomatoes with 2 tbsp tomato paste and the onions, garlic and spices to the boiling lamb pieces. Do not use the yoghurt and pine nut topping.

● *Fatta* is made by layering 1 1/2 cups cooked rice over the bread. If using rice, add another cup of water to the cooking chicken or meat to later saturate the bread and rice.

CURRIED CHICKEN

Salonat al dajaj

Truly a recipe from the Gulf countries. The particular spice combination used in this dish must have migrated to the Arabian peninsula from the sub-continent with the dhows, *trading vessels that criss-crossed the Indian Ocean on the Spice Routes. Baharat, a special spice blend (see glossary), is an essential ingredient of the salonat and contains brown, dried limes (loomi), ginger, cinnamon, turmeric and chilli, sometimes accompanied by nutmeg, coriander, cumin, cloves and cardamom. Ground peppercorns - used as currency during the Middle Ages to pay taxes, dowries and tolls - are included in the spice blend.*

Served on sweet muhammar *rice, or rice with onions,* mashkoul, *the dish is often garnished with slices of boiled egg .*

2 lb (1 kg) chicken, jointed
2 large onions, finely chopped
4 tomatoes, peeled and chopped
3 cloves garlic, crushed
1 *loomi*, pierced twice
1/4 tsp chilli pepper, ground
1/2 tsp cinnamon
1 tsp turmeric
2 tsp *baharat*
oil for sautéing
salt and pepper

1 Coat the chicken pieces with 1 tsp *baharat* and 1/2 tsp turmeric. Leave to stand for 30 minutes.

2 Sauté the chicken with the onions, garlic, chilli powder, cinnamon and the remaining *baharat* and turmeric.

3 Add the tomatoes, *loomi*, water to cover and salt and pepper to taste. Cover and simmer for about 1 1/2 hours or until the chicken is tender and the sauce has thickened.

4 Serve with rice, pickles, Arabic bread and a salad.

CHICKEN AND WHEAT

Hariss bil dajaj

The sight of women seated on the floor, pounding whole wheat grains with pestle and mortar, is still characteristic of the Gulf countries. Hariss, which means 'well cooked' is a wheat purée with added chicken or meat. It is a dish frequently served alongside dates during Ramadan, after the fast is broken at sunset. Occasionally, the paste has a little extra water added, and is sprinkled with sugar or drizzled with honey to make a hearty breakfast.

12 oz (350g) polished whole wheat grains
1 lb (500g) chicken or lamb
1/2-1 tsp cinnamon, ground
2 tbsp butter or *samn*
salt and pepper

1 Soak the wheat in water overnight. Rinse and drain.

2 To make the stock, boil the chicken or lamb in water to cover for 1 hour or until tender and falling apart. Remove from the stock and then the bone.

3 Add the wheat, cinnamon and salt and pepper to the boiling stock. Simmer gently for about 2 hours or until the wheat is very tender.

4 Purée the wheat or pound with a pestle and mortar. Purée the chicken or meat and add to the wheat.

5 Serve hot with *samn* or melted butter and a sprinkling of cinnamon, if preferred.

VARIATIONS

● A chopped onion and a peeled and chopped tomato may be added during the cooking of the wheat.

● Cumin and ground cloves can be used for added flavour.

CHICKEN WITH NOODLES

Dajaj macaroni

Other than vermicelli served mixed with rice, pasta is a rarity in traditional Arab cooking. However, noodles, which incidentally gained in popularity in the west following Marco Polo's visit to China in 1270, found a way into the food of Arabs somewhere along the trading routes. Gadgets for making pasta have been found in the ruins of Pompeii and macaroni is mentioned in writings from as early as 1200.

This recipe is a simpler version of its celebrated Italian counterpart, which also employs the tomato, brought from the New World by Columbus.

2 lb (1 kg) chicken
1 lb (500g) noodles
1 large onion, chopped
3 cloves garlic, crushed
7 oz (200g) tomato purée (see p. 46)
$1/2$ tsp cumin, ground
$1/2$ tsp turmeric
oil for sautéing
salt and pepper
GARNISH
grated cheese
sprigs of parsley

1 Boil the chicken. Leave in quarters or remove the bones if preferred.

2 Sauté the chicken pieces, onions and garlic. Add tomato purée and water to cover well. Season with cumin, turmeric and salt and pepper. Simmer for $1/2$ hour or until the sauce has thickened.

3 Boil the noodles with a drop of oil in salted boiling water for 5 minutes or until tender. Drain in a colander or sieve.

4 Serve the chicken sauce over noodles or combined with the noodles. Sprinkle with cheese and sprigs of parsley.

PIGEON WITH OLIVES

Hamam bil zaytun

Pigeons and other fowl are sometimes raised in Arabs' gardens, primarily for grilling, roasting or frying. Qasr Al Nile, the road which leads to the pyramids, is famous for its restaurants specialising in roast pigeon.

Pigeon-squabs, young birds about four weeks old, and those which have never eaten whole grain, are considered to be the tastiest and most tender. Older birds are considered good only for the stewpot.

For grilling, the small bird is usually split in half, heavily salted and marinated with a little lemon juice and crushed garlic before being placed over the coals.

The Egyptians are also fond of stuffed and baked pigeons or other small birds. The stuffing can be with or without meat and with burgul, rice or farika as in the stuffed chicken recipe on p. 73.

Birds are often stewed to a flavourful tenderness. In this recipe they are cooked with olives - a frequent condiment to a meal, yet rarely added as a cooking ingredient. Here, the tartness of the olives and lemon juice is calmed by the bird and spices. The 'four spice' blend of cinnamon, cloves, nutmeg and ginger is one of the most popular mixtures on a Lebanese kitchen shelf.

5 pigeons or 10 quails
4 tbsp lemon juice
$1/4$ tsp cinnamon, ground
$1/4$ tsp cloves, ground
$1/4$ tsp nutmeg, grated
$1/4$ tsp ginger, ground
1 bay leaf
15 green seedless olives
1 tsp flour
3 tbsp butter or samn
oil for sautéing
salt and pepper

1 Cut the cleaned birds in half. Sauté until browned. Add the bay leaf, cinnamon, cloves, nutmeg, ground ginger, salt and pepper and sauté for a further 2 minutes.

2 Pour 4 cups of water and the lemon juice over the birds and simmer covered for 1 hour or until tender.

3 Stir the flour into the melted butter and add 2 tbsp of the hot sauce from the birds.

4 Add the flour mixture and the olives to the birds to simmer for a further 15 minutes.

5 Remove the bay leaf. Serve the birds and sauce with rice or *burgul*. Accompany with a salad, pickles and Arabic bread.

Maakulat bahria

SEAFOOD

BOUNTIFUL VOYAGES

The warm waters of the Arab world are home to abundant species of fish, from the vast Mediterranean, Red Sea and Arabian Gulf to the roots of civilisation: the Nile, Tigris and Euphrates rivers and the historic Sea of Galilee.

Fishermen and sailors - perhaps even Sindbad himself - invented songs and tales of woe that kept time with the rhythm of the waves. Now only the elderly men, some of whom still gather at the fish market, can still chant the verses, and their lyrics may soon be lost.

One of the first commercial commodities came from the sea - salt. This mineral was vital to life on shore, especially in the desert regions of Arabia. The sea-trading Phoenicians, along with the Southern Arabians, sailed the high seas to firmly establish the Spice Routes, the foundation of maritime history. Phoenicians, from the lands to the north of modern-day Lebanon, ruled the waves and perhaps were best known for their royal dyes - expensive, flaming red and purple. However, some 4,500 years ago the Pharaohs sent ships down the Red Sea to obtain aromatics from the Land of Punt.

However, carbon-dated remains show that people had began to pull their food from the sea, using shallow fish-traps, 6,000 years ago. Later on, boats were used to collect deep-water fish during seasonal harvests.

Today's Middle Eastern fish market, the *souk*, teems with activities. Fishmongers - or the fishermen themselves - hawk the catch of the day by

shouting the names and sometimes even chasing a customer, fish in hand, to demonstrating the freshness by pulling open the gills. Men and their small children are the most frequent visitors to the *souk*, which is filled with watery slabs or woven wire baskets displaying all manner of fish, crustaceans and molluscs.

When buying, choose fish that have clear eyes, bright-red gills and firm, glistening skin. Really fresh fish should have little smell, except perhaps that of the sea. The flesh of fish from the warm Arabian seas is somewhat coarse and therefore excellent for drying, frying, stewing, stuffing, baking or grilling.

Although very simple, whole fried fish are probably the most beloved in the Arab world; they are sometimes served with a side dish of sauce or lemon wedges and accompanied by a crisp salad or whole stalks of spring onions. Almost always available for sale are the most advanced molluscs, including squid, cuttlefish and octopus.

More elaborate recipes can be prepared, from freshwater trout roasted on a stick over charcoal (called *masgouf* near the Tigris and Euphrates Rivers), to the spicy fish stews of the Gulf countries. Each of the recipes here notes the recommendations for species to be used, from tiny anchovies to massive king fish; however, the specified fish can generally be substituted with a fish of similar quality.

FRIED FISH

Samak makli

Arabs prefer their fish fried whole, and eat the head, tail and everything in between. Wee sardines, sprats and anchovies are deep-fried whole in a batter. Medium-sized red mullet, known as Sultan Ibrahim (King Abraham) or grouper fish, hammour, are deep or shallow-fried whole. The flaky white flesh is drenched with lemon, pulled from the bones, and eaten with Arabic bread and salad. Gigantic king fish or habat are sliced into oblong steaks and sometimes deep-fried in a batter. The best fish steaks I ever tasted were simply salted and peppered, shallow-fried, and served on a mound of white rice drizzled with a chilli-hot tomato sauce.

2 lb (1 kg) fish
3 cloves garlic, crushed
1 tsp *baharat*
1/2 tsp turmeric
1 tbsp lemon juice
oil for shallow-frying
salt and pepper

GARNISH
lemon wedges

1 Clean the fish, leaving the head and tail intact. If the fish are large, make 3-4 deep slits (crimps) parallel to the head.

2 Mix the garlic, spices and lemon juice. Rub the fish inside and out with the garlic mixture. Leave to stand for at least 10 minutes.

3 Shallow fry a few pieces at one time in hot oil until golden brown and tender. Drain on absorbent paper.

4 Serve garnished with lemon wedges. Accompany with rice, Arabic bread, and a sauce of garlic mayonnaise (p. 45) *tahina* (p. 46), or coriander (see steps 1 and 2 of *Fish with Coriander*, opposite).

VARIATIONS
● The fish can be dipped into a batter of egg and milk before being dropped into seasoned flour.

● Lebanese coat the fish in seasoned flour (but not usually egg and milk) before frying.

BAKED FISH WITH CUMIN

Samak bil kammun

Prepared as a stew on top of the stove or baked in the oven, this fish recipe exudes the flavour of Arabia by its use of spices - cumin, lemon and garlic. Fresh coriander, which shares a special affinity with fish, is sprinkled on at the last moment for an aromatic flavour. Whole fish are traditionally baked in a covered earthenware dish that seals in the natural liquids.

Flat fish, such as flounder, pomfret or a fish named after the Prophet Moses, samak moosa, can be cooked in a pan. However, more popularly parrot fish, Sultan Ibrahim (red mullet), red fish, hammour (grouper), grey mullet, sea bream or bass, as well as an array of freshwater fish can be oven baked.

2 lb (1 kg) fish
4 cloves garlic, crushed
1/2 tsp cumin, ground
1/4 tsp turmeric
1/4 tsp chilli pepper, ground (opt)
1 tbsp lemon juice
2 tbsp oil
salt and pepper

1 Clean and scale the fish, leaving the head and tail intact.

2 Rub the fish with the cumin, turmeric, lemon juice, garlic, and salt and pepper. Leave to stand for 5 minutes. Add the oil and chilli powder, if preferred.

3 Bake at 350°F (150°C) gas 4 for 20 minutes or until tender.

4 Serve with rice, pickles, salad and a sauce of of garlic mayonnaise (p. 45) *tahina* (p. 46), or coriander (see steps 1 and 2 of *Fish with Coriander*, this page).

VARIATION
● This same recipe can be shallow fried in hot oil and drained on absorbent paper.

FISH WITH CORIANDER

Kuzbara bil samak

In the Arab World, fried or grilled fish are usually eaten simply sprinkled with lemon juice, but occasionally a spicy sauce of fresh coriander and chunky tomatoes is eaten with fried fish steaks and white rice. Kuwait is renowned for its daqous, a rich garlic, lemon and especially hot chilli tomato sauce. Sour tamarind pods are the basis for another Gulf sauce, which sometimes employs cardamom and rose water. Smooth nutty tahina sauce (see page 46) is used as a dip for tiny fish. The following spicy recipe can be used as a basis for baking the fish for 20 minutes in a preheated oven, as a stew or as a sauce served separately.

Almost any firm fish with a large cavity can also be stuffed with the mixture and fried. In the Gulf countries (especially the island state of Bahrain) it used to be customary for the bellies of enormous safi fish to be stuffed with strong spices and rice and secured with tied palm leaves. Freshwater fish from the Sebou River of Morocco are still filled with a date, blanched almond and rice mixture.

1 lb (500g) fish fillet or squid
3 onions, chopped
5 tomatoes, peeled and chopped
2 tbsp parsley, chopped
4 tbsp fresh coriander, chopped
4 cloves garlic, crushed
1/2 tsp cumin, ground
1 tbsp lemon juice
oil for sautéing
salt and pepper

1 Sauté the onions and garlic. Add the tomatoes, parsley and cumin with water to cover. Simmer for 20 minutes or until the sauce has thickened.

2 Add the coriander, lemon juice, season with salt and pepper, and simmer for a further 5 minutes. Adjust the seasoning to taste.

3 Add chunks of cleaned fish or other seafood to stew until tender. Alternatively, serve as a sauce over the grilled or fried fish with rice and salad.

STEWED FISH WITH TOMATOES

Samak bil bandoura

Almost 5,000 years ago the inhabitants of Arabia feasted on the dense flesh of shark, a fish believed to date back about 300 million years (the excavated town of Umm Al Nar, site of the first oil refinery in the United Arab Emirates, produced the evidence). And today long fillets of drying shark still hang, like wind chimes, in the fishing towns along the coast of the Gulf of Oman.

Any coarse-fleshed fish can be stewed on top of the stove or baked in the oven (whole or in pieces) with a strong blend of tomatoes and spices. In the Gulf countries, young shark as well as red-fleshed tuna are stewed with tomatoes and spiced with strong tamarind and tart loomi and served alongside sweet muhammar rice. Sometimes the fish, veg-etables, spices and rice are cooked in the same pot to make machbous. In Iraq, freshwater fish called shabou (a kind of salmon-trout) is baked whole with eight different ground spices and plenty of tomatoes.

1 lb (500g) fish fillet
3 tomatoes, peeled and chopped
2 onions, chopped
3 cloves garlic, crushed
2 tbsp lemon juice
2 tbsp parsley, chopped
1/4 tsp cumin, ground
salt and pepper

1 Sauté the onions and garlic.

2 Add the tomatoes, lemon juice, and water to cover. Simmer for about 10 minutes or until the sauce thickens.

3 Sprinkle the cleaned fish with salt and allow to stand for 5 minutes. Add the pepper and cumin.

4 Drop the fish and parsley into the sauce. Simmer for 10 minutes or until the fish is tender.

5 Serve with rice, a green salad, pickles and Arabic bread.

FISH CURRY

Salonat samak

This curry utilises the seasonings of India, which found their way into the Arab world along the Spice Routes by ocean-going dhows. A coarse, white-fleshed fish, usually stewed in with the spices, can be prepared separately and topped with the fragrant sauce, however both are popularly served with sweet muhammar rice (p.124) or onion mashkoul rice (p. 121).

1 lb (500g) fish fillet
2 tomatoes, peeled and chopped
2 onions, chopped
3 cloves garlic, crushed
1 loomi, pierced twice
2 tsp baharat
1/2 tsp turmeric
1/4 tsp ginger, ground
1/2 tsp chilli pepper, ground
1 tsp lemon juice
oil for sautéing
salt and pepper

1 Sauté the onions and garlic and add the chilli, baharat and turmeric for a further 2 minutes.

2 Add the tomatoes, loomi, lemon juice and salt and pepper with water to cover. Simmer for 15 minutes or until the sauce thickens.

3 Stir-fry pieces of the fish until golden. Place the fish into the sauce. Cover and simmer slowly for a further 15 minutes or until the fish is tender.

4 Remove the loomi; serve with rice, salad, pickles and Arabic bread.

FISH WITH TAHINA

Samak bil tahina

In the Gulf countries, whole fish were once covered with mud to seal in the natural juices, and baked in the ground until the clay began to crack. This distinctive Lebanese version uses a thin paste of tahina *to seal already cooked and reshaped fish, rather like icing on a cake. The head and tail, uncoated, are kept to complete the fish shape.*

The sesame seed that makes tahina *has an ancient history, as sesame oil was traded in the Arabian Peninsula and the Indus Valley by the early inhabitants of Sumeria and Mesopotamia.*

2 lb (1 kg) fish
2 tbsp lemon juice
2 cloves garlic, crushed
1 tbsp oil
salt and pepper

SAUCE
6 fl oz (175ml) *tahina*
2 cloves garlic, crushed
4 tbsp lemon juice
6 tbsp water
salt

GARNISH
2 tbsp pine nuts, fried until golden
fresh coriander or parsley
lemon wedges
olives

1 Clean and scale the fish, leaving the head and tail intact. Rub the fish with lemon juice, garlic, oil and salt and pepper. Bake for 20 minutes at 375°F (180°C) gas 4 Chill and then very carefully remove the skin and bones. Rearrange the head, tail and flesh by re-moulding into a fish shape.

2 To make the sauce, gradually add water and lemon juice alternately to the *tahina* until a thick sauce forms. The water thins and the lemon juice thickens the *tahina*. Stir in the crushed garlic and salt to taste.

3 Coat the body of the moulded fish with the *tahina* mixture and smooth with a spatula, leaving the head and tail uncovered. Garnish with pine nuts that have been lightly fried until golden, sprigs of coriander or parsley, lemon wedges, and an olive to replace the eye.

4 The *tahina* fish is usually served chilled or at room temperature.

FISH WITH RICE

Sayadiah

Similar to machbous or salonat in the Gulf States, this recipe for sayadiah is common in coastal Yemen, where fish are plentiful. The common fish to use are slices of the chanad or the darak, which is said to be similar to the white flesh of fresh tuna. Almost any coarse-textured fish can be used in this rice dish. The quantity of chilli has been reduced from the Yemeni version to make the dish milder.

The fillets of fish are lightly marinated in chilli before being fried and then layered into rice with a tomato and onion sauce called kushna.

In Lebanon and other countries of the Levant, the boneless fish is grilled or fried and tossed into cooked yellow rice.

2 lb (1 kg) fish fillets
1 tbsp chilli paste - *bisbas* (see p. 44)
2 potatoes, sliced (opt)
2 cups long-grain rice, washed
salt

SAUCE
2 large onions, chopped
3 cloves garlic, crushed
2 cardamom, cracked
$^1/_2$ tsp turmeric
1 tsp cumin, ground
1 green chilli pepper, chopped
2 tomatoes, peeled and chopped
oil for shallow-frying

1 To make a *kushna* sauce, sauté the onions, garlic and green chilli pepper. Add the tomatoes, cardamom, cumin and turmeric with water to cover. Simmer for about 15 minutes or until the sauce thickens.

2 Rub the cleaned fish with the *bisbas* (chilli paste) and salt. Leave to stand for 20 minutes.

3 Place the rice in salted boiling water to simmer for 10 minutes. Strain the rice.

4 Shallow fry the fish and the potato slices.

5 Layer half the rice, fish, *kushna* sauce, potatoes and the remaining rice. Place a clean tea towel between the pot and the lid. Cover and leave on a low heat for 30 minutes or until the rice is tender and fluffy.

6 Serve the rice as a bed for the fish pieces.

DRIED FISH

Fesiekh

In the past, sun-dried fish were used out of season, or transported far inland from the coastal villages. Today, dried fish has become a beloved acquired taste. Any spot of beach may be covered with thousands of tiny drying fish, while men dressed in long, skirt-like wazra, squat down, tending the catch. The dried fish are sorted, sacked and sent to market.

Dried whole anchovies, a treat for children in fishing areas, can also be ground and used as a marinade for grilling or to top thin rounds of bread. Shrimp are dried, then soaked prior to cooking out of season. Huge planks of young shark or other fish are dehydrated, only to end up later in juicy stews.

The method is simple, especially in areas with an abundance of sunshine. The fish is cleaned, washed and split open. It is heavily salted inside and out and left on a porous surface, or hung to dry, in the sun for a few days. Sometimes the fish is buried in the hot sand or mud for several days until matured. When required the dried fish can be reconstituted by soaking in water, and then used in the recipe.

CLAMS

Mahar

Crustaceans and molluscs are inherent to the Arab world, and include shrimp, crab, cigale, and clams, as well as the famous Omani lobster. Oysters, a native of the Arabian Gulf, have now sadly become a rarity, and the once-thriving pearl-diving industry is no more.

Clams thrive in the shallow, sandy areas of the Gulf and Red Sea, but are available in the souk only during the cooler months of the year. The smooth-shelled cherry clam species are succulent, while the larger, ribbed varieties are meatier. Although readily available, clams are not usually highly prized because of the effort involved in collecting the scant portion of fish from each shell. Frequently the clams are opened and eaten raw with lemons and a tomato sauce, and occasionally they are sautéed in butter with crushed garlic and pepper until they open.

SQUID

Habbar

Squid is abundant and inexpensive in the Arabian fish market, or souk. Fishmongers - often the fishermen themselves - gather at seaside stalls, sometimes just next to their vessels, and hawk their fresh catch of the day. The fish are displayed in woven wire baskets or on slabs, and the market advertised by fishy smells on the breeze.

Squid, with about 350 species, are the most numerous of all the cephalopods, and generally look like a torpedo with a fin on either side. Squid can be fried in rings with or without a batter, but most Arabs prefer it without. The pockets in small squid (called the mantle) are also stuffed with a mixture of rice, onion, saffron, and the tentacles, seasoned with salt and pepper. (Alternatively, the squid can be cubed and used in place of the fish in the tomato stew on p. 86 or to stew in the coriander sauce on p. 85.)

Much larger, shield-shaped cuttlefish are prepared by first making a slit in one end and removing the bone. The fish is turned inside out, cleaned of entrails, the head and parrot-like beak removed. Skin and wash well before cooking. The body can be left whole and stuffed. Octopus, bulbous in shape, are highly regarded in most warm sea coastal towns, but may be considered by some as unpresentable to guests because of the tough texture. Boiling first can tenderise octopus for the grill or for further cooking procedures.

2 lb (1 kg) squid
2 cloves garlic, crushed
1 tbsp vinegar
butter or *samn* for shallow-frying
salt and pepper

GARNISH
parsley
lemon wedges

1 Clean the squid (your fishmonger may do this) by removing the outer reddish-violet skin. Remove the head and pull the contents from the body section (mantle cavity). Make a slit and pull out the transparent hard piece. Pat dry, and cut the body into rings, removing the eyes and beak. The tentacles and arms may be used for a stew or fried alongside the body rings.

2 Marinate the rings for 5-10 minutes in garlic, vinegar and salt and pepper.

3 Fry gently for 5-10 minutes or until brown. Do not over-cook or the squid will become tough.

4 Drain on absorbent paper. Garnish with chopped parsley and serve with lemon wedges.

SHRIMP/PRAWNS

Robian

The most available of all crustaceans native to Arabian waters, shrimp or prawns are simply grilled, fried with or without a batter, stewed or cooked with rice in machbous.

To prepare prawns or shrimp for frying, simply shell and de-vein. Then, either sauté in butter with crushed garlic, shallow-fry in samn, *or deep-fry after coating first in beaten egg and then seasoned flour. Prawns or shrimp can also be dropped whole, unshelled (heads and all), into boiling water with spices, garlic and a quartered onion for 2-3 minutes.*

Whether sautéing, shallow-frying, deep-frying, or boiling, be careful to avoid over-cooking.

SPICED PRAWNS AND RICE

Machbous robianne

A favourite in the Gulf countries of Oman, Qatar, Saudi Arabia, Bahrain and the United Arab Emirates, this machbous *has shrimp and rice cooked in the same pot. The dish is slightly reminiscent of Chinese prawn fried rice, but the spice blend is more powerful. Dried or frozen shrimp can be substituted for fresh, and an equal amount of cracked wheat for the rice. The spicy prawn rice is most often served with a chilli tomato sauce called* daqous, *famous in Kuwait. (See p. 67 for a lamb* machbous *recipe.)*

2 lb (1 kg) prawns/shrimp
2 cloves garlic, crushed
1 large onion, chopped
2 cups long-grain rice, washed
1 tomato, peeled and chopped
1 tbsp *baharat*
1/4 tsp turmeric

2 *loomi*, pierced twice
1 tsp fresh coriander, chopped
oil for sautéing
salt and pepper

1 Sauté the onions and garlic. Add tomatoes, *baharat*, turmeric, *loomi*, coriander, pepper and 2 cups water. Cover and simmer for 10 minutes. Shell and de-vein the prawns or shrimp. Add them to the boiling sauce for 1 minute. Strain, reserving the liquid.

2 Return the liquid to the boil, add the washed rice and salt to taste. Simmer slowly for 15 minutes.

3 Gently turn the prawns into the rice. Place a clean tea towel between the pot and the lid. Tightly cover and simmer over a low heat for 5 minutes or until the liquid has been absorbed and the rice is tender and fluffy.

4 Serve with Arabic bread, pickles and a salad.

SEA ANTS

Cigale

Almost all fish of the sea are eaten in Arabian coastal towns. Cigale, *lobster and crab are the seasonal delicacies of the Gulf, available only in the cooler months, usually between October and February.*

The sea ant has a tail that looks and tastes almost like lobster or crayfish, but the head of a giant ant. The tail, used for propulsion to swim backwards, is about 5 inches (12 cm) long and slightly brown with a few brightly coloured spots.

Cigale *should be bought alive, to ensure freshness. The heads can be removed if preferred, but should be left on for grilling. The shell may be split away from the underside, but this is much easier to remove after cooking. Various methods are used to prepare this shellfish: boiling, baking,*

Cigale

and grilling - which can also apply to the lobster that pop-ulates the water of the Sultanate of Oman. Any of the three, whether spicy or plain, produces a simply delicious cigale. This recipe comes from the island of Bahrain (the dates may be omitted).

2 lb (1 kg) *cigale*
2 tsp turmeric
2 cloves garlic
1 onion, quartered
2 dates, chopped
salt and pepper

GARNISH
butter
lemon wedges

1 Boil a few inches of salted water in a large pan. Add the turmeric, garlic, onions, dates. Season with a dash of pepper and boil for 5 minutes. Add 3-4 cleaned *cigale* at a time and boil each batch for 2-3 minutes.

2 To remove the shell, place the *cigale* on its back. Cut the shell down both sides. Prise apart to remove the flesh.

3 The flesh of the *cigale* can be returned to the cleaned shell with a pat of butter and served on a bed of lettuce with lemon wedges. Alternatively the flesh can be drizzled with butter and lemon and served on a bed of rice.

Mashawi

OUTDOOR COOKING

Arabian barbecues commonly take place on Fridays, the Moslem holy day and weekend, when friends and families nestle together on tranquil beaches, grassy knolls in the parks or stark desert dunes, or huddle around a charcoal fire tucked between the mountains in a *wadi*, a dried-up river bed.

Mashawi, the art of cooking over the heat of dying embers, is the highlight of any weekend outing; the excitement and pleasure of cooking with spits and skewers or the traditional clay pot or oven captures the true spirit of Arabia.

Although some people prefer to stay at home for the day and cook indoors using an electric or gas grill or oven, others prepare everyday food indoors and then take the pots out with them for a picnic.

The techniques for barbecuing are varied and make use of some special utensils. Long skewers are used to thread *kebab*, bite-size morsels of meat, seafood, chicken and vegetables. *Kofta*, spicy minced meat, is pressed into oblong shapes around flattened thin steel blades, which distribute the heat during cooking and prevent the meat from sliding off into the coals.

Other traditional methods of cooking outdoors are to use the spit to suspend the thinly sliced *shawarma* (see p.104), whole chicken, fish, or lamb; to bury traditional clay ovens and jars filled with lamb in the coals to bake; or to slowly cook beans and boil eggs over an outdoor fire in a wide-bellied pot with a slender neck - a *damassa*. When preparing any grilled dish, select the best cuts of meat and remove fat, tendons, membranes and ligaments. Tender, as well as tough, meats and fish are marinated in one of many sauces (see p. 106). Minimum marinating times are given, but overnight in the refrigerator yields the most flavourful meats for grilling.

Throughout the Arab World, the aroma of the grilled food is also enhanced by burning the fragrant wood of the region on the barbecue.

GRILLED LAMB ON A SKEWER

Shish kebab

Spicy cubes of marinated lamb are threaded onto skewers, sometimes alternating with chunks of tomatoes, onions, sweet peppers and cloves of garlic for an attractively colourful and probably the most familiar of all Arab grills.

The pieces of lamb (beef can be substituted) can be soaked in marinades of ivory yoghurt and garlic, rich red tomato, golden honey or fiery-hot chermoula *(see p. 107)*

1 lb (500g) meat, cubed
2 onions, quartered
$^1/_2$ red capsicum pepper, cubed
$^1/_2$ green capsicum pepper, cubed
$^1/_2$ yellow capsicum pepper, cubed
4 cloves garlic (opt)
4 chilli peppers (opt)
marinade

1 Marinate the meat for at least 6 hours or overnight in the refrigerator.

2 Thread the meat and vegetables alternately onto skewers. A clove of garlic or chilli can be added to each end of the skewer. Baste with the excess marinade.

3 Grill over the dying embers for 10-15 minutes.

4 Cover with Arabic bread to keep warm. Serve accompanied by lemon wedges.

CHICKEN ON A STICK

Shish taouk

Tender chunks of chicken are marinated, placed on grilling rods, then roasted over a low flame. Chicken, like lamb, can be marinated in a tomato mixture, but its white flesh has a special affinity for an ivory-coloured sauce of yoghurt mixed with pressed garlic (see p. 106). Frequently chicken cubes are tenderised by marinading (overnight in the refrigerator) in a mixture of equal quantities of tomato and yoghurt. The chicken has a marvellous flavour when grilled. The key to grilling shish taouk is in the cooking time. Tender chicken will grill in a hurry and has a tendency to dry out easily. The chicken should be grilled over dying embers and can be kept moist by basting with a little of the leftover marinade.

2 lb (1 kg) chicken, cubed
1 capsicum pepper, cubed
2 onions, quartered
marinade

1 Marinate the chicken for at least 2 hours or overnight in the refrigerator.

2 Thread the chicken and vegetables alternately onto skewers.

3 Grill over dying embers for 8-10 minutes, basting with the leftover marinade and turning often.

4 Arabic bread can be placed beneath and above the *kebab* until serving.

MINCED MEAT ON SKEWERS

Kofta kebab

Finely minced meat is mixed with a special combination of seasonings, squeezed into shape around metal rods, and grilled over coals for a sausage-shape roll that is the Arab world's answer to hot dogs. Street-side stalls specialise in this grilled meat, their long troughs of coals often kept glowing with an electric fan or a more traditional, woven hand-held model. Skilful hands shape the minced meat around skewers that are then laid across the charcoal fire to brown, removed, sprinkled with the tart sumac and served on rounds of soft Arabic bread with shredded lettuce, chopped tomato and sometimes onion and cucumber.

1 lb (500g) minced lamb
2 onions, finely chopped
2 tbsp parsley, finely chopped
2 tbsp mint, finely chopped
1 tsp *baharat*
pinch of cayenne pepper (opt)
salt and pepper

GARNISH
parsley
lemon wedges
sumac

1 Combine the minced lamb with the other ingredients. Blend to a smooth sticky paste.

2 With oiled hands, press the lamb tightly around the skewer, shaping into a sausage about 5 in (12 cm) long.

3 Grill over dying embers for 8-10 minutes.

4 Sprinkle with *sumac* and serve garnished with lemon wedges and parsley. Arabic bread can be placed under and over the *kebab* until serving.

LAMB CHOPS

Riyash

Bordered on one side by bone and the other by fat, which seals in the juices, lamb chops seem to have been specially designed for grilling! Chops come from the neck end of the spine of a lamb, and should be soaked in a lemon or vinegar based tenderising marinade (see pages 106-107).

12 lamb chops
marinade

1 Marinate the lamb chops for at least 6 hours or overnight in the refrigerator.

2 Grill slowly over dying embers for 10-15 minutes or until tender, basting with the leftover marinade.

GRILLED FISH

Samak mashawi

Whole grilled fish, sea ants (cigale), and jumbo shrimp are specialities of Arabian fishing villages and coastal cities. In Umm Al Quwain, one of the seven states of the United Arab Emirates, a type of grey mullet called biyah is left whole (entrails untouched), rubbed with salt, then grilled. Residents say the best part of the fish is the tender roe.

Generally Arabs gut fish before grilling, but then leave their fish whole, with the outer skin serving as a natural protective seal for the juicy inner flesh. We have also eaten a tender fish, which was sealed in clay and buried in a fire until the mud began to crack. Abundant dates are puréed and the mixture spread over fish before grilling. The most widely used is whole fish, rubbed with salt and grilled until the skin has a crispy toughness and can be easily pulled away.

Any firm-fleshed variety of fish can be used on the barbecue. The fish can be marinated overnight or just before grilling simply rubbed inside and out with a mixture of salt, pepper and cumin. Onions, garlic and chilli peppers can be added to the marinade, depending on the flavour to be achieved. When the barbecue is ready, place the whole fish directly on the grill. For smaller varieties, a long skewer can be pushed through the fish from head to tail before it is placed on the barbecue. Brush lightly with oil and turn occasionally.

Jumbo shrimp or prawns, as well as other shellfish, are also placed on the grill whole, with head, tail and shell intact. Omani lobster are grilled, as well as a strange-looking sea ant called a cigale, which has a brown lobster-like tail almost in the shape of a fan. Barbecue the shellfish over dying embers until the shells are slightly charred. Overcooking will make the flesh tough. Serve with butter or samn and lemon wedges. See p. 90 for more details about sea ants.

SKEWERED SEAFOOD

Mashawi bahria

Although Arabs generally grill seafood whole, fish, cuttlefish or large squid can be cleaned and cubed and finally skewered before being placed over dying embers. Small squid and fish can be placed on the grill directly or skewered. Any coarse-fleshed fish can be used, including shark, tuna, hammour (grouper), barracuda or king fish.

Yoghurt, tomato, herb and lemon, or spicy hot chermoula marinades can be used on the fish cubes before grilling (see pages 106-107).

2 lb (1 kg) fish, cuttlefish, or squid, cubed
3 onions, quartered
1 capsicum pepper, cubed
marinade

GARNISH
sprigs of parsley
lemon wedges

1 Clean the squid or cuttlefish by removing the outer reddish-violet skin under running water. Remove the head and pull the contents from the body. The thin cuttle-bone is pulled from the tail section of the cuttlefish. Cut the body into cubes. If using fish, clean, fillet and cube.

2 Marinate the cubes for at least 1 hour or overnight in the refrigerator.

3 Thread the cubes and vegetables alternately onto the skewers.

4 Grill over dying embers for about 10 minutes or until tender, basting with the leftover marinade.

5 Garnish with parsley and lemon wedges.

GRILLED LIVER

Kibdah mashwiyak

Arabs love liver, which is generally considered as a strength booster. Liver should be marinated briefly prior to grilling as the meat can dry out quickly. Tomato or honey marinades (see pages 106-107) can be applied; however, in the Levant a special liver dish is prepared with a marinade of garlic paste, crumbled dried mint, olive oil and salt and pepper. Note that vinegar or lemon juice marinades should not be used for more than an hour or the liver will become too soft.

1 lb (500g) liver, cubed
5 small onions
6 cloves garlic
marinade
GARNISH
2 tbsp parsley, finely chopped
lemon wedges

1 Marinate the liver for at least 30 minutes.

2 Thread the liver, peeled garlic and onions alternately onto a skewer.

3 Grill over dying embers for 10-12 minutes.

4 Serve garnished with parsley and lemon wedges. Accompany with spring onions and radishes.

GRILL TRIMMINGS

Kudar mashwiya

Even outdoors, Arabs lavishly complement their richly marinated meats and tender grilled fish with a vast array of pickles and olives, dates, cheese, bread, vegetables, fresh fruit, sweets and always a bottle or two of mai (water) to wash it all down. The feast-like spread usually includes vegetables that are added to the grill: aubergine, bite-sized or quartered onions, and whole or quartered tomatoes. An Arab friend, who is particularly fond of garlic, has been seen stalking his hosts' kitchens in search of the powerful bulbs, which can be thrown on the grill whole, until the skins are black and the insides creamy. Vegetables can be added to the skewered meats, chicken and seafoods, or alternatively placed directly on the grill. Cheese can be added to the grill for a brown-spotted, blistered nibbler. The cheese must be extremely firm to endure the intense heat of a grill. Hard, dry goat's cheese is preferred, as well as nabulsia, haloum or kaskawan - which should first be soaked in several changes of water before grilling. Large pieces can be placed directly on the grill or chunks of cheese can be wrapped in foil and placed over the fire until it begins to glow.

SPECIAL GRILLS

Grilled and roasted meat and poultry are found more in street side cafés or desert barbecues in the Middle East than in the kitchen. In busy areas, where traffic surges to and fro, tiny kiosks are tucked safely away in corners, grilling the evening fare for passers-by.

Upright spits rotate with their layers and layers of mildly spiced lamb or chicken called shawarma. Every few minutes a long blade passes over the cone of meat, dropping slices into a pocket of bread, which is drizzled with tahina sauce and herbs and rolled into a big cigar-shaped sandwich. The shawarma sandwich is the classic Arab fast-food - the equivalent of the hamburger in America.

Rows and rows of brown chickens turn behind glass cases on motor-driven rôtisseries. Whole chickens are sold, but free trimmings are provided: garlic mayonnaise, pickles, salad and sometimes a special chickpea dip, hummos.

Huge flat paddles are covered with miniature pizzas - flat rounds of bread topped with cheese, meat or zaatar - and slid into arched ovens made of clay or bricks.

A true Arabian feast would be incomplete without a whole roast lamb, the most treasured dish in the Middle East. A task to prepare, qouzi is served only on auspicious occasions and either stuffed with a rice mixture or served on a bed of elaborately decorated rice.

A few of these street-side recipes and festive dishes have been included here to give an idea of the flavour of outdoor eating in the Middle East. Cooks with a flair for adventure can improvise with the equipment and give the recipes a try.

WHOLE LAMB ON A SPIT is a ceremonial dish in the Middle East. Qouzi is prepared for special occasions such as holy days, births, weddings, the arrival of an important guest or someone departing for or returning from a long journey. A whole lamb is slaughtered and roasted for family and guests. Well-to-do families are expected to divide half of the meat with the poor or less fortunate.

After being slaughtered in the especially religious halal method, the lamb is rinsed, wiped dry, rubbed inside and out with salt, pepper and crushed onion and garlic (see p. 60 for more details). The lamb is pushed onto a rod from head to tail and the legs bound together. To celebrate the circumcision of our son, our family roasted a whole lamb.

My husband built a metal spit and we dug a hole in the back garden and filled it with charcoal. Two adjustable poles, V-shaped at the top, were erected so that the lamb could be suspended horizontally between them. The spit was turned occasionally and the poles moved up and down to roast the lamb evenly on all sides. The meat was basted quite often with marinade throughout the cooking process to prevent dryness.

The lamb was sampled for tenderness from time to time, but after about 4-6 hours, the roasting of the lamb [about 20-25 lbs (10-12kg) in size] was complete. The whole lamb was served on a large tray surrounded by rice (see rice section for special recipes)..

LEG OF LAMB is ideal for spit-roasting, marinate at least two hours, but preferably overnight (see pages 106-107 for marinades). A strong metal spit should be driven down the centre of the leg, next to the bone. Roast over dying embers of charcoal, or on a gas or electric grill. Turn the leg and baste occasionally with the marinade. The cooking time depends on the age of the lamb as well as the size of the leg, but the outer layer should be roasted within 30 minutes. As the leg grills, pieces can be sliced off.

The enjoyment of grilling outdoors is to have a group of family and friends around to talk while the lamb is roasting and to sample slices as the meat becomes crusty brown.

CLAY OVENS were traditionally used for communal bakeries as they were seldom owned by individuals. The ovens were used for baking bread as well as roasting lamb. More commonly, clay jars containing small whole lambs were laid on a bed of coals and buried in a grave of sand or mud for long, slow baking.

LARGE POTS are found slowly simmering over an open fire. In preparation for a wedding feast in the Gulf countries jointed lambs, or occasionally a camel, are cooked in huge aluminium pots. Chopped onions, saffron threads, cardamom pods, cinnamon bark, cloves, pierced loomi and peppercorns are added to the pot to stew, and the mixture is occasionally stirred with a long-handled oversized ladle.

FISH ON A STICK is prepared with the freshwater catch at restaurants along the banks of the Tigris River in Baghdad, an ancient city founded by Caliph al Mansur in the year 762. Samak masgouf can be made with any firm, white-fleshed, medium-sized fish.

Clean and scale the fish. Rub with salt, and marinade if desired. Attach the fish, through the gills and out the mouth, to a pointed stick, so that it hangs off the end much as it would dangle from the end of a fishing rod. Place the stick in the ground and lean over the coals at an angle, propped if necessary to keep the impaled fish from falling. Dangle the fish over dying embers until fairly cooked (about one hour) and serve in Iraqi fashion on a platter with onions, tomatoes and plenty of bread.

ROAST CHICKEN can be found grilling in rows on a horizontal rôtisserie at many street-side cafés. Buy one quickly because every evening at least 20-30 vanish from each glass case. Otherwise, roasted chicken is simple to prepare at home, especially with the help of an oven with a built-in rôtisserie.

The cleaned and washed chicken can be soaked in a light marinade of olive oil, garlic, lemon juice or vinegar, and salt and pepper. However, more spices can be added, including turmeric, cumin, coriander, baharat and dried mint. After marinating, the chicken is fed onto the spit from neck to tail, then roasted in the oven on a medium heat or over charcoals. The chicken can be basted occasionally with the excess marinade. Roast for about 20 minutes per pound (500g). If roasting in an oven, turn the oven up to a higher heat for the last 10 minutes, to help the chicken skin to become brown and crisp. Serve with garlic mayonnaise (see p. 45), salad and plenty of Arabic bread.

BEANS IN A POT *simmering overnight on the charcoal fire make the ideal breakfast for a camp-out. Dried beans are always soaked, then simply added to a pot with a tight-fitting lid, with water to cover and spices. A few raw eggs with scrubbed shells can be added to the pot with the beans. Alternatively, bury several eggs around the outer hot perimeters of the camp-fire. Either way, after cooking overnight the eggs are a perfect, firm and almost poached-tasting accompaniment for the beans. For further details see* Foul Medames *on page* $.

SHAWARMA, *the most popular of all street-side Arabian snacks, is virtually impossible to prepare without elaborate equipment. Readers may enjoy knowing how this simple-looking sandwich is prepared from start to finish.*

Start with about 20 lbs of lamb or chicken. The meat is sliced into thin rounds about ¹/4" *(6mm) thick by 7" (18cm) in diameter. The fat should also be cut the same size. The meat and the fat must then be marinated for 24 hours. The meat is then thread (with a layer of fat every so often) onto a huge upright skewer, which is finally topped by an onion, tomato and lemon.*

To make a shawarma sandwich, stuff Arabic bread with thin slices of meat, finely chopped lettuce, tomatoes and onions and dribble with tahina *sauce. Roll tightly and enjoy!*

20 lb (10 kg) lamb or chicken
MARINADE
1 lb (500g) onions chopped
20 cloves garlic, crushed
1 pt (500ml) vinegar
5 tbsp baharat
5 bay leaves
1 tbsp pepper
3 tbsp salt
GARNISH
1 lemon
1 tomato
1 onion

1 Thinly slice the meat and fat.

2 Blend all marinating ingredients.

3 Coat the meat and fat with the marinade and refrigerate for 24 hours.

4 Thread the lemon, tomato, onion and then the meat and fat onto a long rôtisserie skewer. Alternate one slice of fat between every 4 slices of meat. To make a cone shape, thread the small pieces of meat on first, then add larger slices alternately to the opposite sides.

5 Place the rod of meat on the vertical rôtisserie. The edges of the meat will brown while rotating close to the heat. Thinly slice the meat diagonally and place onto a tray beneath the *shawarma*, which keeps the meat warm and holds the drippings.

MARINADES

Manguoa

Arabs marinate both tough and tender meat, chicken and fish in a variety of spices prior to grilling, usually overnight.

The following recipes will each marinate about 2 lb (1 kg) of meat, chicken or seafood. Lamb or beef should be marinated for at least two hours, chicken at least one hour and fish for 20-30 minutes - for best results, marinate overnight in the refrigerator. Marinades with lemon juice will over-soften liver if it is marinated for more than 1 hour.

After marinating, save the leftover sauce for basting the flesh, which often dries, while grilling.

BASIC MARINADE
Great for lamb, chicken or seafood, this marinade should be used overnight, unless marinating liver.

4 tbsp lemon juice
3 cloves garlic, crushed
1 onion, finely chopped (opt)
pinch of cayenne pepper (opt)
pinch of cumin, ground (opt)
pinch of paprika (opt)
2 tbsp oil
salt and pepper

HONEY MARINADE
The sweetness of honey and the Worcester sauce-like spices blend ideally with lamb chops, shish kebab or any other lamb to be grilled, as well as chunks of chicken. This marinade is not recommended for fish or seafood. As a simpler alternative, the anchovies, vinegar, tamarind, cinnamon and cloves can be replaced with 2 tbsp Worcester sauce.

2 tbsp honey
4 cloves garlic, crushed
1 large onion, finely chopped

1 tsp anchovies, ground
1 tsp vinegar
1 tsp lemon juice
1 tsp tamarinds, soaked
pinch of cinnamon, ground
pinch of cloves, ground
2 tbsp oil
salt and pepper

YOGHURT MARINADE
Yoghurt is an ideal tenderiser for any meat that is a little tough, but is also an excellent marinade for chicken shish taouk, fish, liver or lamb kebab and chops. However the maximum time for liver is 1 hour.

$^1/_2$ pt (275ml) yoghurt
4 cloves garlic, crushed
1 onion, finely chopped
2 tbsp mint, finely chopped
1 tbsp lemon juice
1 tbsp paprika (opt)
1 tbsp oil
salt and pepper

TOMATO MARINADE
This red marinade can be used for chicken, lamb or fish and is for those who enjoy a savoury, spicy tomato sauce. The maximum time for liver is 1 hour.

7 tbsp tomato purée
1 tbsp lemon juice
2-3 cloves garlic, crushed
1 onion, finely chopped
$^1/_2$ tsp cinnamon, ground
2 tbsp parsley, finely chopped
4 bay leaves
2 tbsp oil
salt and pepper

HERB AND LEMON MARINADE

The olive oil in this marinade is ideal for sealing the tender flesh of fish for grilling and the lemon and herbs naturally blend with seafood. Any white flesh, such as chicken, is also recommended for soaking in the sauce. Red meat usually contains plenty of fat without the need for additional oil. The maximum time for liver is 1 hour.

5 tbsp olive oil
4 tbsp lemon juice
1 onion, finely chopped
1 tbsp parsley, thyme and dill, finely chopped
salt and pepper

HOT AND SPICY PASTE MARINADE
Chermoula

This tasty Moroccan speciality is used mainly for marinating fish, but sometimes for chicken and lamb. Be warned that the puréed red chilli peppers are not for the faint hearted. All the ingredients are ground to a paste. Sometimes the paste is covered with a thin layer of olive oil to preserve it for later use.

1 onion, puréed
3 cloves garlic, puréed
4 tbsp fresh parsley or coriander, puréed
2-4 red chilli peppers, puréed
4 tsp paprika
3-4 saffron threads (opt)
olive oil to cover
salt and pepper

Kudar

VEGETABLES

EDEN'S OASES

The oasis of the Garden of Eden - thought to have been located between two of the Arab world's most fertile rivers, the Tigris and Euphrates - is considered the earliest source of the wide variety of vegetables still available in the region today.

Some evidence that vegetables have been grown since ancient times was uncovered in Egyptian tombs dating back to 3,500 BC and Mexican caves from as long ago as 7,000 BC. A type of squash or marrow, thought to have originated in Africa, was found in the tombs.

The sights and sounds of today's *souk*, vegetable market, are reminiscent of days gone by. Rows and rows of baskets and boxes are filled to the brim with the colours of the rainbow, plus more. The astounding kaleidoscope of fruit and vegetables lies amidst slanted display shelves, sometimes beneath drooping tented canopies. Arabs demand the freshest of vegetables, which are usually purchased by the crate. The shouts of vendors are commonplace and the active trading enticing. Even the most shy shopper finds the courage to bargain and is only satisfied when a discount is awarded. The sounds are almost deafening early in the morning or after dark, when the marketplace is dominated by men. Women, who seldom frequent the vegetable *souk*, are usually at home preparing the next meal, which employs anything from one to a dozen vegetables.

However, in the Arab world vegetables are never plain boiled, but topped with savoury sauces, blended into stews and soups, stuffed or simply crunched raw.

BASIC STUFFED VEGETABLES

Mahshi

Ordinary vegetables are transformed into a mouthwatering display, neat rows of hollowed and stuffed Arabian delights. Tender young pale green cusa - akin to the courgette (zucchini) - are cored and stuffed with spicy rice, minced meat or a combination of both. Paper-thin vine and cabbage leaves are filled with a similar stuffing and rolled to finger-size perfection. A masterpiece-like pot of mahshi may consist of a layer of flat lamb chops, followed by several rows of stuffed squash and finally topped with intricately placed delicate vine leaves.

Although cusa and leaves are the most commonplace among Arabs, capsicum (bell pepper), mild banana pepper, over-sized chilli pepper, onion, tomato, aubergine and any squash, even large marrow, are also served stuffed.

The artistic presentation of mahshi depends on the selection of even-sized vegetables, which have been neatly and consistently cored. The makwara, a special coring tool, is most effective for scooping. A very slim knife or apple corer, with a tube to pull out the pulp, can be used but is more time consuming. However, care should be taken never to puncture the vegetables, or the stuffing will come tumbling out during the cooking process.

After the inner pulp has been removed, the hollow space is filled with one of a huge variety of stuffings - an infinite number of combinations. The vegetables are placed in a heavy-bottomed pan, side-by-side in neat layered rows, then half-covered with water, stock or a special sauce. Weighted down with a heavy plate, they are slowly simmered until tender.

Presented here is a basic method of making mahshi, with a limited selection of variations for stuffings and sauces. The tomato, stock and yoghurt sauces are used in the cooking process, while uncooked yoghurt sauce is poured over mahshi that has been prepared in stock.

For about 2 lb (1 kg) vegetables

MEAT AND RICE FILLING
8 oz (225g) minced lamb or beef
1/2 cup short-grain rice, washed
1 onion, chopped
2-3 cloves garlic, crushed
2 tsp parsley, finely chopped
1/2 tsp *baharat* (opt)
2 tbsp pine nuts (opt)
salt

MEAT FILLING
Omit the rice and double the meat.

RICE FILLING
Omit the meat and double the rice.

CHICKPEA FILLING
Substitute the meat and/or rice for an equal
quantity of cooked chickpeas.

SAUCES

TOMATO SAUCE
3 tomatoes, peeled and chopped
1 large onion, chopped
2 cloves garlic, crushed
2 tbsp tomato paste
2 tbsp butter, oil or *samn*
1/2 tsp cinnamon, ground
salt and pepper

COOKED YOGHURT SAUCE
1 pt (575ml) stabilised yoghurt (p. 52)
2 cloves garlic, crushed
1 tsp mint, finely chopped (opt)
salt

UNCOOKED YOGHURT SAUCE
1 pt (575ml) yoghurt
3 cloves garlic, crushed
1 tsp mint, finely chopped (opt)
salt

STOCK SAUCE
stock
1 onion, chopped
2 cloves garlic, crushed
salt

METHOD

1 Wash and scrub the vegetables.

2 Remove the stem and scoop out all the pulp
using a *makwara* or apple corer. Avoid puncturing
the skin, or it will fall apart while cooking. Soak
the cored vegetables in mildly salted water for 10
minutes. Rinse well and drain.

3 For the filling, lightly sauté the vegetables
and/or the meat. Add the nuts, rice and spices for
a further 2 minutes. Add 2 tbsp water and gently
simmer until all the liquid has absorbed.

4 Spoon the cooled filling into the vegetable
shell, tapping it lightly after each addition. As rice
expands and meat shrinks, the filling choice dic-
tates the quantity used. For example, a meat and
rice mixture should equal out.

5 Lay the stuffed vegetables side by side, in layers into a heavy-based pot or oven tray.

6 Pour the tomato sauce, cooked yoghurt sauce
or stock sauce over the vegetables. Add water to
half cover the vegetables.

7 Place a heavy plate on top of the vegetables.
Cover and simmer for 20-30 minutes or until tender. Alternatively bake at 300°F (150°C) gas 4 for
30 minutes or until tender.

8 Serve with any remaining sauce or uncooked
yoghurt sauce.

SQUASH MAHSHI: *Follow the basic method in preparing 12-15 squash/courgettes. For a crisper taste, add 1 tsp mint to the salted water when soaking. Stuff with the meat and rice filling, meat filling, or rice filling. Simmer in tomato sauce, cooked yoghurt sauce, or stock sauce. The uncooked yoghurt sauce can be served separately when the squash are cooked in the stock sauce.*

CABBAGE-LEAF MAHSHI: *Follow the basic method for preparing stuffed vegetables. Vary the method by boiling the outer leaves of a cabbage, 2-3 at one time, in water until softened. Cut the large leaves in half. Make the meat and rice filling or rice filling. Omit the onion and pine nuts. Substitute allspice for the baharat and add 1 tsp chopped mint. Roll up 1 tbsp of the filling inside each leaf, tucking in the sides. Squeeze to make a firm parcel. Line the bottom of the pot with the leftover cabbage leaves. Layer the stuffed leaves, sprinkling with 3 tbsp pomegranate juice and 1 tsp lemon juice diluted with 2 tbsp water. Cover with water, tomato sauce or stock sauce and simmer on low heat for 1 hour or until tender. For more information on stuffing leaves, see 'stuffed vine leaves' p, 12.*

In Saudi Arabia, the large outer layers of a blanched onion are stuffed using the same method and ingredients as the cabbage leaves.

CAPSICUM MAHSHI: *Follow the basic method for preparing stuffed vegetables. Five capsicum peppers can be stuffed using the meat and rice filling, meat filling or rice filling. Another alternative is to use the rice filling, omitting the pine nuts and baharat and adding 1 lb (500g) spinach which has been washed, chopped, blanched and drained. Proceed by baking according to the basic method.*

AUBERGINE MAHSHI: *Prepare the stuffed vegetables: First, drain the bitter juices of the aubergine/eggplant by salting the inside, placing in a colander and leaving to stand for one hour. 10-12 small aubergines can be stuffed with the meat filling and simmered in the tomato sauce.*

Alternatively, 4 medium aubergines are cut in half lengthways and stuffed with the rice filling or chickpea filling. Add two peeled and chopped tomatoes to the filling. Following the basic method, bake the stuffed aubergines for 20 minutes or until tender.

FRIED AUBERGINES/EGGPLANT

Badenjan

Almost any vegetable can be shallow or deep fried in samn, olive or vegetable oils. Arabs use olive oil when the food is to be served cold and prefer to shallow fry slender aubergine slices and deep fry individual florets of cauliflower. The Middle Eastern aubergines are much smaller than those usually found in the West, so the quantity should be adjusted accordingly.

Some boil the cauliflower in salted water until just tender and drain before frying. Egyptians boil and deep fry cauliflower, then drop it into a sauce of parsley, garlic and tomato.

Some aubergine/eggplant has a bitter aftertaste and should be sweated as indicated in the recipe prior to frying. For an Iraqi twist to white or purple fried aubergine, try topping each thin-as-possible slice with a spoon of yoghurt which has been sprinkled with crushed raw garlic.

1 large, or 4 small aubergine/eggplant
salt
oil for shallow frying

TO SERVE
2 heaped tbsp yoghurt
1 tsp crushed garlic

1 Slice the aubergine. Sprinkle with salt and place in a colander with a weight on top. Leave for 1 hour to drain the bitter juices.

2 Wash and dry the aubergine and shallow-fry until browned.

3 Drain on absorbent paper and serve topped with yoghurt and crushed garlic.

FRIED POTATOES

Batata makliya

An Englishman saturates 'chips' with malted vinegar, an American plunges 'French fries' into tomato ketchup and an Arab drenches batata makliya *with lemon juice.*

The common white potato is usually sliced or cubed, rather than cut into strips, and fried in sweet olive oil. Another version calls for the addition of garlic and coriander to the potatoes, which are finally sprinkled with crunchy fried pine nuts. In Algeria, spicy mashed potatoes seasoned with cumin, paprika, a dash of cayenne, chopped coriander, parsley and salt and pepper, are shaped into cakes, dipped into beaten eggs and deep-fried until brown.

Potatoes, seldom cooked as a separate dish in the Arab world, are generally integrated into main courses. Even fried potato strips, along with lettuce, tomato and meat, are rolled up in Arabic bread for a sandwich. Potato slices line the bottom of the pot in layered makluba, *and quarters are dropped into savoury stews (see p. 74 for* makluba*).*

1 lb (500g) potatoes
4 cloves garlic, crushed (opt)
2 tbsp fresh coriander, chopped
oil for deep-frying
salt

GARNISH
lemon wedges

1 Peel the potatoes and cut into small cubes. Wash, drain and dry.

2 Deep-fry the potatoes in two batches until golden brown. Drain on absorbent paper.

3 Then stir-fry the potatoes with the garlic and coriander for 3 minutes. Sprinkle with salt.

4 Serve hot or cold garnished with lemon wedges.

SQUASH FRITTERS

Aroug shigar

Any squash, including courgettes, can be grated, added to eggs, thickened with cornflour and fried like pancakes. The mint-flavoured fritters are eaten as a snack in the mezza or as a side dish with the main meal. Any cheese that will melt easily, including haloum, which is much like mozzarella or akawi, but with the flavour of mild cheddar, can be added. If preparing stuffed squash/courgettes (see p. 110) save the cores and freeze for later use in this recipe.

3 eggs, beaten
1 lb (500g) squash/courgettes
4 tbsp mint, finely chopped
4 tbsp cornflour/cornstarch
oil for shallow-frying
salt and pepper

1 Grate the squash. Add the eggs, cornflour, mint, salt and pepper.

2 Shallow-fry a large spoonful of the batter until golden brown. Drain on absorbent paper.

MIXED VEGETABLES

Khodara mushakkaleh

Vegetables alone are seldom a main course dish in the Arab world, but rather are added to meat in stews or casseroles, to be consumed with mounds of rice. Stews are usually sautéed on top of the stove and casseroles cooked slowly in the oven with a little less liquid. In general, no two Middle Eastern casseroles or stews are exactly alike, the contents depending on what is available in the market on any particular day as well as on the imagination of the cook.

This particular Moroccan-style stew, prepared with or without meat, is similar in nature to stew for couscous *(see p. 68) and could combine up to seven vegetables.*

2 carrots, sliced
2 potatoes, peeled and cubed
3 onions, chopped
4 cloves garlic, crushed
1 turnip, cubed
1 aubergine/eggplant, cubed
2 squash/courgettes, cubed
1-2 chilli peppers (opt)
2 tbsp parsley, chopped
1/4 tsp cumin, ground
oil for sautéing
salt and pepper

1 Cover and simmer the carrots, garlic, 2 onions, potatoes, turnips and aubergines in water to cover for 15 minutes.

2 Add the squash/courgettes and simmer for a further 10 minutes.

3 Sauté the remaining onion, and add the chilli peppers, cumin and parsley.

4 Add the sautéed onion-spice mixture to the vegetables and simmer for 5 minutes. Adjust the seasoning to taste.

TURNIPS

Left

Arabs usually pickle turnips, which are coloured pink with a little beetroot. However, the vegetable can be sautéed with onions and coloured with a pinch of yellow turmeric for a savoury combination.

In Tunisia, young turnips are sliced thinly and soaked in a combination of olive oil, the juice of one bitter orange or grapefruit, garlic, salt and pepper and an optional pinch of cayenne.

For those with a sweet tooth, turnip may be boiled with fresh or dried dates or dibbis, the fruit's dark molasses syrup. These roots can also be simply boiled in water and dusted with sugar. Either savoury or sweet, turnips can become a unique side dish for meat, chicken or fish.

7 turnips, peeled and cubed
5-6 dates, soaked and mashed or

4 tbsp date syrup
salt

GARNISH
icing sugar

1 Boil the turnips until tender, with the date syrup or dried dates and sufficient water to cover.

2 Drain the excess liquid.

3 Serve with a dusting of icing sugar.

BEANS WITH TOMATOES

Lubia bil bandoura

Long strings of cut green beans are cooked in two methods in the Arab world - either by sautéing gently in olive oil and garlic to produce a favourite cold dish, or by stewing with tomatoes, onions, garlic (and sometimes meat) for one eaten hot. Two varieties of green beans exist in Arabia, plump fassoulia and slim, almost flat lubia - either of which can be used in the recipe.

1 lb (500g) green beans
1 large onion, finely chopped
2 cloves garlic, crushed
3 large tomatoes, chopped
4 tbsp tomato purée
olive oil for sautéing
salt and pepper

1 Wash and cut the beans.

2 Sauté the onions and the garlic in the olive oil. Add the tomatoes and tomato purée. Simmer until stewed. Finally add the beans and season to taste with salt and pepper.

3 Cover and simmer for 20 minutes or until the beans are tender and the sauce has thickened. Check the consistency occasionally and add water as required.

STEMS WITH TAHINA

Saleq bil tahina

Beetroots are typically used in the pickle-making process and saleq, *much like French sorrel, in salads or soups. Although difficult to obtain, silver beet or saleq stems are used here in a dish of Lebanese origin. The stalks, after being boiled and mashed, are mixed with an especially nutty-flavoured tahina sauce. If saleq stems are unavailable, spinach can be substituted. However, only the hard stems are used in this dish, and the fragile leaves set aside.*

2 lb (1 kg) stems of silver beet, *saleq* or spinach
7 tbsp *tahina*
2 cloves garlic, crushed
4 tbsp lemon juice
1 tbsp mint, chopped
salt and pepper

1 Wash the stems and cut into small lengths. Boil in salted water until tender. Drain and pat dry. Mash to a thick paste.

2 Make a slightly thick *tahina* sauce, as the juice from the stalks will later thin it: alternately add the lemon juice and water to the *tahina*, stirring continually. The lemon juice thickens the *tahina* and the water thins it. Add the garlic to the sauce.

3 Add the mashed stems and mix gently.

4 Sprinkle with mint, and serve cold.

Bukoliyat

GRAINS AND PULSES

THE STAPLES AND SEEDS OF THE SOWN

Since cultivation of wheat and barley first began, probably about 6,000 years ago in Mesopotamia, grains have been a staple in the Middle Eastern diet. Throughout history the success of the grain harvest was crucial: years of plenty were recorded when the storehouses were filled to bursting, and times of famine when supplies were exhausted.

Probably native to the Middle East, pulses - the dried seeds of legumes, peas, beans and lentils - have been found in archaeological digs dating back to the Bronze Age. Pulses were a staple in the ancient diet of Arabian country folk, *fellaheen*. The less celebrated, common pulses, once thought of as food for those who couldn't afford meat, are now unashamedly regarded as favourites in the Arab World.

Broad beans (sometimes called fava), chickpeas, *foul*, pearl haricot and several varieties of lentil are all used in a variety of ways. Pulses can make a main course, side dish or snack and be eaten at any time of day.

THE ANCIENT ART OF COOKING RICE

The staple grain of over half the world's population, rice was originally taken into cultivation somewhere in southern Asia - it has certainly been in use in India and China for over 5,000 years. A comparative newcomer to Mediterranean civilisations, rice passed through or around Persia into Arabia and arrived in Egypt between 300 and 400 BC, gradually becoming established in the Middle East. Arabs transported it via their caravan trails through the fertile crescent and around North Africa to their colonies in Europe in about 1000 AD. The ancient word *'aruz'* forms the base of the grain's name in many languages,

116

reflecting its spread: 'arroz' in Spanish, 'oryza' in Latin, 'rizi' in Greek and 'roz' to Arabs.

Middle Easterners have elevated rice cooking to an art. Worthy of a place in the world's finest cuisines, rice is cooked delicately and perfectly so that each spoonful is light, fluffy - never sticky - with each grain firm and separate.

Arabs swear by their rice-cooking methods: absorption - using just enough water to saturate the grains - and an extended technique by which the rice is part cooked, strained, then steamed in an oil base.

Though rice cooked in water is almost exclusively prepared by the absorption and extended methods in the Arab world, the ingredients for cooking vary, as does the procedure. For example, some cooks boil water, add rice, cook and then finally add butter, *samn* or oil. Others prefer to add butter or a stock cube to the boiling water before adding the rice. Yet another method involves sautéing the rice in oil before adding water (in some parts of Arabia, long ago, oils were very expensive and sold by the spoonful so rice was most often simply boiled).

Cooking the grains may require a little experimentation with the amount of water to be used, as one bag of rice may differ from another.

Instructions are given here for both the general and extended methods for plain rice, as well as for grains cooked with other ingredients to produce an array of colours, variety of textures, unusual shapes and unbelievable flavours - that reflect the diversity of Arabia itself. (Further dishes using rice are to be found in the meat, poultry, and seafood sections.)

TIPS FOR COOKING RICE

1 Always use the same pot, with a tight-fitting lid. If the lid does not fit tightly, place a clean, folded tea towel between the pot and lid - be careful not to let the cloth burn. A heavy pot is best, but a lighter weight pot with a heat-diffuser underneath can also be used.

2 Basmati rice, a long-grained and fragrant rice, is most widely preferred. Although finer grades of rice are available in the Middle East, the long, slender grains of basmati rice are recommended for all recipes, except for stuffings where a shorter grain is required. If basmati is unavailable, other long-grained rice may be substituted, although requiring a little more water, varied cooking times and rendering different textures and flavours. Easy-cook rice will not work successfully in these recipes.

3 Wash all rice - some bought in sacks can contain tiny stones. Usually rice is clean and only needs to be rinsed to remove the starch which can make it stick together when cooked, so washing is essential for a consistent texture.

4 Rice is measured by volume, never weight, and the water-to-rice ratio is the key to mastering perfect rice. (Approximately $1\frac{3}{4}$ volume of water to 2 of rice.) Remember, not enough water is better than too much. A little water can be added if the rice dries out before becoming tender. However, trying to absorb too much water by lengthy cooking only makes the grains begin to disintegrate.

5 After the water and rice have been brought back to the boil, lower the heat and simmer slowly until tender. Timing varies, according to the type and dryness of the rice, although it usually about 20 minutes.

6 Do not stir rice during cooking, except when it is first poured into the boiling water - stirring will break the grains and make the rice glutinous. If necessary, the rice can be fluffed with a fork at the end of cooking.

7 Always leave the rice to stand for a few minutes before serving. The longer the rice dries, the fluffier and more fragrant it becomes.

PLAIN RICE BY ABSORPTION METHOD

Roz abaid

2 cups long-grain rice
1³/₄ cups water
1 tsp salt

1 Clean and wash the rice until the water runs clear. Drain.

2 Add the rice to salted boiling water.

3 When the water returns to the boil, cover and reduce the heat to a slow simmer for 15 minutes.

4 Check the rice for tenderness and absorption. Do not stir! If the water has not been absorbed, simmer for a further 5 minutes. If the rice is not tender, add a little water, if required, and continue to simmer.

5 Leave to stand for a few minutes before serving.

VARIATIONS
● Stock can be substituted for water or a stock cube can be added to the water.

● Add 2 tbsp oil, butter or *samn* to the boiling water.

EXTENDED METHOD

Rice is cooked following the absorption method, but is removed from the stove when half cooked. It is then strained and slowly steamed in butter, samn or oil until tender.

2 cups long-grain rice
4 cups water
4 tbsp butter, *samn* or oil
1 tsp salt

1 Clean and wash the rice until the water runs clear. Drain.

2 Add the rice to the boiling water.

3 When the water returns to the boil, cover and reduce the heat to a slow simmer for 6 minutes. The grains will then be under-cooked but slightly tender.

4 Strain, wash and drain the rice. Swirl 2 tbsp oil, *samn*, or butter in the bottom of the rice cooking pot. Return the rice to the oiled pot, adding salt. Add 2 more tablespoons of butter or *samn* over the rice.

5 Cover tightly and allow to steam on a very low heat for 20-30 minutes or until tender and fluffy.

6 Leave the rice to stand for 10 minutes before serving.

RICE IN A MOULD

To most Arabs the presentation of food is almost as important as the cooking methods or ingredients used in preparation. Food should look beautiful. Cooked rice can became more decorative when pressed into a mould of any shape - the most popular is a ring. For individual servings, try pushing rice into small bowls to mould it.

To shape rice, line an oiled mould with nuts, browned onions, sultanas, pulses or a combination of fruit and nuts. Press the cooked rice very tightly into the mould and turn out carefully onto a serving dish.

CRISP-CRUST RICE

Timman

A favourite way of cooking rice is by this traditional recipe, in which a crisp crust forms at the bottom of the pot. To achieve this crunchy texture, return the rice to steam over a very low heat for 5-15 minutes (2 tbsp oil added to the bottom of the cooking pot will help the crust form in about 5 minutes - otherwise it will take much longer).

GREEN RICE

Roz bil khodara

White rice with hints of green is popularly served alongside stews or fried fish. Commonly, a cup of chopped fresh dill is gently turned into the rice during the last 10 minutes of cooking. Other herbs, including mint, tarragon, chives or parsley can be experimented with. Timman bagella (see p. 66) is a dill rice which also has broad, or fava beans and is usually topped with lamb.

YELLOW RICE

Roz asfar

Yellow-coloured rice is an attractive as well as aromatic and tasty dish popular in the Middle East. The faint colouring can be attained by adding saffron, the expensive tiny red crocus stigmas, or - less costly but also less aromatic - turmeric, the roots of a plant of the lily family.

The rice can be tinted yellow throughout, or a patchwork of yellow and white can be made. For a batch of completely yellow rice, add $1/2$ tsp powdered turmeric or saffron to the boiling water before adding rice. For the spotted version, make 4-5 small wells in the cooked rice and fill them with saffron or turmeric that has been soaked in a few spoons of warm water.

RED RICE

Roz ahmar

Rice coloured red or orange with tomatoes or tomato sauce or purée (see p. 46) can provide a uniquely enticing bed for tender cubes of lamb, for chicken legs or for any meat, poultry or seafood stewed with tomatoes. Tomato sauce can be substituted for some of the cooking water and a few peeled, chopped and seeded tomatoes can be added to the boiling water. For a strong, reddish rice, add 8 tbsp tomato sauce, or extra fresh tomatoes, and a pinch of sugar to cut the acidity. For a soft, pinkish rice, lessen the amount of tomato sauce to 2 tbsp.

2 cups long-grain rice, washed
1 3/4 cups water
6 onions, chopped
1/2 cup pomegranate juice with 1 tsp sugar or
1/2 cup pomegranate syrup
1 tbsp tomato purée
1 cup walnuts, chopped (opt)
oil for sautéing
1 tsp salt

1 Sauté the onions. Boil the water, pomegranate juice, onions and salt.

2 Add the rice and walnuts. Cover and slowly simmer for about 20 minutes or until the liquid has been absorbed and the rice has become light and tender.

3 To form a crispy crust on the bottom, return to a very low heat for about 10 minutes.

PINK RICE

Sharab al ruman

Pomegranate, among the most ancient of fruits, is the source of sweetness for this rice dish. Use either the slightly tart juice from the shiny red seeds of the fresh fruit along with some sugar, or a prepared grenadine syrup known as dibs ruman.

Roast chicken legs are sometimes served on a platter of this slightly sweet rice.

ONION RICE

Mashkoul, or Roz bil basal

Mounds of rice topped by a heap of golden-fried onions are a popular accompaniment for stews, but sometimes serve as a bed for lamb pieces. Simply sauté chopped onions until golden, add water and bring to the boil before adding the rice (proportions of rice to water as for absorption method). Garnish with more onions that have been fried until caramel coloured. (In some of the Gulf States onion rice is drizzled with clarified butter, samn.)

YOGHURT RICE

Roz bil laban

Yoghurt is an essential element in the Middle Eastern diet, and is often prepared daily (see p. 50). Fresh yoghurt should be stabilised (see p. 52) before being cooked with rice, though unstabilised yoghurt can be added to warm rice after cooking. A Middle Eastern speciality calls for dried yoghurt balls (jameed) which are crumbled and cooked in stock to pour over the rice (see p. 52)

Generally, the absorption method is used, with plain home-made or bought yoghurt simply take the place of an equal volume of the cooking water.

For a spicier rice, add 1 tbsp dried mint and 2 cloves crushed garlic to plain yoghurt and allow to stand for 1 1/2 hours before adding to cooked rice.

CREAMY RICE

Roz maslouk

A speciality of the Kingdom of Saudi Arabia, in which rice is cooked slowly in milk for a long time until a smooth consistency is achieved. In other regions of the Arab World milk or stabilised yoghurt (see p. 52) is added to stock and poured over the rice dish as a sauce. This creamed rice or rice with sauce is used to form a bed for a whole roast lamb.

Creamy rice is popular with children, who sometimes eat it for breakfast with a little honey, but can also be trickled with rich samn, clarified butter. Rose water or cinnamon can also be used to flavour the rice.

In the Levant roz bil haleeb is cooked with milk, sugar, rose water and a pinch of baking powder and served cold as a sweet resembling rice pudding.

For the Saudi speciality, the milk rice is cooked using the absorption method on p.119, with the addition of sautéed onions. Milk and rice are added to the boiling water in equal quantities. If cooking 2 cups rice, add 3/4 cup of water and 2 cups of milk together with the salt before adding the rice. Boil until soft and purée-like.

RICE WITH FRUIT

Roz bil fawakeh

For over 5,000 years Arabs have dried fruit in the sun, including indigenous dates and figs, plucked from the finest orchards of the ancient world, and apricots - which must have been transported along the Silk Road from China .

Rice made with fruit and nuts, though a savoury dish, seems slightly sweet because of the fruit. However, this can be left out for a nutty rice (see facing page). Availability determines which fruit will be used, but keep in mind that dried fruit is much sweeter and richer than fresh. Typically, Arabian fruit-sweetened rice includes sultanas, raisins or berries - but sometimes apricots, pomegranate seeds or one of the hundreds of varieties of native dates are included. Dates can be accompanied by almonds and/or pistachios, while apricots are usually combined with walnuts.

The rose water gives the rice a delicate aroma.

2 cups long-grain rice, washed
1/2 cup dates or apricots, soaked and chopped (opt)
3 tbsp raisins, sultanas or
1/2 cup pitted sour cherries or barbaries
1 onion, finely chopped
1/2 cup almonds, pistachios or walnuts (opt)
5-6 saffron threads
2 tbsp rose water (opt)
oil for sautéing
1 tsp salt

1 Soak the saffron in the rose water.

2 Sauté the onions. Add the dried fruit of choice.

3 Add 1¾ cups salted water, bring to the boil, and then add the rice. Simmer slowly over low heat for 15 minutes.

4 To remove the thin skin from the nuts, pour boiling water (salted for pistachios) over them and rinse in cold water. The skin should come away easily. Add the blanched nuts and saffron rose water to simmer with the rice for a further 5 minutes or until the rice is dry and fluffy. Leave to stand for about 10 minutes before serving.

and sprinkled over the cooked rice before serving. Alternatively the nuts can be steamed along with the rice for 20 minutes, using the extended method for cooking rice (see p. 119).

RICE WITH NOODLES

Roz bil shariyah

Golden vermicelli noodles and ivory rice contrast in a dish that should be presented on a platter to look its very best. The unusual texture of thin broken strings of pasta and fluffy rice is pleasing to the palate, especially when served alongside the smooth green melokhiya *stew (see p. 77) or the nutty meatballs in tomato sauce (p. 64).*

2 cups long-grain rice, washed
¹/₂ cup vermicelli noodles
1¾ cup water
oil for sautéing
1 tsp salt

1 Break up the vermicelli noodles into pieces about ²/₃ inch (2 cm) long. Sauté in a little oil until lightly browned, taking care as the noodles can burn easily.

2 Boil the water with the salt and add the rice. Simmer slowly for 15 minutes.

3 Before the rice is tender, toss in the sautéed noodles to simmer for a further 5 minutes. Serve on a large dish or platter.

RICE WITH NUTS

Roz ma mucasarat

Nuts were collected by the food-gatherers long before the birth of agriculture, and today are still an important feature of Middle Eastern cooking. In fact, medieval Europe probably learned the art of cooking with nuts from the Arabs. Six varieties of nut figure prominently in Arabian cooking: pine nut kernels, pistachios, almonds, cashews, hazelnuts and walnuts. A decorative dish, Roz ma mucasarat is served mainly at parties and celebrations, and to dinner guests.

The nutty rice can be prepared either with one variety or with a mixture of nuts, and can be left white or coloured yellow with saffron. Use 1 cup pistachios, almonds, cashews and/or pine nuts to 2 cups uncooked rice. The skins of almonds can be easily removed by pouring boiling water over the nuts and then rinsing in cold water. To remove the skins of pistachios and leave the nut with its green colour, blanch first in salted water then treat as you would almonds. Nuts can be sautéed in a little oil until golden

RICE WITH PULSES

Mujadara

Tiny brown lentils or plump green broad beans (fava) dot white rice in a dish that can be served alone or as a base for stew. The amount of lentils or beans can be varied considerably, according to taste, but be careful not to skimp on the mound of crispy brown onion garnish. If using broad beans, add a bunch of freshly chopped dill to produce a dish called timman bagella *(see p. 66).*

2 cups long-grain rice, washed
$^1/2$-2 cups brown lentils
1 onion, chopped
oil for sautéing
1 tsp salt

GARNISH
3 onions, quartered and sliced
oil for shallow frying

1 Soak the lentils overnight. Drain and wash. Boil the cleaned lentils until almost tender.

2 Sauté the chopped onion.

3 Add the washed rice, onions, and salt to $1^3/4$ cups boiling water. Return to the boil, carefully folding the lentils into the rice.

4 Cover and simmer gently for about 20 minutes or until the rice is tender, adding a little water if required.

5 Place a clean, folded tea towel between the lid and pot. Allow to stand for 10 minutes.

6 Meanwhile, fry the onions until they have turned to a caramel colour.

7 Serve garnished with the browned onions.

VARIATIONS

● Cook the rice and lentils separately, combining when both are tender.

● Add $^1/2$ tsp ground cumin or 1 tsp ground coriander with the salt.

SWEET RICE

Muḥammar

Long before the advent of cultured pearls in the Far East, the Arabian Gulf was a natural pearling area. The divers, who plunged into unknown seas with only a nose clip and rope tied around the waist, produced their own rice dish. This sweet rice, muhammar, *would raise the divers' blood-sugar levels, allowing them to stay under the water for longer periods of time without the aid of modern equipment. To the astonishment of today's scuba divers, the pearlers claimed to have reached depths of 130 ft (40 m). This rice is a favourite of those with a sweet tooth, who savour the aromatic rose water, saffron and cardamom. For a rice with a more subtle sweetness, reduce the honey to 2 tbsp.*

This rice was traditionally served with fish, the food most easily obtained by the pearl divers.

2 cups long-grain rice, washed
3 cups water
$^1/2$ tsp saffron threads
3 cardamom pods, cracked
2 tbsp rose water (opt)
$^1/2$ cup honey or date syrup (opt)
2 tbsp butter, *samn* or oil
1 tsp salt

1 Soak the saffron and cracked cardamom pods in the rose water for at least 10 minutes.

2 Add the rice and salt to the boiling water. Cover and simmer for 6 minutes. Drain well.

3 Carefully turn the honey into the drained rice.

4 Swirl the oil or *samn* around the bottom and sides of the rice pot and add the honeyed rice. Sprinkle with the rose water mixture.

5 Place a clean tea towel between the pot and the lid. Steam the rice on very low heat for 10-15 minutes or until tender.

WHEAT DISH

Hariss

Wheat, which is thought to have been first cultivated in the region of the Tigris and Euphrates and was spread throughout the Middle Eastern civilisations by merchants' caravans, forms the basis of this wholesome dish. The word hariss, *meaning 'well cooked', is a good description of wheat grains which are most often puréed and sometimes mixed with pulverised chicken or lamb (see p. 79). However, the cooked grains can be left intact, prepared without meat and drizzled with honey for a warm soothing porridge, which is a favourite among children. Hariss is also served for breakfast in the Arab world, topped with milk, melted butter or samn.*

The savoury version here is wheat cooked in stock with a touch of cinnamon. In the Gulf, thickened hariss *is served along with the main course.*

Kisk, a Lebanese and Syrian breakfast dish, is similar to hariss. *A soured mixture of wheat and milk - which has*

been dried to a powder - is mixed with water, laced with onions and garlic and fried in mutton which has been rendered in its own fat, qawwrama.

12 oz (350g) whole wheat grains
1 tsp cinnamon
1 1/2 tsp salt

TO SERVE
2 tbsp butter or *samn*

1 Soak the wheat overnight in water. Wash and drain.

2 Boil the wheat in sufficient salted water or stock to cover for about 3-4 hours or until very soft. Remove any scum as it rises.

3 Add the cinnamon and seasoning to taste.Blend to a purée or pound with a pestle and mortar.

4 To serve, spoon butter or *samn* over the wheat.

VARIATION
● For the grains to remain whole, boil for about 1 hour.

CRACKED, OR BULGUR WHEAT

Burgul

Grains are boiled, dried and finally cracked or roughly ground to yield a processed wheat call burgul. *A prominent staple food throughout the Middle East, the cracked wheat is featured in* tabouleh, *a salad of finely chopped parsley (see p. 32), and in* kibbah, *shaped spicy minced meat (see pages 20-22), or is simply served in the place of rice to accompany any stew.* Burgul *can also be drizzled with butter or* samn *as a breakfast cereal.*

Farika, an unripened cracked wheat similar to burgul, *is used to replace rice in stuffing vine leaves (see p. 12) and stuffed chicken (see p. 73).*

Burgul *is like rice in that it is cooked by volume and not by weight. The previous rice recipes, including most ingredients, can also be used to prepare bulgur wheat, using equal amounts of water to* burgul - *a one-to-one ratio.*

Bulgur wheat can be found in most healthfood shops and large supermarkets, (sometimes graded coarse, medium and fine) but can be made at home. To make your own, take good quality whole wheat and, if necessary, pick out any stones or roughage, rinse and strain. Place the wheat in a saucepan of boiling water. Boil until the wheat is somewhat soft and begins to crack open. Then drain well and dry in the sun or in a very low oven. The dried burgul *must then be coarsely ground in a hand grinder or coffee mill and sieved.*

2 cups coarse *burgul*
2 cups stock or water
1/4 cup butter or *samn*
1 tsp salt

1 Clean and wash the *burgul* until the water runs clear.

2 Add the *burgul* with salt to the boiling stock or water. Cover and simmer for 10-15 minutes or until tender and the liquid has been absorbed, adding water if required.

3 Pour the butter or *samn* over the *burgul*.

4 Place a clean, folded tea towel between the pot and lid. Allow to steam over very low heat for a further 5-10 minutes, or until each grain is firm and separate.

VARIATIONS

● Steam 3 tbsp toasted pine nuts, slivered almonds and/or raisins with the *burgul*.

● Rather than butter or *samn*, cubes of cheese can be added to the *burgul*.

COUSCOUS

Couscous, or Maghrebiya

A cereal processed from semolina into tiny pellets, couscous is best known for its use with traditional North African stews which go by the same name (see p. 68). In Morocco, especially on festive occasions, the cereal is steamed, shaped into a cone, covered with the stew which contains at least seven vegetables and meat pieces, and served in a special earthenware dish called a tagine.

Expert North Africans own a couscousier, a special steamer, or simply perch the grain atop the cooking vapours of the stew or broth in a sieve or double steamer. For more details about couscous and the stew see p. 68.

Although couscous can be bought in packets usually pre-cooked and requiring minimal steaming) it can also be made at home by the adventurous. A half-and-half mixture of coarse and fine semolina is required, both preferably

Moroccan clay pots, *tagine*

from hard wheat. The simplest way is to prepare a basin of water, a shallow dish of mixed semolina, and a clean cloth spread on the table. Dampen the palm of the hand in the basin, then lay it on the semolina mixture so that some of it sticks. Lightly rub one palm against the other in a circular motion to round the grains. Allow the grains to naturally fall on the cloth. The fine particles of semolina make the coarser ones stick together. Finally let the couscous dry and sieve out any surplus flour

2 cups *couscous*
3-4 tbsp *samn* or oil
salt

1 Moisten the *couscous* by sprinkling with salty water, gently mixing to allow the grains to swell. Rub the grains between the fingers to remove any lumps. Let stand for 10 minutes. Coat evenly with the *samn* or oil.

2 Cover and steam in a sieve or steamer over a simmering stew, raking the grains occasionally to help them swell. Pre-cooked *couscous* only needs to be steamed for about 15 minutes, other *couscous* for 30-45 minutes,

3 Strain the stew and place the meat and vegetables in the centre of a serving dish surrounded with *couscous*. Serve the sauce separately.

PULSES

Fassoulia

Visualise a steaming pot-bellied vessel perched on a bed of glowing coals, the fire dancing round the edges. This is the age-old way of cooking pulses in the Arab world. In traditional kitchens and outdoors, pulses are cooked in a kidra or damassa, a special bean-cooking, wide-bottomed and narrow-necked pot with handles. The shape allows steam to condense on the upper sloping sides and forces flavoursome vapours back into the pot. However, any pot with a tight-fitting lid can be used in its place.

Pulses can be pressure cooked if time is a factor, but will vary in taste and texture from those cooked slowly over a low heat. Dried pulses should be soaked in water before cooking. Although preparation methods for pulses may vary, one steadfast rule should be observed: never add salt until near the end of cooking time, or the beans, peas and some lentils will harden.

Cooking beans in a *damassa*

TIPS FOR COOKING PULSES

1 Soak all pulses - except soft red or yellow lentils - overnight before cooking.

2 Most beans are cooked in water, 1 1/2 times their volume.

3 Salt is added to pulses after they are tender. With red or yellow lentils, salt can be added at any time.

4 For best results, slowly cook pulses over low heat for many hours. An electric slow cooker is ideal. If cooked too quickly, beans will fall apart.

5 We do not recommend adding bicarbonate of soda to pulses - although it may shorten cooking time it also destroys some of the nutrients.

6 Addition of cumin to pulses is said to decrease their flatulent effects.

WHITE BEANS

Fassoulia baida

Served with white rice, dried haricot beans cooked slowly in a red sauce with a few pieces of browned meat and plenty of spices are a main course in Arabia. Pearl haricots, sometimes called navy beans, are the ones used in our familiar baked beans. However, the larger creamy-white flat variety can also be used in this recipe.

1 cup dry haricot beans
6 oz (175g) meat, cubed
1 1/2 cup water
2 onions, chopped
3 cloves garlic, crushed
2 tomatoes, peeled and chopped
6 oz (175g) tomato purée
2 tbsp parsley, chopped
2 bay leaves
1 tsp paprika
pinch of cayenne pepper
oil for sautéing
salt and pepper

GARNISH
lemon wedges
sprigs of parsley

1 Soak the beans overnight. Wash and drain.

2 Sauté the onions and the garlic. Add all the ingredients except the salt to the pot, and add water to cover.

3 Boil for 2-3 hours or until the beans are tender. The cooking time depends on the size and dryness of the beans.

4 Adjust the seasoning to taste by adding salt. Simmer for a further 10 minutes.

5 Serve hot with lemon wedges and garnished with parsley.

LENTILS

Adas

Lentils are a type of pulse that came originally from the Middle East and are still grown in Egypt and North Africa. At least half a dozen types of dried lentils, both whole and split, are used in Middle Eastern soups, stews, mixed with rice, puréed to a dip or simply cooked to perfect spicy consistency and eaten with pieces of Arabic bread. The most popular lentils in the Arab world are the yellow split lentils, adas asfar, which are only made into soups and stews. The brown variety, adas bil gibba 'lentils in a cloak' or adas hub 'whole lentils', retain their shape much better for simmering, although require soaking and longer cooking. Red-orange lentils can be used but become very soft when cooked.

Most lentils are available ready washed. If you need to clean the lentils, first pick through to remove grit and stones. Wash the lentils several times in fresh water, making sure to remove all the impurities that float to the top or small stones that sink to the bottom. A simple method for washing the seeds is to shake water in a tilted pan until the stones, which are heavier, slid down to the bottom corner. The clean lentils can be easily scooped out. In the Orient, lentils bought in the bazaars are often stone-ridden, and housewives often become expert at removing the unwanted matter by tossing the lentils in baskets or with mats.

Whole lentils take from 45 minutes to one and a half hours to cook, depending on age and variety, but with a pressure cooker can take as little as 15 or 20 minutes. The pot should be watched closely as the tiny seeds absorb vast amounts of water. Any excess water can be used as a great stock!

1 cup lentils
1 1/2 cups water
1 large onion, chopped
3 cloves garlic, crushed
1/4 tsp cumin, ground
1/2 tsp coriander, ground
2 tbsp olive oil
salt and pepper

1 Brown lentils should be soaked overnight, while red and yellow lentils require little or no soaking. Wash and drain.

2 Combine the lentils onion, garlic, cumin, coriander, pepper, 1 tsp oil and water. Cover and simmer the red or yellow lentils for about 20 minutes and the brown lentils for 1 to 1 1/2 hours or until tender, adding water as required. The lentils should remain suspended in a thick rich sauce.

3 Add salt to taste and simmer for a further 5 minutes.

4 Garnish with the remaining olive oil and chopped herbs. Serve over rice as a bed for stew or meat.

VARIATION

● For a lentil purée, boil the lentils until they begin to disintegrate, adding water as required. Serve mashed to a paste and garnished with onions, fried until caramel coloured.

BROWN BEANS

Foul medames

This typically Egyptian dish must be one of the oldest in recorded history. Still today, it is beloved by all. Foul is both served from brass pots in the finest five-star hotels and ladled from huge pots perched on the back of wagons.

When cooking this dish, Arabs use the damassa, *the wide-bellied pot dedicated to the cooking of beans.*

The secret of this dish is the long, slow cooking. The best we ever tasted had been cooked over a dying fire all night, out in the desert where wood was scarce so it had to be burned slowly. When dawn came and the sun was peeking over the sand dunes, we were presented with a bowl of these beans with an egg on top. The egg had been wrapped in foil and had sat in the ashes all night. Although firm it was creamier than the typical boiled egg. (The mood was enhanced as we were served by a tall slender Arab in his long, flowing, pure white kandura!)

2 cups *foul medames*, brown beans
3 cups water

TO SERVE
3 cloves garlic, crushed
5 tbsp fresh lemon juice
1/4 tsp cumin, ground
2 tbsp parsley, chopped
3 tbsp olive oil
1 green chilli pepper, chopped (opt)
1 tomato, chopped
salt and pepper
4 eggs

1 Soak the beans overnight. Wash and drain. Carefully scrub the eggs in their shells.

2 Cover and simmer the beans and eggs covered with the water on very low heat for 6 hours or until the beans are tender, adding water as required. Shell the hard boiled eggs and put aside to garnish.

3 Mash a few of the beans to a crumbly paste and add back to the bean pot.

4 Crush the garlic with 1 tsp salt. Add the lemon juice, cumin, parsley, olive oil, and chilli pepper to the beans. Leave to stand until the flavour has been absorbed. Adjust the seasoning to taste by adding more olive oil or lemon juice. Add the tomato and eggs to garnish.

5 When served as a traditional Arabian breakfast, the bowl of beans is placed in the centre of the floor mat. Each individual scoops up the beans using Arabic bread.

VARIATION
● For a 'quick' version, the beans can be boiled for 90 minutes or until tender. However, long, slow simmering enhances the flavour.

BROAD, OR FAVA BEANS

Foul nabet, Bagella

Green shelled beans, fresh or frozen, along with dill are added to rice for timman bagella (*see p. 66*). *The beans can also be simmered slowly for a delicious dish that Middle Easterners eat by scooping up with pieces of Arabic bread. Arabs eat the dried giant variety of the bean, some at least an inch long and dark brown in colour, which are simply boiled, salted and have their skins removed for snacking. Dried broad beans should be soaked overnight and the skins squeezed off before cooking. Either fresh or frozen beans can be used.*

2 cups dried broad beans
1 onion, chopped
4 cloves garlic, crushed
$1/4$ tsp cumin, ground
$1/4$ tsp coriander, ground
oil for sautéing
2 tbsp dill, chopped
salt and pepper

GARNISH
lemon wedges

1 Soak the beans overnight. Wash and drain. Remove skins.

2 Sauté the onions and garlic until soft. Add the coriander and sauté for a further 2 minutes.

3 Cover and simmer the broad beans with the onion, garlic, coriander, cumin, pepper and water to cover for about 30 minutes or until tender.

4 Add the dill and salt to taste. Simmer for a further 10 minutes.

5 Serve garnished with lemon wedges.

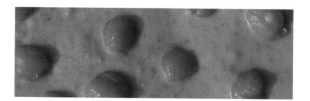

CHICKPEA PURÉE

Musabaha

Considered a native of the Middle East, chickpeas are a staple in Arabic cooking and are used in snacks, soups, salads, stuffings and stews. These large peas, sometimes called garbanzo beans, are shaped like hazelnuts, and are usually beige or golden, although there is also a small, dark brown variety.

Chickpeas are served throughout the Arab world for breakfast, especially on Friday, the day off work. Palestinian in origin, Musabaha is a flavourful chickpea breakfast dish, similar to the hummos *dish served in the mezza, and is eaten scooped up with pieces of Arabic bread. Fatta hummos - a thinner version of* musabaha *- is served over broken Arabic bread, topped with a layer of sautéed meat pieces and sprinkled with pine nuts and sumac.*

8 oz (225g) dried chickpeas
3 fl oz (75ml) *tahina*
3 tbsp lemon juice
2 tsp yoghurt
3 cloves garlic, crushed
1 green chilli pepper, chopped (opt)
$1/4$ tsp cumin, ground
salt
1 tbsp *samn* or butter

1 Soak the chickpeas overnight. Drain and wash.

2 Boil the chickpeas in water to cover with the cumin for 1 hour or until tender. Add salt to taste and boil for a further 5 minutes. Drain and reserve 1 cup of the tender chickpeas and $1/4$ cup of the cooking liquid.

3 Add the reserved stock and the lemon juice

alternately to the *tahina*, one spoon at a time until a creamy thick sauce forms. (The stock thins *tahina* and the lemon juice thickens it.)

4 In a food processor, blend the remaining chickpeas with the garlic, chilli pepper, yoghurt and the *tahina* mixture until puréed. Adjust seasoning to taste. Scoop out into a bowl.

5 Decorate with the reserved whole chickpeas. Drizzle the *samn* or butter over the top.

6 Traditionally served for breakfast with Arabic bread, olives, chilli peppers and pickles, this can also form a pre-dinner snack or hors d'oeuvre.

Khoubz
BREAD

THE STAFF OF LIFE

Throughout the Arab World, bread has always been associated with life. The Arabic word for life is *aisha*. The ancient Egyptians mastered the art of fermenting dough in 1500 BC, baking round flat loaves of *aish*. One Arab's analysis of the similarity in words is that 'God gives life by providing the wheat to make the bread.'

Wheat was cultivated in Mesopotamia at the beginning of civilisation, some 6,000 years ago, but barley was perhaps the first grain to be made into unleavened cakes. Also once made into flat bread, millet - associated today with fodder for animals - was grown by the Romans and, with alfalfa, passed along the Silk Road to China.

Traditionally, bread was baked on a flat stone or iron plate or sent for baking at the community oven (*tanour* or *furun*). A friend told me of his experience as a young boy in Jerusalem when children, usually girls, were sent running to the neighbourhood bakery balancing heavy trays of dough on their heads. The mothers marked their dough with a fingerprint, or two, and the children played while the bread was baked.

The ovens of modern Middle Eastern bakeries vary in size and shape. Some look almost like a hooded wishing well, the sides and top covered with plaster or hardened clay mud. Skilled bakers whirl the dough in the air like a pizza before slapping it onto the inner sides of the oven. Upright, front-opening ovens, constructed of brick, have arched or domed openings and a chimney at the back. The dough is placed on flattened paddles and slid into the oven to bake.

The names of bread, and their spellings, are as varied as their shapes and forms. *Khoubz*, pitta bread, is a flat pocket-bread baked in small

rounds of about 6 inches (15 cm) across, or in larger 8-10 inch (20-25 cm) loaves. The rounds can be made of white or brown wheat flour or a combination of both. *Shraak* and *rukak* are paper-thin breads used for layering foods or for wrapping chickens or whole roast lambs. The dough is sometimes pulled over a *saj*, an inverted cast-iron wok-like implement, to cook an ultra-thin bread.

A thick, oily Egyptian bread with many fine layers, *fatir mushaltet*, is eaten with chunks of cheese, *mish* - seemingly aged forever - or drizzled with honey. *Khoubz al tabon* has two layers - one thick and one thin - but they cannot be separated to make a pocket. This special bread is baked in a *tabon*, a clay oven with agate stones, which retain the heat during the cooking.

Bread is also flavoured before baking: *manakish* is a standard *khoubz* dough brushed liberally with a mixture of olive oil and *zaatar*. Syrians top the dough with raw onions mixed with a little ground cumin, coriander and dried mint before baking. In Yemen, a hot chilli and fenugreek paste is spread over the dough.

Bread baked to a crunchy hardness, *kaak*, with a touch of a special spice called *mahlab* and sometimes coated with sesame seeds, is dunked in tea or warmed camel's, goat's, sheep's or cow's milk for breakfast. *Samit*, also a rusk-like bread, is Cairo's answer to pretzels. Street vendors or bakeries hawk the hoops of bread on long sticks.

An Arabic meal would not be complete without plenty of *khoubz*. To many people it replaces the knife and fork; bread is torn off into small pieces and held as a utensil for gently collecting the food and conveying it to the mouth. For convenience, urbanised Arabs and restaurants cut their bread neatly into pie-like slices before serving.

The making of Arabic bread is only recommended for those seeking a new cooking challenge. Speciality shops usually carry a few fresh loaves, a packet of which is more than can be eaten at an average size meal, and pitta is readily available through Greek shops and supermarkets. The flat loaves take up little room in the freezer, can be defrosted in a few seconds in the microwave and still taste almost fresh-baked. The bread can also be warmed in the oven or over a gas flame. Before warming, sprinkle a little water on each loaf to prevent the bread from drying. However, for the adventurous, here are the recipes for the main types of bread.

LEAVENED POCKET BREAD

Khoubz arabi

1 lb (500g) plain flour, sifted
1 tbsp fresh yeast or
1 tsp dried yeast
$^1/_2$ tsp salt
$^1/_2$ tsp sugar
10 fl oz (275ml) lukewarm water
oil for coating

1 Combine the yeast with 3-4 tbsp warm water. Add the sugar and leave to stand in a warm place for about 10-15 minutes or until it begins to bubble.

2 Sift the flour and salt into a warmed mixing bowl.

3 Make a well in the centre of the flour and pour in the yeast mixture. Gradually add enough warm water to make a soft firm dough.

4 On a lightly floured surface, knead the dough vigorously for about 15 minutes or until smooth and pliable. For a softer bread add 1 tbsp of oil.

5 With oiled hands, slightly coat the surface of the dough to prevent a crust forming as it rises.

6 Cover with a damp cloth and leave to rise in a warm place for 2 hours or until double in size.

7 Punch down the dough and knead for a few minutes. Separate the dough into about 6 balls. Roll until round and smooth.

8 On a lightly floured surface, flatten each ball into a disc about 1/4" (0.5 cm) thick. Dust with a little flour and cover with a cloth. Leave to stand. To make a pocket bread, fold the flattened disc in half. Once again roll into a disc.

9 Carefully slide the discs onto hot baking sheets. Sprinkle with a few drops of water to prevent rapid browning. Bake in a pre-heated oven at 400°F (200°C) gas 6 for 10 minutes or until puffed up. Do not open the oven door during this time.

VARIATIONS

● Prepare one piece of bread and put aside. Place another on the heat, immediately spread with a topping of cream cheese, egg or anchovy paste. Quickly cover with the first piece of bread.

THIN UNLEAVENED BREAD

Rukak

1 lb (500g) plain flour, sifted
1/2 tsp salt
lukewarm water
oil for frying

1 Add enough water to the flour and salt to make a very moist, sticky dough. It should almost resemble a batter but still hold together as a dough.

2 Rub a wok, saj, with an oiled cloth.

3 Pick up a handful of the very sticky dough and roll with a circular motion around the inside surface of an oiled wok. As you push the dough around, a thin layer will stick to the wok. Return the remaining dough to the bowl.

4 The bread will become crisp very quickly. To lift the bread, lightly loosen the edges with a sharp instrument.

5 To serve, roll up and drizzle with butter or samn or break into small pieces to use for soaked-bread dishes (see pages 69, 78).

THIN CRISPY UNLEAVENED BREAD

Shraak

MAKES 8 ROUNDS
1 lb (500g) plain flour, sifted
1/2 tsp salt
lukewarm water

1 Add enough water to the flour and salt to make a firm dough.

2 On a lightly floured surface, knead until well combined.

3 Cover and leave to stand for 30 minutes. The dough will not rise but will become more pliable.

4 Divide the dough into eight pieces. Roll into balls and flatten into thin disc shapes. Place on floured baking sheets.

5 Bake for 10-12 minutes in a pre-heated oven at 400°F (200°C) gas 6. Alternatively, spread over a greased top of an inverted cast-iron wok, saj, and

HARD BREAD

Kaak

Early one chilly Jordanian winter morning, we sat wrapped in blankets next to the window and watched the ever-greying sky and gently drifting snow. Our gracious hosts soon delivered a dish of hard rusks covered with sesame seeds, and demonstrated how the kaak was dunked in steaming mugs of sweetened goat's milk.

Shaped in rings, rectangular planks, blocks or sticks, this hard bread's secret flavour of is the pale-brown pepper-corn-sized kernel of the black cherry called mahlab. *The bread is long-baked until any hint of moisture disappears. Arabs dunk the dry crusty bread into extra-sweet tea, or coffee, as well as milk.*

1 lb (500g) plain flour, sifted

2 tbsp fresh yeast or

^{1}/$_2$ tbsp dried yeast

4 fl oz (100ml) lukewarm water

^{1}/$_2$ tsp sugar

4 fl oz (100ml) *samn* or melted butter

^{1}/$_2$ tsp salt

^{1}/$_2$ tsp *mahlab*, ground

1 egg, beaten

sesame seeds

1 Put the yeast into a small bowl with 3-4 tbsp of the lukewarm water. Add the sugar and leave to stand in a warm place for about 10-15 minutes or until it becomes frothy.

2 Mix the flour, salt and *mahlab*.

3 Make a well in the centre and slowly pour in the yeast and butter or *samn*, working well between each addition.

4 Add enough water to make a stiff dough. Knead vigorously for 10 minutes.

5 Roll pieces of the dough into walnut-size balls or other desired shapes.

6 Brush with the egg mixed with 2 tbsp water. Dip into or sprinkle with the sesame seeds.

7 Leave to rise on an oiled baking sheet in a warm place for 2 hours.

8 Bake at 350°F (175°C) gas 4 for 20 minutes. Lower the heat to 300°F (150°C) gas 2 for a further 1 hour. Once again lower the heat 225°F (100°C) gas ^{1}/$_4$ for 2-3 hours. The *kaak* should be brown, dry, hard and crunchy.

9 Store for several months in an airtight container. Serve to be 'dunked' in tea, milk or coffee.

VARIATIONS

● *Kaak Ramadan*, a sweet cake, is made by mixing 8 tbsp sesame seeds and 8 tbsp sugar with a little oil to make a paste. Spread on top of the dough.

● *Kaak bil tamer* is made with dates.

Muajeenot

SAVOURY PASTRIES

PARCELS OF TREASURE

Hidden in the mysterious packaging of fillings, doughs and shapes of parcelled savoury pastries are the traditions of a thousand and one years of Arabian cooking. An attempt is made here to provide a key to unlock the treasure chest of delicacies, revealing a few of the secrets of generations.

Reflecting the diversity of the regions in the Arab world, the varieties of savoury pastries are almost uncountable - and their combinations of ingredients make their flavours hard to describe.

Trying to pin-point the names is virtually impossible, too, as one person may name the pastry for its ingredients, another for its shape and another simply 'because my mother called it that.' Asking my Arab friends, 'What do you call this?', would always send the conversation into

chaos! For that reason, Arabic names have been omitted here, in most cases, and savoury pastries are classified by the type of dough, filling and shape. The chart on p. 147 gives some traditional combinations.

Thin-crispy, flaky and crunchy crusts are filled or topped with nutty-meats, creamy chicken, mint-flavoured cheese, a tangy/oily blend of *zaatar*, mild brains or biting aubergine.

The parcels are packaged in dough - in squares, triangles, cylinders, semi-circles, flat discs and spheres - but creative and imaginative thinking are encouraged. Sizes can range from one-inch (2.5 cm) to half a foot (l5 cm) and they can be served in the *mezza* or alongside the main course.

The difficulty of dough-making lies in the fact that most Arab cooks describe the recipe very

An array of *Muajeenot*

generally. Butter, water and oil are loosely measured by the tiny Arabic 'coffee cupful,' with a sprinkling of salt, and 'enough' flour to make a pliable dough.

Savoury pastries are typically deep-fried, but can be baked after being brushed with a beaten egg at 375°F (190°C) gas 3 until golden brown.

In accordance with the Arab tradition that guests should be offered an extensive array of treats, try preparing several fillings at a time, but using only one dough. The varied shapes can be frozen in airtight containers, then later thawed - and a beautiful tray of diverse savoury pastries presented to astonish visitors.

A FEW TRADITIONAL SAVOURY PASTRIES

The diversity of possibilities may baffle beginners, therefore this section begins with a few recommended, traditional pastry recipes that have been in constant use for countless years.

ARABIC PIZZA

Lahma bil ajeen

To the chagrin of Italians, Arabs lay claim to the invention of pizza. At the height of the Byzantine era, which at that time included Syria, this dish probably was popularised from the capital Constantinople (Istanbul) to the far reaches of the Empire. The word 'pizza' is strikingly similar to the Greek 'pitta' and Turkish 'pide', unleavened breads.

In Levant cafés, the spicy meat filling is spread over the ajeen pastry, which is then placed on huge flat paddles to bake in an arched oven called a furun. Still warm from the oven, the little pizzas are folded over and usually devoured on the spot with a glass of freshly squeezed juice. For diagrams of how to make the shapes see pages 148-149.

MAKES ABOUT 12 PIZZAS

YEAST BREAD DOUGH
1 lb (500g) plain flour, sifted
1 tbsp fresh yeast or
1 tsp dried yeast
¹/₂ tsp salt
¹/₂ tsp sugar
1 egg, beaten
10 fl oz (280ml) lukewarm water
2 tbsp oil

LAMB FILLING
2 lb (1 kg) minced lamb
2 tomatoes, peeled and finely chopped
1 large onion, finely chopped
¹/₄ tsp allspice, ground
¹/₄ tsp cinnamon, ground

3 tsp pomegranate juice, lemon juice or 1 tsp
sumac
salt and pepper

1 To make the filling, mix all the filling ingredients together.

2 To make the dough, combine the yeast with 6-8 tbsp warm water. Add the sugar and leave to stand in a warm place for about 10-15 minutes or until it begins to bubble.

3 Sift the flour and salt into a warmed mixing bowl.

4 Make a well in the centre of the flour and pour in the yeast mixture, egg and the oil. Gradually add enough warm water to make a soft firm dough.

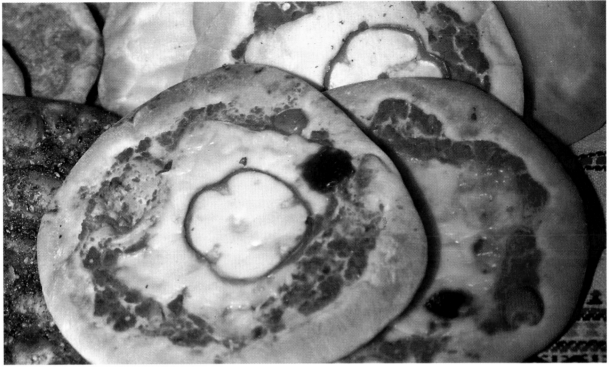

Arabic pizza with egg

5 On a lightly floured surface, knead the dough vigorously for about 15 minutes or until smooth and pliable.

6 With oiled hands, slightly coat the surface of the dough to prevent cracking or a crust forming as it rises.

7 Cover with a damp cloth and leave to rise in a warm place for 2-3 hours or until double in size.

8 Take off a piece of dough about the size of an egg and roll or press into rounds about 4" (10 cm) diameter.

9 Spread a thin layer of filling onto each round and leave to rest for 10 minutes.

10 Carefully slide the discs onto oiled baking sheets. Sprinkle the edges of the dough with a few drops of water to prevent rapid browning.

Bake in a pre-heated oven at 400°F (200°C) gas 6 for 8-10 minutes. The pastries should be well done but not brown as they should be soft enough to fold over.

VARIATIONS

● An Iraqi version calls for mixing minced meat directly in with the dough before cooking.

● *Manakish bil zaatar* is the same dough as *lahma bil ajeen* but topped with olive oil and sprinkled with *zaatar* instead of the lamb filling.

● Sometimes a broken egg is placed in the centre of the dough, which is then sprinkled with tangy *sumac* and slid into an open-faced brick oven to bake - both the bread and the egg cook at the same time!

145

CIGAR-SHAPED CHEESE PASTRY

Fatayer jibnah

Commercial or home-made filo dough or puff pastry is cut into long rectangles and rolled up around the tangy cheese and mint filling into cylinders 2-3 inches (5-8 cm) long. For diagrams of how to make the shapes see pages 148-149.

MAKES ABOUT 20-30 PASTRIES
8 oz (225g) white cheese
1 tbsp mint, finely chopped
2 eggs, beaten
oil for deep-frying
filo dough (p. 151)

1 To make the filling, crumble the cheese and add the mint and half the beaten egg. Mash until well blended.

2 One piece of dough is cut into long rectangular shapes. Keep the unused dough covered with a damp cloth, as it dries quickly.

3 Place $1/2$ tsp of the cheese mixture into the lower portion of one rectangle. Flip the end over the cheese and roll into a tight cylindrical shape, tucking in the sides.

4 To seal the shape closed, brush the loose end of the dough with a little of the remaining beaten egg. Deep-fry until golden. Drain on absorbent paper.

SPINACH TURNOVER

Fatayer sabaneq

Spinach is thought to be of Persian origin, introduced to Europe by the Arabs. Here, circular-shaped discs are filled with tangy spinach and folded into a triangle. The sumac and lemon juice combine for a tangy-tasting turnover.

MAKES ABOUT 30 PIECES

LEAVENED DOUGH
8 oz (225g) plain flour, sifted
1 tsp dry yeast
$1/2$ tsp salt
4 fl oz (100ml) lukewarm water
2 tbsp olive oil
1 egg, beaten

SPINACH FILLING
8 oz (225g) spinach
1 onion, finely chopped
1 tbsp lemon juice or
$1/2$ tsp *sumac*
1 tsp olive oil
salt and pepper

GARNISH
sprigs of parsley

1 Dissolve the yeast in $1/4$ cup lukewarm water and leave for about 10 minutes or until a froth forms.

2 Gradually add the oil, yeast liquid, egg and remaining warm water to a well in the centre of the flour and salt to make a firm dough. Knead well.

3 On a lightly floured surface, knead until a soft ball forms. Roll the dough into a ball. With oiled hands, slightly coat the surface of the dough to prevent cracking or a crust forming. Cover and leave to stand for 1-1$1/2$ hours or until it rises.

4 Meanwhile, prepare the filling by cleaning and washing the fresh spinach, or defrosting frozen spinach. Steam the spinach for 7-8 minutes or

until wilted. Squeeze out excess moisture and chop finely. Sauté the onion. Add the chopped spinach, lemon juice, *sumac*, salt and pepper, then simmer until the liquid is absorbed. Adjust the seasoning to taste.

5 Punch down and pull off pieces of the dough to form balls about golf ball sized. Flatten each ball into a disc.

6 Add 1 heaping teaspoon of the filling into each disc. Fold three edges of the disc over the filling to form a triangle. Lightly press the edges together by brushing with beaten egg.

7 Deep-fry for a crisp outer crust and succulent filling. Alternately, brush with oil and bake on a oiled baking sheet at 450°F (230°C) gas 6 for 20 minutes or until golden.

8 Serve hot or cold, garnished with sprigs of parsley.

SAVOURY PASTRIES - THE BASICS

TRADITIONAL COMBINATIONS

Described below are doughs, fillings and traditional shapes used for savoury pastries. The combinations are almost limitless, but some traditional combinations are listed below, as a starting point.

FILLING	SHAPE	PASTRY
spinach	triangular	unleavened dough
cheese and mint	cigar	filo
minced meat	disc	leavened dough
minced meat	square	unleavened dough
chicken	square	filo
zaatar	disc	leavened dough
cheese	square	unleavened dough

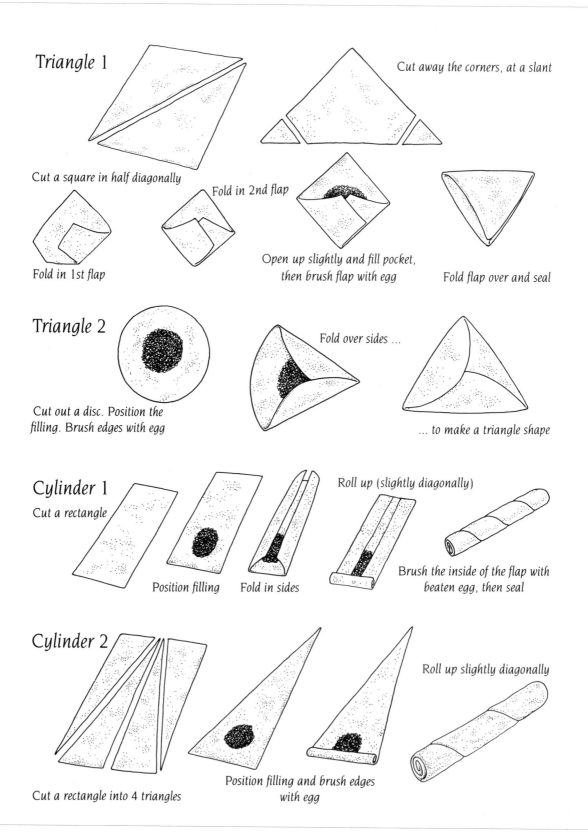

Triangle 1

Cut a square in half diagonally

Cut away the corners, at a slant

Fold in 1st flap

Fold in 2nd flap

Open up slightly and fill pocket, then brush flap with egg

Fold flap over and seal

Triangle 2

Cut out a disc. Position the filling. Brush edges with egg

Fold over sides ...

... to make a triangle shape

Cylinder 1

Cut a rectangle

Position filling

Fold in sides

Roll up (slightly diagonally)

Brush the inside of the flap with beaten egg, then seal

Cylinder 2

Cut a rectangle into 4 triangles

Position filling and brush edges with egg

Roll up slightly diagonally

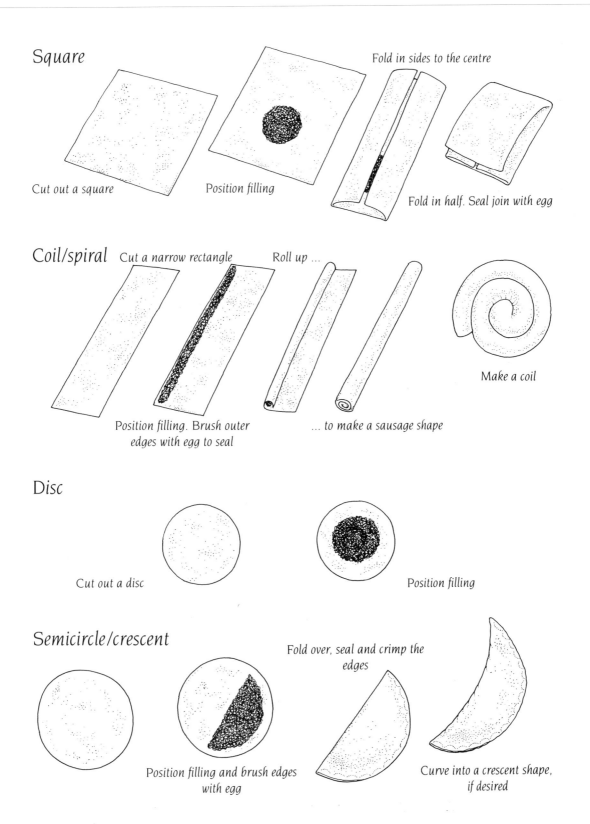

Square

Cut out a square

Position filling

Fold in sides to the centre

Fold in half. Seal join with egg

Coil/spiral

Cut a narrow rectangle

Position filling. Brush outer edges with egg to seal

Roll up ...

... to make a sausage shape

Make a coil

Disc

Cut out a disc

Position filling

Semicircle/crescent

Position filling and brush edges with egg

Fold over, seal and crimp the edges

Curve into a crescent shape, if desired

DOUGHS

The dough recipes can be used in combination with any of the fillings (see next page) and shapes (previous page).

BASIC UNLEAVENED DOUGH

Traditionally the unleavened bread dough is shaped into a half-moon, crescent, or triangular shape, commonly called sambusa or fatayer, and are filled with cheese, meat or spinach.

1 lb (500g) plain flour, sifted
$^1/_2$ tsp salt
4 fl oz (100ml) lukewarm water
4 tbsp butter or *samn*
1 tsp sugar
1 egg, beaten
oil for deep frying

1 Gradually add the water, egg and oil or *samn* to a well in the centre of the flour, sugar and salt to make a firm dough.

2 On a lightly floured surface, knead until a soft ball forms, working as little as possible.

3 With oiled hands, slightly coat the surface of the dough to prevent cracking or a crust forming.

4 Cover and leave to stand for 30 minutes. The dough will not rise but become more pliable.

5 Roll out the dough on a lightly floured surface until thin. Cut into the desired shapes. Add the filling and roll to the desired shape.

6 Deep-fry in hot oil until golden brown for a crisp outer crust and succulent filling.

YEAST BREAD DOUGH

Akin to a miniature pizza, this Arabic pastry can be topped with meat filling to make Lahma bil ajeen *(see p. 144), with grated cheese to give* Manakish bil jibnah; *or* zaatar *and oil, for* Manakish bil zaatar.

1 lb (500g) plain flour, sifted
1 tbsp fresh yeast or
1 tsp dried yeast
$^1/_2$ tsp salt
$^1/_2$ tsp sugar
1 egg, beaten
$^1/_2$ pt (275ml) lukewarm water
2 tbsp oil

1 Combine the yeast with 3-4 tbsp warm water. Add the sugar and leave to stand in a warm place for about 10-15 minutes or until it begins to bubble.

2 Sift the flour and salt into a warmed mixing bowl.

3 Make a well in the centre of the flour and pour in the yeast mixture, egg and oil. Gradually add enough warm water to make a soft firm dough.

4 On a lightly floured surface, knead the dough vigorously for about 15 minutes or until smooth and pliable.

5 With oiled hands, lightly coat the surface of the dough to prevent cracking or a crust forming, as it rises.

6 Cover with a damp cloth and leave to rise in a warm place for 2-3 hours or until double in size.

7 Roll out the dough until thin. Cut or roll into flat round shapes and spread the filling on top.

8 Carefully slide the discs onto hot baking sheets. Sprinkle the edges of the dough with a few drops of water to prevent rapid browning. Bake in a pre-heated oven at 400°F (200°C) gas 6 for 10 minutes or until browned.

HOME-MADE FILO PASTRY

Ready-made filo dough is available at delicatessens and in good supermarkets. However, for those with great stamina or a desire to be challenged, the home-made version is achievable. Endurance is the key because the dough must be pulled and punched non-stop for about 30 minutes, left to rise for three hours and then stretched again. Finally, the sheets are cut and wrapped. For most, including this author, a quick stop at the shops is a time-saving alternative. Home-made filo dough is never as thin as the expert commercial version, therefore, if you have made your own, use half as many layers as the recipe states.

To make 20 sheets, 12x16 in (30x36cm)

2 lb (1 kg) plain flour, sifted
1 pt (575ml) lukewarm water
4 tbsp olive oil
2 tsp salt
cornflour/cornstarch

1 Sift the plain flour and salt into a mixing bowl. Pour the water slowly into the flour, beating continually.

2 Knead the dough for about 5-10 minutes, or until the dough pulls away from the sides of the bowl and forms a ball.

3 Slowly add the oil, kneading after the addition of each tablespoonful. Continue kneading for about 30 minutes, or until the dough is satiny and smooth.

4 Cover with a damp cloth. Leave to stand for at least 3 hours but no longer than 12 hours.

5 Shape the dough into 'golf balls', flatten into a disc and place on a cloth which has been sprinkled with cornflour.

6 Stretch the dough over the back of both hands and pull the hands apart, again and again. Place between layers of wax paper.

7 Cover with a damp cloth and leave to stand for 30 minutes.

8 To make a paper-thin sheet, again stretch the dough over the back of both hands and pull the hands apart, again and again.

9 Trim off any thick edges and cut into the desired shape. Wrap each sheet in plastic and use immediately, as paper-thin home-made filo dough dries out very quickly.

PASTRY SHAPES

triangular
square
cylinder
cigar
coil
semicircle, crescent or half-moon
disc

FILLINGS

CHEESE AND MINT

Any semi-soft white cheese, including haloum, kaskawan, fetta, *cottage, Gouda, Swiss or* mozzarella *are adaptable. The salty cheeses may need soaking in several changes of water prior to preparation.*

8 oz (225g) white cheese
1 tbsp mint, finely chopped
1 egg, beaten (opt)

1 Crumble the cheese. If the cheese is too salty, wash under running water.

2 Add the beaten egg and mint to the cheese.

3 Prepare the desired dough and fill and shape. Deep fry or bake.

MINCED MEAT FILLING

1 lb (500g) minced lamb or beef
1 large onion, chopped
2 tbsp parsley, finely chopped
1 tsp *baharat* (opt)
oil for sautéing
2 tbsp pine nuts (opt)
salt and pepper

1 Sauté the onion and meat. Remove the excess oil. Add the *baharat*, pine nuts, parsley, and salt and pepper and cook for a further 2 minutes or until the parsley is wilted.

2 To keep the meat moist for filling, add about 4 tbsp water. Simmer slowly until the liquid has been absorbed.

3 Prepare the desired dough and fill and shape. Deep fry or bake.

VARIATIONS

● For Arabic pizza, *lahma bil ajeen*, the meat is sometimes not sautéed but is spread raw on top of the unbaked dough. After baking the pizza is folded in half to be eaten.

● Tomato juice with a pinch of sugar can be substituted for the water.

● Cumin, coriander and other herbs and spices are used instead of *baharat*.

SPINACH FILLING

1 lb (500g) fresh spinach or
8 oz (225g) frozen spinach
1 onion, finely chopped
1 tbsp lemon juice or
$1/2$ tsp *sumac*
1 tsp olive oil
2 tbsp pine nuts, roasted (opt)
salt and pepper

1 Clean and wash the fresh spinach. Thaw frozen spinach.

2 Steam the spinach for 7-8 minutes or until wilted. Squeeze out excess moisture, and chop finely

3 Add the onions with the oil, pine nuts, lemon juice or *sumac*, and salt and pepper to the spinach. Simmer until the liquid is absorbed. Adjust seasoning to taste.

4 Prepare the desired dough and fill and shape. Deep fry or bake.

AUBERGINE/EGGPLANT FILLING

1 lb (500g) aubergine/eggplant
3 tomatoes, finely chopped
1 onion, finely chopped
olive oil for sautéing
salt and pepper

1 Sprinkle the peeled and chopped aubergine with salt. Drain in a colander with a heavy weight on top for 1 hour. Rinse and squeeze out the excess moisture.

2 Sauté the onion and add the aubergine. Continue cooking until soft and lightly browned.

3 Add the tomatoes and salt and pepper. Simmer until tender. Adjust the seasoning to taste. Blend to a paste.

4 Prepare the desired dough and fill and shape. Deep fry or bake.

CHICKEN FILLING

1 lb (500g) chicken
1 clove garlic, crushed
1/4 tsp lemon juice
1 tsp mint or coriander, finely chopped
1 tsp tomato purée (opt)
pinch of nutmeg, grated
butter or *samn* for sautéing
salt and pepper

1 Boil and bone the chicken. Cut into very small cubes or strips or crush to a paste.

2 Sauté the garlic in the *samn* or melted butter. Add the spices, chicken and the herbs to sauté for a further 2 minutes. Add the lemon juice and tomato purée if preferred. Season with salt and pepper.

3 Prepare the desired dough and fill and shape. Deep fry or bake.

SEAFOOD FILLING

Shrimp, crab, flaky fish or any combination of seafood may be used with lemon juice to make a tasty filling. Shrimp are lightly chopped and accompanied with finely chopped vegetables like cabbage, capsicum pepper, and sometimes mashed potatoes. Crab meat and finely chopped fish pieces are commonly accompanied with garlic but not vegetables. Spices are optional according to preference in taste.

1 lb (500g) seafood, chopped
2 cloves garlic, crushed (opt)
3 tbsp lemon juice
1/4 tsp cumin, ground
1/2 tsp paprika
1 tbsp parsley or coriander, finely chopped
pinch of cayenne pepper (opt)
oil for sautéing
salt and pepper

1 Sauté the garlic.

2 Simmer the garlic, seafood, lemon juice, spices and coriander or parsley in a little water until tender and the liquid has absorbed.

3 Prepare the desired dough and fill and shape. Deep fry or bake.

Baad al wajbeh

AFTER THE MEAL

DRINKS, TOBACCO AND FRAGRANCES

Long summer nights in Arabia are charac-
terised by groups of men sitting cross-legged
on a mat or carpet, relishing the enjoyment of a
meal. As they sip tiny cups of strong coffee, one
after another, the conversation about the day's
events begins to unfold. The rhythm of the parley
is accompanied by the methodical tugging at the
water-filtered tobacco pipe. Other entertainment,
such as jokes, riddles or story-telling, may enter
the otherwise serene setting. The ambience surrounding the after-dinner setting is heightened
by the use of special scents, an Arabian speciality
from along the Frankincense Trail. Slotted scent
burners and ornate sweet water decanters are
passed around the room to remove any smells of
food that still linger.

A meal in the Arab world is incomplete until
trays of colourful fruit, followed by warm, soothing tea and delicate syrupy confections are consumed. Fragrant custards, layered pastries
doused in sweet syrup, thin pancakes topped by
thick clotted cream, candy swirls or a waffle treat
called "lovers' windows" provide the perfect end-
ing to a perfect meal (see the chapter on sweets
for recipes).

Baad al wajbeh

COFFEE

Qahwah

Although coffee originated in Ethiopia, the plant was first cultivated in 575AD in neighbouring southern Arabia. By the fifteenth century 'coffee arabica' was grown extensively and began to spread along the caravan trail and ocean-going dhow routes to countries bordering the Indian Ocean and the Mediterranean. One of the world's finest coffees, mocha, found its beginnings from the old Arabian port of Mocha in Yemen.

Coffee drinking became, and remains, a valued activity in the Arab world. Business is seldom conducted or guests entertained without cups and cups of strong, thick, black coffee or the weaker, fragrant coffee of the Gulf. Guests are obliged to sip two or three cups of the top half of the strong coffee, as the lower part is unpalatable sludge. To drink less could be an insult and to drink more may keep one awake all day and night! When finished, one notifies the host by shaking the cup from side to side or turning it upside down.

The occasion may determine the amount of sugar: on happy occasions, coffee should always be sweet, while in times of mourning the coffee should be bitter, with no sugar at all. Otherwise, guests are asked how they prefer the brew - sweet, medium or black - as the sugar is actually boiled along with the coffee. Traditionally, men would always be served first, but today in many homes women take precedence. Young people are almost always held responsible for serving their elders.

The coffee and the pot of the Gulf region differ from ones in other parts of the Arab world. The light coffee of the Arabian Peninsula is heavily scented with cardamom and rose water. The pots, known as dallah, are intricately designed, and have long spouts that curve downward. Originally hewn from durable copper or bronze, the dallah was placed directly on burning coals.

In other regions, the beans are ground (traditionally they were pounded) to a fine powder and each pot freshly brewed in a qulla, a non-filtering, long-handled pot. Arabic coffee cups are always small, even tinier than a demi-tasse. Most are the shape of a Chinese tea cup (some with handles, others without). The strong black coffee - sometimes called Turkish coffee - is drunk from ones with handles, and the weaker fragrant type, brewed with the lightly roasted beans is drunk from small round cups without handles. Some cups are made to fit into small metal holders that match the serving tray - this is usually decorated with inscriptions of Arabic calligraphy (often text in praise of Allah) and is carved or inlaid in copper, brass or silver.

Arabic coffee can be bought dark, medium or light roasted and comes with 1 tsp ground cardamom seeds or 4 tbsp ground cardamom pods already added to each kilo of coffee. The strength, spices and sweetness of either brew is up to regional and individual tastes. The following ratio yields four tiny Arabic cups of coffee:

STRONG BLACK COFFEE
8 oz water (4 Arabic coffee cups)
dark roasted coffee (2 tsp for strong, 1 tsp for medium)
sugar (1 heaped tsp for very sweet, 1 level tsp for sweet, 1/2 tsp for medium)

1 Boil the water.

2 Stir in the quantity of coffee for strong or medium and add sugar for very sweet, medium sweet or medium. Return to the boil.

3 When the froth begins to rise, remove from the heat and stir. Return to the heat until the froth rises once again.

4 Cover and leave the coffee to stand for a few minutes, or until most of the grounds have settled. Serve in small cups.

FRAGRANT GULF COFFEE
8 oz water (4 Arabic coffee cups)
1 tbsp lightly roasted coffee
1 tsp crushed cardamom
4-5 saffron threads (opt)
1/2 tsp rose water

1 The ground coffee is added with the cardamom and saffron to boiling water for 3 minutes.

2 The rose water is added and then the coffee is served in small rounded cups without handles.

VARIATION
● The coffee of some regions has 1/4 tsp ground ginger or a little cinnamon added with the boiling water.

READING THE CUP

Kiraat al fi:jan

Arabian mysticism is exemplified with the practice of unveiling one's past, present and future by peering into a tiny coffee cup.

Seldom seriously practised, the jest of cup reading must have originated from the long hours spent drinking coffee after a meal. By turning the cup upside down on the saucer, a guest signifies that he has had enough. The reading of the cup begins after the sediment has oozed down the sides and an 'enlightened' reader examines the shapes formed by the residue. Like a fortune-teller, the reader begins to relay the eerie message portrayed in the bottom of the cup.

TEA

Shy

Strong tea steeped with mint, shy bil naana, is the soothing finale to an Arabian feast and some would say is imperative to the digestive process. In Morocco, peppermint or spearmint are popular tea additives, while businessmen in the Gulf greet their guests with pitcher-shaped flasks filled with weak, delicate saffron tea.

Native to south-west China, tea probably first made its way westwards along the Silk Road. The East India Company was known as a famous transporter of the drink that took Europe by storm. In 1640, when tea was first brought to Britain and France, the warm soothing drink was thought to have medicinal properties associated with banishing fevers and curing head and stomach aches.

Imported tea and native coffee became the favoured drinks in the Arab World and both are usually drunk rather strong, with regional tastes demanding the type and

Qahwah

amount of spices added. Generally, boiling water is poured over the tea leaves and spices and allowed to sit and steep in the brew for 5-10 minutes, depending on the strength desired. As well as mint and saffron, popular spices for tea include sage, cinnamon, lemon and dried lime, loomi. After the tea has been steeped, sugar is usually added to the whole pot. The tea is almost always served (without milk) in small glasses with handles.

Infusions do not include any tea at all, but are simply warm drinks produced by brewing spices, flowers or herbs - jasmine, mint, sweet basil, sweet marjoram, rose petals, or black elder - in boiling water, sometimes with a little sugar added. One such infusion, meramiya (sage), noted for its curative effects on upset stomachs, is popularly stocked in school clinics. Another, mati, a wild herb from the mountains of Lebanon and Syria, is sipped through a filtered straw from a pot in which the sweet infusion is brewed.

DRINKS

Sharbat

Juice bars in the Middle East - resembling ice-cream parlours - feature menus listing dozens of freshly squeezed juices. On display in refrigerated glass cases is a brilliant selection of fruits, ranging from always-available oranges to more exotic varieties, all of which can be custom-blended with water and a little sugar.

Perhaps because of the Moslem prohibition of alcohol, Arabs have attained a passion for fruit drinks, and they are prepared with fervour. Intricate cocktails, blends of fruit with sweet cream, or with milk and sugar, are swirled into tall, handled glasses and topped with almond halves, ground pistachios or whole pine nuts. Sometimes whole strawberries, slices of banana or of chunky fresh pineapple are added, producing a 'drink' that has to be accompanied by a long-handled spoon.

The ancient pomegranate, originally brought along the Silk Route from southern or western Asia, has found a home in Middle Eastern gardens and produces a tangy drink. Tamarind, probably native of tropical East Africa, but cultivated extensively in the warm climate of India, provides the basis for a mellow drink.

Almost any fresh fruit or vegetable is juiced, including lemon, watermelon, passion fruit, carrots, grapes and apples. As they did in the past, juice vendors in the street

still beckon the thirsty with gigantic glass jars of drinks - the slightly sour, purple jallab; pink rose water; green-coloured violet water; brown tamarind and black liquorice water. Almonds, orange-blossom water and cornflour make a traditional milky blend.

Prior to the advent of refrigeration, fresh fruit was dried or combined with sugar into thick syrups or pastes that could later be added to cool water - which in the remote areas was sometimes purchased from the backs of donkeys laden with clay jugs. The fruit drinks were also made from berries and roots.

Below are instructions for some of the drinks in the Arab juice-making tradition.

SYRUPS

Syrups must be diluted with chilled water before drinking. These are usually prepared in enormous quantities, with proportions of fruit to sugar varying to taste, and on the natural sweetness of the fruit. As a rough guide, try 3 tbsp sugar to 1/2 pint juice, or 5 tbsp to 1/2 litre.

ORANGE: Sugar added to orange juice, is boiled with a little lemon juice to produce a syrup. To serve, dilute with water.

MULBERRY: Sugar added to Mulberry juice, is boiled with a little lemon juice until the syrup thickens. To serve, dilute with water.

APRICOT: Dried apricots or the paste, *qamar addine* are soaked in a little water for several hours. Purée and dilute with water, adding sugar to taste. A few pine nuts are usually added to each glass.

TAMARIND: Soak the tamarind overnight in water. Purée and then sieve before adding sugar. Bring to the boil and simmer until the syrup thickens. To serve, dilute with water and add a few pine nuts to each glass.

LIQUORICE: The root is steeped as in making tea. Remove the root and add sugar for a drink or thicken to make a syrup.

YOGHURT DRINK

Laban

Almost a cross between a milk shake and buttermilk, laban - made sweet or salty - is a healthy thirst quencher enjoyed in the Arab world by children and adults alike. Simply stir 3 tablespoons of yoghurt into a glass of milk, or add 1/4 glass of cold water to 3/4 glass of yoghurt. If preferred, sprinkle with crushed mint. Salt or sugar may be added to taste. Serve chilled. Some regions of the Middle East make this drink using 1/3 glass yoghurt with 1/3 glass of still or carbonated water and 1/3 glass crushed ice. Iraqis use fresh basil instead of mint.

TOBACCO

Tabgh

Long, tranquil Arabian nights are marked by an atmosphere of drifting, repetitive rhythms and the wafting, sweet aroma of the water pipe.

As the sun begins to set and prayer-time is finished, men begin to gather at the majlis, *the meeting place. Typically, the most prominent man of the community serves as the host - the outdoor coffee-house is also a frequent rendezvous. The men chat about business, politics, the weather or religion, while sipping at strong coffee and tugging gently on the water pipe. Their shoes set aside, they sit cross-legged on a carpet or mat, or on a long bench, telling jokes, playing cards or perhaps simply sitting quietly while poetry is recited or a story is told.*

The gurgling water pipe is known by different names, sometimes called a hookah or hubble bubble in the West, a shesha in Egypt, argila in the Levant countries, nargila in Iraq and qudu in the Gulf. The pipe of the Gulf countries differs, as the hose through which the smoke flows to the mouth is stiff rather than the flexible type of other regions.

Tobacco blends are left to individual preference. Some smoke plain leaves, while others opt for a sweeter version blended with honey or date syrup.

For the plain variety, crush or cut the dried tobacco leaves into small pieces. Wash the tobacco and squeeze out excess moisture before using it in the bowl of the water pipe. For the sweet variety, add the date molasses syrup, maasel, to the plain tobacco.

Smoking the water pipe after dinner

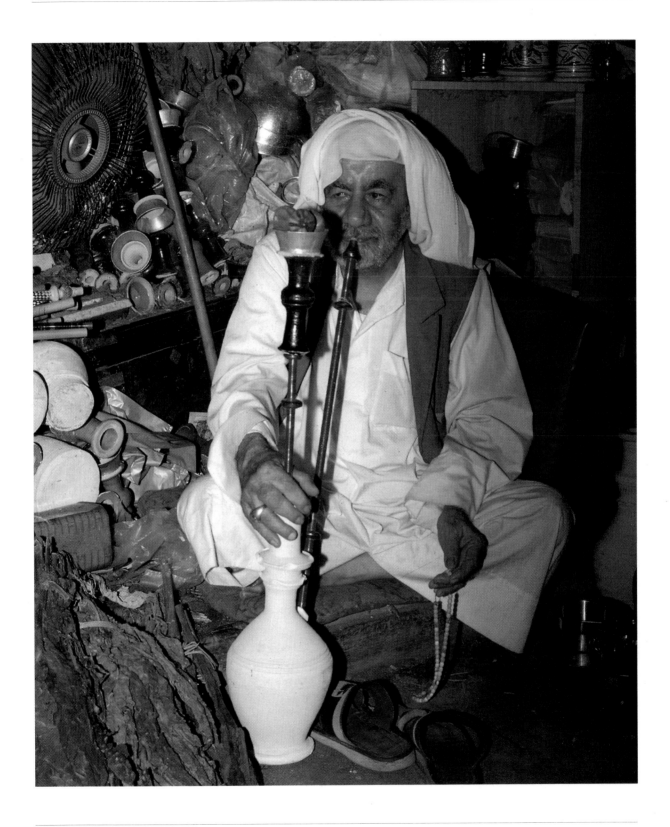

SWEET FRAGRANCES

Bakhour

During the 10th century an Arabian doctor and philosopher called Avicenna discovered how to extract the aromatic properties of flowers. The original formula, in which he used the sweetly scented cabbage rose, can still be found in his book on chemistry. The use of rose water - for culinary purposes, for washing hands (for especially respected persons) and for sprinkling on clothes - gained in popularity in the Arab world and was brought to the West by the Crusaders.

Frankincense, globules of aromatic resin, embodies some of the historical essence of Arabia. Still used today for incense and perfumes, the fragrant sap is harvested from trees whose prickly branches ooze drops of the white substance when scarred. The process that Marco Polo described more than 700 years ago is still practised, though the frankincense tree grows only in Dhofar and northern Somalia.

Myrrh, the dark, fragrant resin obtained from the small thorny trees of the genus commiphora, has been used to embalm and perfume the royal mummies of Egypt, in medicines and as incense, but is today an important ingredient of some perfumes.

Ornate decanters filled with perfumes, orange-blossom or rose water, are passed from person to person to help obliterate lingering food smells. In the Gulf countries, particularly at special occasions like weddings, strong fragrant chunks of incense called bakhour are burned, and the smoke spirals out through slotted holes of the burner. Some burners are made of sun-baked red clay, while others are hewn of wood or stone, or beaten out of brass. The latest in aromatic technology is the production of metal, electric-powered burners.

Treasured oud, fragrant aloe wood for burning, can cost anywhere from $300 to $3,000 for only a sixteenth of a ounce. Yet, the smoke of these extravagant fumes are passed fleetingly beneath the skirt tails, and carefully between the layers of clothing.

Bakhour

Halawiyat
SWEET PASTRIES AND DESSERTS

At the end of a meal in the Middle East, tea is usually served, followed by a tray piled high with a colourful display of fruit, then tiny cups of thick, black coffee, then finally the moment all have been waiting for ... pastries and desserts.

Legends suggest that Polynesians were the first to use sugar cane as a source of sweetness, but it was probably Arabs who first introduced 'sukar' to Europe. In 510 BC, the Persians discovered sugar cane in the Indus Valley, but it wasn't until the 7th Century AD that the Arabs set up the first sugar refineries.

Sweets have become a part of Arabian life - served almost every day - but in abundance during particularly important occasions to celebrate new beginnings, such as the birth of a child, or sad endings following the burial of a loved one. Special sweets are prepared during the Eid feast and Ramadan, the month-long period of fasting from dusk to dawn.

Arabic sweets, *halawiyat*, are more than simple desserts. Pastries, cookies, puddings, sweetmeats and fruit exude the beautiful Arabian tradition of family and friendship. To say that a woman is *halwa* (sweet) is more than a mere kind compliment, but an expression of her inner beauty (*helwa*).

It is virtually impossible to describe the astonishing shelves of a Middle Eastern bakery - with their striking arrays of trays piled high with oozing sweets - nor truly describe the aromatic yet delicate flavours, without recommending a visit to the Arab World. Yet, even if they are available for purchase in speciality shops, these 'sweet things' can be home-made - inexpensively and with little effort.

FRUITS

Fawakeh

As plentiful as in the Garden of Eden and colourful as a painter's palette, Arabian fruit markets are a feast for the eye and the taste buds. Imported American apples and New Zealand kiwi are displayed in crates alongside Middle Eastern dates and figs. They are bought in large quantitites, and guests in Arab households are presented with masterfully stacked trays, a veritable cornucopia of fruit, and tiny paring knives.

Middle Eastern merchants have long been known for their savvy with the fruit trade. In 500 BC, King Darius commended one of his governors for the transportation of fruit trees along the Persian Royal Road, a section of the Silk Road. Peaches, for example, originally cultivated in China, were given the scientific name 'prunus persica', perhaps because the fruit passed through the vast Persian Empire along trading routes.

From the East came apricots and oranges, while the Middle East exported grapes, figs and pomegranates. Over the years, species have been gathered from abroad which grow easily in the Arab world, including grapefruit, mangoes, limes, melons and strawberries. One of the first fruits to be brought to cultivation, bananas were grown in the region (Assyria) over 3,000 years ago, but must then have died out - for the armies of Alexander the Great were surprised at the sight of the strange fruit growing in the Indus Valley in 327 BC. A thousand years later, Arabs brought bananas into Egypt and Palestine. Figs, a very ancient fruit, which must have flourished in Eden itself, were discovered growing wild in Arabia.

By the 2nd Century AD, fruit was shipped in all directions, including the dried versions from the lush orchards of Damascus along the Silk Road. This dried fruit compote, Ramadaniya, is particularly favoured during Ramadan (the month-long period of fasting from sunrise to sunset) and can contain any dried fruit.

Apricot paste, kamardine, is used in some recipes, and is available from specialist stores.

The fruit market

FRUIT COMPOTE

Ramadaniya

4 oz (100g) dried apricots, figs, and plums
5 tbsp almonds, pistachio and pine nuts
1 tsp orange blossom water
4 oz (100g) apricot paste/*kamardine*, soaked

1 Soak the apricot paste overnight in 1 cup of water.

2 Soak the dried fruit overnight in water to cover.

3 To remove the skins, pour boiling water over the almonds and pistachios, then rinse in cold water.

4 Drain the reconstituted fruit. Stir the apricot paste to blend well and add the fruit, orange water, almonds, pistachio and pine nuts.

DATES

Tamer

Without doubt a fruit of Arabic origin, dates are synonymous with Western images of the Middle East - mirages of swaying palms tucked away in a secluded desert oasis. Date palms were once the sustenance of the Gulf's economy and are still cultivated in the desert oases throughout the Arab world, including southern Algeria and Tunisia. In the days before oil transformed their lives, the Bedouin of Arabia virtually lived on dates and the products of their camels and flocks of sheep. The fruit was also bartered. Even today the fronds are used for making baskets and mats, and as a building material for traditional fences or thatched roofs, and almost every garden in the Arab world contains a palm drooping with clusters of dates. During the late summer months, wrapped in protective sacks to deter insects and speed ripening, dates are harvested and eaten fresh or dried for later use.

Golden, red, brown or even black, there are over 300 varieties of date. Some are dried for export, while other, more delicate, varieties are eaten fresh. Iraqi dates are commonly made into a syrup, heated with butter or *samn*, or served on squares of Arabic bread with *gammer*, thick buffalo's cream.

This special affection for dates is reflected throughout the Arab world during Ramadan, when the fast is broken with a plate of sweet dates and a bowl of fresh yoghurt. In Oman, fresh dates are dipped in clarified butter or eaten with camel milk curds. In other regions, dates are dipped in *tahina* to produce a flavour akin to peanut butter.

DATE SWEETMEAT

Al batheeth

Chopped dates mixed with coarse flour and samn *(clarified butter) make one of the oldest dishes in the Arabian Peninsula. A 10-year-old schoolgirl from the United Arab Emirates taught me how to prepare this sweet. Young Hessa had been told how to prepare the dish by her mother, who had been given the recipe from her own mother. Hessa said her grandfather relayed to her stories of pearl-diving trips - it turns out that* batheeth, *unaffected by the hot sun, was traditionally taken on these trips as well as aboard the* dhows *that crossed the Indian Ocean and Arabian Gulf in pursuit of trading opportunities.*

5 oz (150g) wholemeal flour
8 oz (225g) pitted dates, chopped
8 tbsp *samn*
2 cardamom pods, cracked

1 Sauté the cardamom in the *samn* for 5 minutes.

2 Separately heat the flour until slightly browned. Add the chopped dates until softened, stirring continually.

3 Mix the *samn* into the flour and dates.

4 Leave to cool.

5 *Batheeth* can be stored in an airtight container for several months.

SYRUP

Qater, or Ater

An Arabic pastry without a soaking of qater is like a day without sunshine! Qater, which varies in fluidity depending on the amount of water used and the cooking time, can be prepared with or without fragrant rose water. This recipe makes a large quantity, which can be covered and stored for many weeks.

Another traditional syrup, dibs, is made by boiling down dates, raisins, carob beans or sweet grapes to a thick sugary solution that can be used as a sweetener.

This qater recipe makes a very thick syrup, which can be thinned as required with 10 oz (275g) syrup to 1 pt (500ml) water.

1 lb (500g) sugar
10 fl oz (275ml) water
1/2 tsp lemon juice
1-5 tbsp rose water (opt)

1 Dissolve the sugar in the water and boil for about 5-12 minutes or until thickened. The usual test for thickness is to see if the syrup coats a metal spoon.

2 Add rose water and lemon juice and simmer gently for a further 2 minutes.

3 Cool and store until required.

4 For better absorption, pour cold syrup over hot pastries (hot syrup will also soften the pastry).

VARIATION
● Non-traditional, yet a quick and easy substitute for qater, is 1/4 pt (150ml) golden syrup, 2 fl oz (50ml) honey and 2 tbsp lemon juice.

THICK CLOTTED CREAM

Kishta/Eishta

Thicker than cream and tastier too, cow's milk kishta or buffalo's milk gammer is a perfect accompaniment for pastries. In Egypt, kishta is the topping for aish saraya, half a loaf of Arabic bread soaked in sugar syrup or in honey and samn, then baked to a cake-like texture.

English clotted cream can be eaten in its place, and a reasonable substitute for kishta can be made with double cream and milk, but be warned that homogenised milk, without the separate rich fat, will never yield the sweet clotted cream. Whipped double cream can also be used as an alternative to kishta.

1/2 pt (275ml) double cream
2 pt (1 litre) non-homogenised milk

1 Add double cream to the milk.

2 Pour into a wide and shallow tray, thus giving the cream the largest possible upper surface.

3 Bring slowly to the boil, simmering gently over a very low heat for 1 1/2 hours. Leave to stand for 7 hours and chill overnight.

4 A thick layer of cream should have formed on the surface of the milk. Detach the cream, using a sharp knife. Slice and serve.

MILK PUDDING

Muhaballiya

Thickened with flour, this milk pudding is a favourite dessert throughout the Middle East. Delicately fragranced with rose water, the not-so-sweet pudding looks and tastes luxurious. Muhallabiya can be made creamier by using milk as a base instead of water, and cornflour/cornstarch to give a firmer pudding.

The pistachio garnish - sometimes called 'green almonds' - give a distinctive flavour, one which has been treasured for centuries. Of Asian origin, the nuts were brought to the

Mediterranean regions many thousands of years ago, reaching Italy from Syria during the reign of the Emperor Tiberius.

32 fl oz (1 litre) whole milk
4 tbsp cornflour/cornstarch
6 tbsp sugar
1 tbsp rose water (opt)
1 cardamom pod, cracked (opt)

GARNISH
4 tbsp almonds and/or pistachios, ground

1 Add a little milk to the cornflour/cornstarch to form a paste.

2 Boil the remainder of the milk with the sugar and cardamom, if preferred.

3 Gradually add the paste, stirring continually with a wooden spoon. Simmer slowly over a low heat until the mixture has thickened. If using rose water, add it and simmer for a further 2 minutes, stirring continually.

4 Pour into a serving dish or mould. Chill for 2 hours before serving. Garnish with ground nuts.

VARIATIONS
● A few saffron threads will add a delicate flavour and colour.

● For added sweetness, *qater* syrup can be poured over the cold *muhallabiya* (see opposite).

● For a firmer cream, double the cornflour and add an equal quantity of rice flour, or add 1 tsp unflavoured gelatine.

MOTHER OF ALI

Umm Ali

Asian pistachio nuts, Middle Eastern dates, and raisins and spices from trading routes link up with milk from the herdsmen to unite into a creamy, nutty bread-and-butter pudding.

Umm *is the Arabic name for 'mother' and Ali, a name as typical as John - the 'mother of John' must have creatively put her leftover bread to good use with the discovery of this dessert. Filo dough, Arabic bread or typical loaf bread is baked with nuts, dates, raisins and gentle spices and served warm in a bowl. The sweetness is a matter of preference.*

7 oz (200g) bread or filo dough
6 tbsp almonds, walnuts, or pistachios, chopped
8 tbsp raisins and/or chopped dates
1/2 tsp cloves, ground
1/2 tsp cinnamon, ground
1/2 tsp cardamom, ground
4-8 oz (100-225g) sugar
2 pt (1 litre) milk
cream for serving

1 Layer the toasted and chipped bread or filo dough with nuts, raisins, and/or dates in a baking dish.

2 Heat the sugar and spices with the milk until dissolved. Pour over the bread.

3 Bake at 400°F (200°C) gas 6 for 15-20 minutes or until golden. Add more milk as required to keep the pudding moist and creamy.

4 Serve hot, topped with a swirl of cream.

SWEET COUSCOUS WITH NUTS

Couscous hilu

A Moroccan dish, couscous - semolina coated with flour - sounds an unlikely dessert. However, steamed and then mixed with nuts, then moulded into a pyramid and streamed with tears of icing sugar, the dish takes on a fluffy sweetness. The nutmeg passed along the Spice Route and found its way into this dessert.

1 lb (500g) couscous
6 tbsp butter or *samn*

GARNISH
6 tbsp almonds
4 tbsp raisins
2 tsp cinnamon, ground
1 tsp. nutmeg, grated
3 tbsp icing sugar

1 Soak the raisins for several hours or until softened.

2 Moisten the *couscous* slightly with water, rubbing the grains between the fingers to prevent lumps forming. Leave to stand for 10 minutes. Coat evenly with the butter or *samn*.

3 Cover and steam the *couscous* in a sieve or steamer over boiling water, raking the grains occasionally to promote swelling. Pre-cooked *couscous* is steamed for about 15 minutes to become tender, otherwise allow 30-45 minutes.

4 Serve warm sprinkled with the nuts, raisins and with icing sugar which has been mixed with the cinnamon and nutmeg.

SESAME SEED BRITTLE

Simsimiya

The sesame plant, which probably was first grown in Africa, has been cultivated in India and China since ancient times. The first written history of the Sumerians in Mesopotamia tells of trading the seeds for goods with other Gulf civilisations.

A hard candy plank loaded with whole sesame seeds is probably most admired by children, but is also a healthy snack for adults.

The simplest way to make the brittle is to place the nuts and sugar in a copper pan - copper is good conductor of heat - and to stir the mixture over heat until the sugar starts to caramelise, by which time, if heated slowly, the nuts will roast at the same time. Turn out on a marble slab and allow to cool.

The following recipe is a more traditional way of preparing a brittle.

4 oz (100g) sesame seeds, roasted
5 oz (150g) honey
9 oz (250g) sugar
$1/4$ tsp rose water (opt)
$1/4$ tsp lemon juice

1 Gently simmer the sugar with $1/2$ cup water until the mixture reaches the hard ball stage, stirring continually. Test by dropping a small amount into a cop of cold water. The drops should separate into hard and brittle threads. Hard crack temperature is 289°F (143°C)

2 Add the lemon juice, honey and rose water, and cook for a further 2 minutes. Leave to cool until the candy can be handled.

3 Meanwhile spread the sesame seeds in a pan and bake until golden brown.

4 Roll the warm, soft brittle into the sesame seeds. Keep rolling back and forth until the seeds are evenly distributed.

5 Spread, about $1/4$ inch thick, onto a warm, greased baking sheet.

6 Leave to cool and chop or break into squares for serving.

Trays of pastries

ALMOND BISCUITS

Ghoraïybah

These shortbread sweets, just as popular as chocolate chip cookies are in the West, can be found piled high, in all different shapes and sizes, on the shelves of bakeries throughout the Middle East. Usually dotted with an almond, these tasty treats are attractive served with coffee or tea.

MAKES ABOUT 35 BISCUITS.
1 lb (500g) plain flour, sifted
8 oz (225g) unsalted butter or *samn*
8 oz (225g) icing sugar, sifted
1/2 tsp cardamom, ground
17 almonds, halved

1 Slowly add the icing sugar to the melted butter or *samn*, stirring continually. Add the flour and cardamom, mixing well.

2 Knead until a smooth, pliable paste forms.

3 To make a ring-shaped biscuit, roll a small section of the dough into a coil and join both ends. Place a half almond over the joint.

4 Bake on a greased baking sheet at 300°F (150°C) gas 2 for 20 minutes. The biscuit should remain white, but the almond should turn lightly brown.

LOVERS' WINDOWS

Shubbak al habayb

These little fried waffles require a special tool, a hand-held iron rosette waffle maker, and a great deal of patience while frying, as the tiny iron must constantly be dipped in the batter and dropped in the hot oil. The thickness of the batter will determine whether the waffle is hollow or solid. However, an imaginative source of conversation after a meal or at a party, "lovers' windows", dusted with icing sugar, look and taste much like miniature funnel cakes.

10 tbsp self-raising flour, sifted
7 tbsp cornflour/cornstarch
10 fl oz (275ml) milk
2 eggs, beaten
oil for deep-frying
icing sugar for dusting

1 Add the egg and milk to both of the flours, beating until smooth and creamy. The thickness of the batter determines the texture of the waffle, either crisp or spongey.

2 Heat the oil for frying and place the waffle iron or rosette maker into the oil.

3 Dip the rosette end of the hot waffle iron into the batter, making sure to bring the batter up to the rim. Do not submerge. The iron should stay in the batter until it stops sizzling, thus allowing the batter to gather on the iron.

4 Dip the filled waffle iron into the hot oil. A quick pop (or a sharp pointed knife) will free the waffle from the iron. Leave the waffle in the hot oil for about 20-25 seconds or until golden.

5 Remove the waffle to drain on absorbent paper.

6 After frying one waffle, adjust the texture by adding one more tbsp of flour or a little water to the mixture. It may take a couple of tries to get the texture of the batter just right.

7 Dust with icing sugar.

DATE OR NUT-FILLED PASTRY

Maamoul, or Klacha

The ingredients in this sweet pastry passed along trading routes to converge with Middle Eastern dates. Wheat was probably first grown in Mesopotamia and has been culti-vated in Eurasia for 6,000 years, milk and butter (samn) came from the herdsmen, pistachios down the Silk Road and cinnamon and nutmeg along the Spice Routes.

During an traditional afternoon with the ladies, we sat on the floor and visited while making maamoul *two days before the Eid celebration. Some impressed patterns into the dough with the help of a qalib, a small wooden mould carved with deep engravings. Others created their own 'family' designs, moulding and marking the dough like a coat-of-arms. While the women chatted, the rhythmic rounding and shaping of the balls and thump of the qalib, like beating drums, produced the final result. The ladies left the hostess with hundreds of* maamoul, *which were placed on baking sheets and popped in the oven.*

DOUGH

2 lb (1 kg) coarse semolina

1 lb (500g) fine semolina

4 oz (100g) plain flour

1 1/2 lb (675g) unsalted butter or samn

4 fl oz (100ml) milk

6 tbsp sugar

1 tbsp *mahlab*, ground

4 tbsp rose water (opt)

4 tbsp orange blossom water

4 fl oz (100ml) *samn* or oil

icing sugar for coating

DATE FILLING

8 oz (225g) pitted dates, chopped and mashed

4 tbsp walnuts, ground

2 tbsp butter or *samn*

2 tbsp milk

1 tsp cinnamon, ground

1/2 tsp nutmeg, grated

NUT FILLING

8 oz (225g) pistachios, almonds or walnuts, chopped

1 tbsp sugar

1 tsp cinnamon, ground or 2 tbsp rose water (opt)

1 For the dough, mix both semolinas, *mahlab*, sugar, rose water, orange blossom water and *samn* or softened butter. Blend to a cream and leave for 12 hours or overnight in the refrigerator.

2 To prepare the date filling, blend the dates, walnuts, cinnamon, nutmeg, butter and milk to a paste. To prepare the nut filling, add sugar and cinnamon to the chopped nuts; add rose water if using chopped almonds and/or pistachios.

3 Heat the milk until tepid. Put a little into a cup and mix in the yeast. Leave to stand for 10 minutes or until it begins to form a froth.

4 Add the yeast mixture and remaining tepid milk to the dough. Knead thoroughly adding the plain flour and oil.

5 Shape the dough into walnut-size balls. Make a big grove with the thumb into the centre of each ball. Place a spoonful of the filling into the dough and close the top.

6 Reshape into an oval or round ball and make a pattern across the top or press into the *qalib* mould.

7 Bake on a greased oven tray at 300°F (150°C) gas 2 for about 10 minutes. Do not brown the nut-filled *maamoul* - they will appear soft and uncooked yet will become firm when cooled. The date-filled pastries, unlike the nut-filled, are usually left in the oven until brown.

8 Sprinkle nut-filled pastries with icing sugar, but not the browned, date-filled pastries, which are left plain.

SWEET CRISP PASTRIES

Baklawa

Cinnamon, the essential flavouring of baklawa, was brought along the Spice Routes from across the Indian Ocean to the Middle East where Arabs acted as middlemen, and caravaned it along the Frankincense Trail to the Nile Valley. East Africa was called 'Cinnamon Land,' perhaps because Arab Traders wanted to protect their monopoly on the trade and conjured up wild tales to conceal the actual source.

Probably the best known of all Arab pastries, the diamonds of ultra-thin buttered pastry, layer upon layer, are filled with chopped nuts and doused with streams of syrup. These sticky irresistible delights are for festive occasions when calories are not counted.

Baklawa can be stored in the refrigerator for 3-4 days before baking and 3-4 days after baking.

1 lb (500g) filo dough (p. 151)
6 fl oz (150ml) unsalted butter or *samn*
9 oz (250g) pistachios, finely chopped
1 tsp cinnamon, ground (opt)
qater syrup (p. 168)
2 tbsp pistachios, ground

1 Grease an oven tray [about 12x10in (30 x 25cm) with sides at least 2 inches (5cm) high] with melted butter or samn.

2 Cut all the filo dough into the size of the oven tray. To keep the filo dough moist, constantly cover with a damp cloth; as it dries quickly.

3 Gently layer 5 sheets of the filo dough into the oven tray, lightly brushing each layer with melted butter or *samn*. Sprinkle with the mixed cinnamon and nuts.

4 Continue layering by repeating step 3 three

times; thus using all the sheets of dough and nut mixture.

5 Partially cut the *baklawa* into squares or diamond shapes leaving a few bottom layers uncut.

6 Bake at 350°F (180°C) gas 4 for 30 minutes or until pale gold. Increase the temperature to 425°F (220°C) gas 5 and bake for a further 10-15 minutes or until golden brown.

7 Pour the cold *qater* syrup over the hot pastry. Cut the *baklawa* all the way through. Leave to cool. Sprinkle with the ground nuts.

VARIATION

● A ground cardamom pod can be substituted for the cinnamon.

● Walnuts, hazelnuts, or almonds can be used with the pistachios.

SHREDDED PASTRY

Kanafa

The dough for this cream or cheese-filled pastry looks like finely shredded filo or uncooked vermicelli noodles. Several variations of the creamy white or orange pastry exist, though it is virtually impossible to make at home. Watered-down filo mix is poured swiftly through a sieve, in spirals onto a hot griddle. An unusual version, borma, is the shredded dough stuffed with walnuts or pistachios rolled into a log shape, coated with qater and sliced into tasty rounds. Though the dough is readily available in the Middle East, especially during Ramadan, it will probably be difficult to locate in the West.

1 lb (500g) *kanafa* pastry
8 fl oz (225ml) unsalted butter or *samn*
qater syrup (p. 168)

CHEESE FILLING

2 lb (1 kg) ricotta, unsalted fetta, mozzarella, *haloum* or any sweet white cheese
1 tsp lemon rind, grated
1 tbsp sugar

Kataif assafir with *qater*

NUT FILLING

12 oz (350g) pistachios or walnuts, coarsely ground

1 tsp cinnamon

2 tbsp sugar

CREAM FILLING

6 tbsp ground rice or rice flour

2 pt (1 litre) milk

1/2 pt (275ml) double cream

4 tbsp sugar

FILLINGS

CHEESE: Beat the cheese until soft, adding sugar and grated lemon rind to taste.

NUT: Mix the chopped nuts with the cinnamon and sugar.

CREAM: Mix the sugar and ground rice with enough milk to make a paste. Boil the remainder of the milk, and gradually add the paste, stirring continually. Simmer and continue stirring until very thick. Leave to cool and mix in the cream.

1 Pull the strands of the *kanafa* dough, separating them as much as possible. Pour the melted butter or *samn* over the *kanafa*. By hand, work the butter into each strand.

2 Gently spread half the dough over the bottom of an oven tray. Spread the preferred filling over the dough. Gently place the remaining dough on top.

3 Bake at 325°F (160°C) gas 3 for 1 hour or until pale gold. Increase the temperature to 425°F (220°C) gas 5 for about 10-15 minutes, or until golden brown.

4 Pour the cold *qater* syrup over the hot pastry.

5 Serve warm cut into individual portions.

VARIATION

● *Borma*, small rolled pastries, are made by wrapping the strands of dough around the nut filling. The rolls are baked in long strips (logs), dipped in syrup and sliced.

SWEET FRIED PANCAKES

Kataif

Pancakes, layered with cream, or stuffed with creamed cheese or nuts and dripping with syrup, are specially prepared throughout the Islamic world during Ramadan, the month-long period of fasting from dawn to dusk. Just before sunset, kataif-making begins, when the stuffed version is folded into a semi-circle, pinched together, deep fried and finally drenched with qater.

Arabian pancakes are a little thicker and spongier than the western version, and about 6 inches/15 cm in diameter. Though they are easy to make at home, many Arabs buy pancakes ready-made and layer or stuff them at home.

Layered kataif are fried on both sides and piled with mounds of kishta, thick clotted cream, or whipped double cream and sprinkled with chopped nuts. However, another version calls for stuffing the centre of the pancake with nuts or soft cheese; pinching the sides together in a semi-circle and deep frying. Yet another kataif is miniature pancakes (about 4 inches/10 cm in diameter) shaped into triangular pockets by pinching together one end, stuffing with fresh cream and drizzling with syrup. These kataif assafir translated mean 'little birds,' and were traditionally garnished with the red-coloured sweet pickled flower of the lemon tree.

MAKES ABOUT 30 PANCAKES

1 lb (500g) plain flour, sifted
1 tsp dried yeast or
1 tbsp fresh yeast
16 fl oz (500ml) lukewarm water
1 tsp sugar
oil for shallow-frying
oil for deep-frying
1 portion cheese filling or 2 portions nut filling
(see pages 174-175))
qater syrup (p. 168)

1 Dissolve the yeast and sugar in a cup of the lukewarm water. Leave to stand for 10 minutes or until it begins to bubble.

2 Gradually add the yeast mixture and the remaining water to the flour, stirring continually until the batter is smooth and creamy

3 Cover with a damp cloth and leave to stand for 1 hour or until batter rises and bubbles.

4 Pour about 3 tbsp of batter onto a hot greased frying pan or griddle. Fry until bubbly and the pancake easily comes away from the pan. Only fry one side of the pancake, thus allowing the uncooked side to stick together after stuffing.

5 Choose the preferred cheese or nut filling. In the centre of the un-fried side of the pancake place a tablespoon of the filling (depending on the size of the pancake).

6 Fold the pancake in half over the filling. Seal by pinching the edges together.

7 Deep-fry for 2-3 minutes or until golden brown.

8 Immediately dip each hot *kataif* in the cold *qater* syrup.

VARIATION

● To make miniature pancakes pour 2 tbsp of the batter [about 3in (7cm) round] onto a hot greased frying pan or griddle. Fry until golden brown on one side only. Pinch the bottom half of the edges to make a triangular pocket in which to stuff thick cream, *kishta* (p. 168) or cream filling (p. 175). Garnish with a sliver of red cherry or sweetly preserved lemon flower, *zahra al lemon* and top with *qater* syrup (p.168).

PASTRY BALLS

Awama

Fried bite-sized balls, soaked in a bowl of qater *and drained, take on the appearance of miniature doughnuts. Awama are served warm on almost any occasion.*

1 lb (500g) plain flour, sifted
1 pt (575ml) yoghurt
1 tsp lemon juice
$^1/_2$ tbsp bicarbonate/baking soda
1 tsp salt
oil for deep-frying
qater syrup (p. 168)

1 Gradually add the yoghurt and lemon juice to the flour, soda and salt. Knead well.

2 With a spoon, cut out marble-size balls of dough. Deep-fry until golden.

3 Immerse the hot balls into the cold syrup and remove to drain.

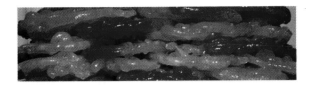

CANDY SWIRLS

Mushabbak

Bright orange-red and transparent-coloured chewy candy, looking almost like an intricate pretzel, is made by interweaving liquid dough swirled from a teapot or decorating tube into sizzling hot oil. The fried dough has a taste somewhat like taffy, after it has soaked up the sweet syrup of qater.

awama dough (previous recipe)
2-3 drops red food colouring
water
oil for deep-frying
qater syrup (p.168)

1 Add water, drop by drop, into the dough until a thick batter forms. Add a few drops of red food colouring, but do not stir.

2 Place the batter into a tea pot or decorating tube, then stream the batter into hot oil, forming a disc (around 4 inches/10cm across and $^1/_2$

inch/1 cm thick)with a swirled twisted knot or flower design. Fry until crispy but not brown.

3 Immerse the hot candy swirls into *qater* syrup.

SEMOLINA CAKES

Namura, or Basbousa

In one of the richest-tasting Arabic sweets, coarse semolina is mixed with tender coconut to make a thick, concentrated cake. The syrupy squares are dotted with almond halves.

12 oz (350g) semolina
4 oz (100g) self-raising flour, sifted
4 oz (100g) dessicated coconut
4 tbsp sugar
4 fl oz (100ml) yoghurt
4 fl oz (100ml) unsalted butter or *samn*
1 tsp baking powder
1 tbsp rose water (opt)
6 tbsp almonds, halved
qater syrup (p. 168)

1 Mix the melted butter or *samn* to the semolina, flour, coconut, sugar, and baking powder.

2 Add the yoghurt, rose water and $^1/_2$ cup warm water to make a thick batter.

3 Pour and spread the batter until about $^1/_2$ inch thick onto an oiled baking tray. Leave to stand for 20 minutes.

4 Score diamond shapes into the surface. Press an almond into the centre of each diamond.

5 Bake at 375°F (190°C) gas 5 for 20 minutes or until golden and firm.

6 Drench the hot cake with cold *qater* syrup. Slice each diamond shape all the way through.

GLOSSARY OF
SPICES & HERBS

When Stone Age cooks learned to wrap meat in leaves to protect it from dirt and ash before cooking it over a fire, they would have discovered that certain leaves exuded special flavours. This may well have been the first chapter in the history of seasoning.

Aromatic sacks of sweet cinnamon, perfumed cloves, delicate saffron, strong cardamom, harsh cumin, and overpowering coriander were transported westward along the caravan trails and by the ocean-going dhows that crisscrossed the Indian Ocean and Arabian Gulf. Spices were the first objects of commerce between the East and West, traded even more often than gold or precious stones!

Southern Arabia became the spice kingdom. Fortunes were made in the Arabian Peninsula and the coast of East Africa, particularly Zanzibar, which was once called 'Cinnamon Land.' The origins of spices - especially of the highly desirable and costly barks of cassia and cinnamon - were trade secrets. Arab merchants were eager to protect their sources and the monopoly they held on the spice trade.

A visit to the narrow, dark passageways of an Arabian spice market, with its heady, aromatic atmosphere, reveals some of the hidden Eastern treasures of the region's heritage. Yet though spices are no longer luxury items, they are still highly valued in Arabian cooking.

Ready-ground spices quickly lose their savour. Try to buy them whole, then grind small batches of whole spices or dried herbs and store in screw top jars - do not prepare large quantities as the spices will eventually lose their pungency and aroma.

ENGLISH NAME   *Botanical name*   ARABIC NAME

ALLSPICE   *Pimenta officinalis, dioica*   BAHAR HILU
Allspice berries are round, aromatic and dark brown, similar in appearance to an oversized peppercorn. Columbus discovered the spice in Jamaica and gave it the botanical name Pimenta, which is the Spanish word for 'pepper'. To date, confusion remains as allspice is not related to the pimento family. The name 'allspice' is far more descriptive because it closely resembles the fragrance of cloves, cinnamon, and nutmeg. Commonly used in Middle Eastern stuffings, allspice adds a delicate flavour to lamb and chicken.

ANISE   *Pimpinella anisum*   YANSOON
Small grey-green oil bearing seeds were cultivated in Egypt since the days of the Pharaohs. Anise is occasionally used in drinks and savouries, as well as sweet cakes to add a sweetly scented flavour. Although many do not like its flavour, anise blends delightfully with figs and with the addition of garlic to fish soup, shellfish, chicken and game birds. The seeds (aniseed) are sometimes chewed after a meal to sweeten the breath and as a digestive agent.

BARBERRY   *Berberidacae*   BARBARIS
Reddish brown berries resembling raisins when dried, barbaries are very sour and used in some Gulf nations when cooking rice.

BASIL   *Ocimum basilicum*   RAYHAN
Easily grown in any moderate climate, basil has white flowers and tender, light green leaves. The herb is known to have a great affinity with tomatoes and is best fresh. Iraqis add basil to a yoghurt drink, while other Arabs prefer to eat the fresh leaves as an accompaniment to meals.

BAY LEAF   *Laurus nobilis*   WARAQ AL GAR, KENYA
Green spear-shaped leaves, also called sweet bay and laurel, are used world-wide to flavour soups and stews. The tree came originally from Asia Minor. The leaf can be used green, or is more commonly dried.

CARDAMOM *Elettaria cardamomum* HAIL
Strong green, and milder black, aromatic cardamom pods, from a plant related to ginger, can be freshly ground or cracked open and added to stews and rice. Whole cardamom pods or the seeds inside the pod are a distinctive ingredient of Arabic coffee.

In the past, the highly valued pods of cardamom were sent to friends and family as an invitation to a wedding.

The Middle East today is the largest importer of the expensive pods, which are a native of the wet tropical jungles of India. The tiny seeds contained in the pods may be dark brown or black, while the outer husk of the pod may be coloured cream, brown, pale green or white. Much larger, dark brown, often hairy pods of cardamom, a more inferior species, are commonly sold as black.

Although more expensive, cardamom should be bought as whole pods, cracked open and then ground for each use. Ground pods quickly loose their essence.

CHILLI PEPPER *Capsicum frutescens* FILFIL HAR
Fresh chilli peppers can be red or green depending on ripeness. Arabs say that the small peppers are more fiery than the larger varieties. The peppers are used heavily in the North African countries and Yemen, but in moderation in the other Arab countries. We met an Arab who carried a pepper or two in his pocket just in case any meal was too mild. Whole chilli peppers are usually added to the relish tray or salad bowl at meal time or ground into a paste called *harissa* in the Maghreb, *bisbas* in Yemen or *shatta* in other regions.

CINNAMON *Cinnamonum zeylanicum* QIRFA

CASSIA *Cinnamonum cassia* QIRFA
Cassia and cinnamon can be easily confused - both come from the inner bark of an evergreen tree and are closely related but from different species; cassia originates from Burma and cinnamon from Sri Lanka. Cinnamon is considered to be of better quality and is used in sweets, rice dishes and as a spice for fish, chicken and lamb. The popular flavour is an essential ingredient of *baharat*, a spice blend used in cooking a wide variety of Arabic dishes.

Cinnamon has the more delicate taste and cassia is more pungent. Buy ground cinnamon in small quantities, as it quickly loses its aroma and becomes stale.

CLOVES *Eugenia aromatica* QURNFUL
Dried flower buds of an evergreen tree, which flourish only near the sea and is native to the Spice Islands of Southeast Asia, cloves are powerfully scented. Their English name comes from the Latin word 'clavus' which means nail - and they are indeed shaped like small nails.

Cloves are picked when they are pink flower buds, and are then spread out to dry on mats.

The spice was used in the tombs of the pharaohs, probably because they contain the essential oil which is powerfully antiseptic and has a preservative action. Historically, when washing the body was more difficult, a little bag, full of a clove blend, was carried as an aromatic perfume.

The powerful flavour of cloves should be used sparingly to add to but not overwhelm the other flavours of the food.

CORIANDER *Coriandrum sativum* KUZBARA
Coriander leaves, used as an herb, render a totally different flavour from the pale brown, round seeds which are usually ground. The overpowering flavour and aroma of fresh coriander helps calm the fishy flavour of seafood.

Coriander, a native of Mesopotamia, was said to have been cultivated in the hanging gardens of Babylon - today the ground seeds are prominently used in a spice blend called *baharat*.

In Middle Eastern cooking, a special spice blend called 'taklia' is prepared by mixing a teaspoon of ground coriander with three cloves of salted and fried garlic. 'Taklia' is added at the end of cooking to spinach, chickpeas or meatballs for an aromatic and unusual flavouring.

CRESS *Arabis caucasica* BARBEEN
A dark green leaf of the mustard family, used in salads.

CUMIN *Cuminum cyminum* KAMMUN
Small pale brown seeds of an annual related to parsley, cumin is used whole or powdered. The spice is believed by Arabs to calm any flatulence and for that reason a dash is usually added to pulses. Cumin must be used sparingly as it will have a bitter taste if used in large quantities.

The origins of cumin are debatable - some say the spice originally came from the Orient but was grown in the Mediterranean region well over 2,000 years ago. The Romans used it as a substitute for pepper and even ground it to a paste for spreading on bread. Others say cumin is a native to the Middle East - specifically indigenous to the upper Nile.

DILL *Anethum graveolens* SHIBITT
A dark green member of the parsley family, this herb is sometimes called dill weed. When crushed, dill has a distinctive aroma and is used fresh in salads, sauces, fish and rice dishes. Dill seeds are rarely used in Arabic cooking.

Dill is native to Asia, but has been grown in Mediterranean countries since ancient times and is now naturalised over most of Europe.

FENUGREEK *Trigonella foenum-graceum* HILBEH
A native to Europe and Asia and related to clover, the name means 'Greek hay'. These rock-hard, golden brown, irregularly shaped seeds are bitter - bitterness can be reduced with soaking and cooking.

Fenugreek seeds are an essential ingredient for dried beef, called *bastirma*. In Yemen, the green leaves or the pungent ground seeds are made into a dip, spread on bread or generally used as an accompaniment to a meal.

GARLIC *Allium sativum* TOUM
Usually considered a vegetable in Arabian cooking, garlic is present in almost every savoury dish or sauce. Sometimes whole cloves of garlic are placed on a grill until the husks are brown and insides soft and creamy. The whole cloves are eaten with grilled meats and fish.

GINGER *Zingiber officinale* ZANZABIL
An irregularly shaped rhizome, ginger will keep well for a long time in dry conditions and has a thin skin that needs to be removed before use. Except in the southern Gulf Countries, ginger is not used frequently in Arabic cooking today, but was noted in the Holy *Quran* for its medicinal value.

Indigenous to the tropical jungles of southern Asia, ginger has also been used extensively in China for thousands of years. It was brought along trading routes into Europe long before Roman times.

WATERCRESS *Nasturtium officinale* JIRJEAR
A green leafy type of watercress only eaten raw, *jirjear* is almost sweet but slightly pungent and peppery in taste. Usually the leaf and tender stem are eaten plain. *Jirjear* is commonly served with fish.

DRIED LIME *Citrus aurantifolia* LOOMI
Dried lime, closely related to the lemon, must be pierced twice with a skewer or ground before use.

If *loomi* is not available, the rind of ¹/₂ fresh lime or lemon can be substituted, although altering the flavour. For the ambitious, fresh lime can be dried.

MARJORAM *Origanum majorana* ETRA
An aromatic herb with small delicate leaves, marjoram has been used for centuries. The sweet or cultivated variety is combined with wild marjoram or oregano (*Origanum vulgare*) in a spice blend, *zaatar*, which is used as a dry dip.

MAHLAB *Prunus* MAHLAB
The kernel of the black cherry, *mahlab* is added to dough when baking bread for an almost vanilla fragrance. Bought whole, to be ground just before use, *mahlab* quickly looses its potency.

MELOKHIYA *Corchorus olitorius* MELOKHIYA
A member of the mallow family, which includes okra and cotton, *melokhiya* was originally grown in Egypt. The leaves can have a viscous property similar to okra/lady's finger. *Melokhiya* is made into stew or soup.

MINT *Mentha* NAANA
The Arabic name *naana* means 'the gift of Allah'. Dried crisp mint is a herb used diversely throughout the Arab world. Yoghurt-mint drinks whet the appetite for the meal to follow and mint tea seems to sooth after a heavy feast. The fresh leaves can be placed on a tray along with other greenery and consumed whole. Mint also has a great affinity for yoghurt when used in sauces and marinades.

The herb is considered to be native to the temperate regions of the Old World, but the ease with which the plant grows has resulted in a range of 25 or so species, some of which even grow in the wild.

NUTMEG *Myristica fragrans* JOZET AL TAYIB
An extremely hard brown ball, nutmeg is the dried kernel of the fruit from an evergreen tree of the myrtle family.

Ancient societies used nutmeg as a remedy for intestinal disorders. Today it is used in many spice blends, such as *baharat*, and as flavouring for desserts, including U*mm Ali*.

Native of the Molucca Islands of Indonesia, nutmeg should be bought whole (the white-coloured nutmeg balls have been treated with lime), as the powdered version quickly loses its fragrance. The thin layer around the nutmeg seed is mace, also used as a spice.

PAPRIKA *Capsicum tetragonum* FILFIL HILU
A bright red powder made from ripened and dried peppers, in Arabic paprika literally means 'sweet pepper'. Paprika is one ingredient in *baharat*, a frequently used spice blend, and is occasionally used as a garnish.

PARSLEY *Petroselinum crispum* BAQDOUNIS
In the Arab world, the flat-leaf variety of parsley is regarded as having the best flavour, perhaps because of its abundance in the Middle East. Flat-leaf parsley is considered adaptable to temperatures - whether hot or cold. Believed to be of Mediterranean origin, the herb has many varieties and is used in stews and with meats and poultry. Parsley is the primary ingredient in a finely-chopped salad called *tabouleh*. A bunch of parsley - chopped quickly and added at the last moment of cooking or as a garnish to retain its flavour - is a necessity in every Arab kitchen.

PEPPER *Piper nigrum* FILFIL
The world's most popular spice is found as white or black peppercorns. The black variety are plucked while still green and unripe and then sun dried. The white peppercorns are allowed to ripen on the vine and then the skin is removed. In Arabic recipes, black pepper is more common. White pepper, though less intense and more sparse on grocer's shelves, is believed to be easily digested. Pepper freshly ground in a mill is recommended to preserve its volatile and easily lost flavour.

POMEGRANATE *Punica granatum* RUMAN
The succulent, red seeds of the large, thick-skinned pomegranate fruit are used raw, in cooking, or as a garnish. The juice is extracted for a drink or made into a syrup, grenadine. Pomegranate syrup is commonly used to give a sweet and sour balance. To juice the fruit, separate the compartmentalized seeds from the tough, bitter inner membranes. Place a handful of the shiny seeds in muslin cloth and squeeze the juice into a bowl, or place the seeds into a sieve and press out the juice. Freeze in ice-cube trays, then pack cubes in plastic bags to be stored in the freezer. The cubes can be defrosted for any recipes that call for the juice or used frozen to drop into drinks or use as a garnish. (Dried seeds are often used as a garnish in the Middle East.) The colour - which ranges from transparent to dark purple-red - is no indicator of taste.

POPPY SEEDS *Papaver somniferum* KASHAKISH
The prime use of grey or white poppy seeds in ancient Arabic cookery was to garnish breads and cakes. The Egyptians formerly fed their athletes on honey and poppy seed cakes in the belief that their strength and endurance would be increased.

PURSLANE *Portulaca oleracea* RIJLA/BAGLI
A spreading annual plant with fleshy leaves, purslane resembles samphire, though has a different flavour.

The taste of purslane is mild, though slightly sour with a mucilaginous texture - somewhat like okra. The leaves can be gritty and should be washed thoroughly before use. The tender shoots can be dressed with oil and vinegar to be eaten raw in an array of salads. This vegetable, which is thought to be an unsightly weed in the United States and is unrecognised in other parts of the world, is considered an essential salad ingredient in areas of the Arab World - especially in Lebanese *fattoush*.

SAFFRON *Crocus sativus* ZAFFARAN
The world's most expensive spice comes from the dried stigmas of the saffron crocus flower. As there are only three stigmas to each plant, it takes over 75,000 of the hand-picked strands to produce 1 lb. But, only a few threads (a pinch) of this spice will give a beautiful yellowish glow to rice and poultry dishes. Deep-red saffron is even more precious and costlier. The flavour of saffron is delicate and should not undergo any lengthy cooking. A few dried stigmas can either be soaked in a little milk or water for about 15 minutes to loosen the dye or ground with one teaspoon of sugar and added to food at the last minute. Turmeric is a cheaper substitute for colouring, but with less flavour and aroma. Powdered saffron is almost always a dye used as a food cosmetic, not a flavour enhancer.

SESAME SEEDS *Sesamum indicum* SIMSIM
The pale ivory nutritious seeds from an annual sesame plant are one of the world's oldest spices and oil seed crops. Once, highly valued sesame seeds were used for barter and are probably best remembered for their role played in the story of Ali Baba and the forty thieves when he uttered the words *iftah ya simsim* (open sesame). The seeds are used raw or roasted to flavour many dishes and breads. A sweet sesame seed brittle is called *simsimiya*. The oily paste made from grinding the seed, *tahina*, is used uncooked in many Arabic recipes, particularly in dips and with chickpeas. This paste is not to be confused with the more refined sesame seed oil.

SUMAC *Rhus coriaria* SUMAG
Dried dark red to purple clusters of seeded hairy fruit of the cashew family is ground to a coarse powder. The fruit is noted for the material used in tanning and dyeing. In the Middle East, *sumac* is used as a spice which is slightly sour with an almost lemon flavour. This eccentrically Eastern spice can be used uncooked, to give a tartness when sprinkled into salads or over grilled meats.

TAMARIND *Tamarindus indica* TAMER HINDI
Tamarind is a large acidic bean pod from a tropical tree. The pods are sold as a dried yet sticky, consolidated chunk. In appearance only, tamarind resembles dates; thus, the Arabic name *tamer hindi*, which means 'date of India'.

Tamarind is soaked, seeds removed and then most commonly made into a tart drink by the same name, or is used in cooking many Gulf dishes. It can also be used in a Worcester sauce-like marinade.

TURMERIC *Curcuma longa* KURKUM
A bright yellow rhizome from the same family as ginger, turmeric comes from a plant indigenous to the humid, hilly districts of south and southwest Asia. The root-like spice is prepared by first boiling, peeling and then drying in the hot sun for several weeks. Whole dried roots are hard, so purchase of the ground version is recommended. Though a cheaper alternative to saffron, turmeric is no substitute for taste and should be used sparingly, as too much will give a slightly bitter flavour. The colour of turmeric is probably most recognised in the yellow prepared jars of mustard or an Indian curry dish.

THYME *Thymus vulgaris* ZAATAR
In Arabic, *zaatar* literally means thyme. However, most Arabs when using the word *zaatar*, are normally referring to the spice blend (see opposite) which cheese balls are rolled into, as a coating for bread which has been dipped in olive oil, or as a filling or topping for savoury pastries. Thyme belongs to the family of labiates, along with mint, sage, oregano and basil. The garden herb is easily grown in soil that is dry, stony and lime-rich. The spice's aromatic flavouring is conducive to long, slow cooking in a casserole or stew.

SPICE BLENDS

Recipes for each spice mixture vary from house-to-house and each region has its own particular blend of freshly ground fragrant spices, but all are called baharat *(a mixture of spices). North African blends are fiery-hot; the northern Levant version heavier on cinnamon, and the Egyptian mix leans toward cumin. Gulf blends, with close proximity and trading ties to the Indian sub-continent, have a tendency to be sweetly aromatic, almost like the spices used in curry.*

In the Middle East, narrow shops specialise in stocking a vast selection of spices to be ground, mixed and blended to personalised perfection.

Zaatar

An Arabic word meaning thyme, zaatar is also a blend of herbs and spices, which has a flavour akin to oregano. Wild marjoram, which is oregano (Origanum vulgare), is a herb closely related to sweet marjoram but with more pungency according to the area where it is grown. Oregano dries well and is seldom used fresh. Dried rigani from Greece includes both the leaves and flower buds.

Zaatar - slightly oily yet dry and a crumbly blend of roasted sesame seeds, wild marjoram, thyme and sumac - is a frequent component of an Arabic breakfast. Blended with drizzled oil, the mixture serves as a tangy bread topping or as a dry dip in which to plunge torn off pieces of thin warm bread. It can be sprinkled over a tangy drained yoghurt or used to coat a zesty cheese ball called shankalis.

1 part thyme, dried
$1/2$ part wild marjoram
$1/4$ part sesame seeds, roasted
$1/8$ part *sumac*
oil (opt)

1 Grind the thyme, wild marjoram and sumac. Add the roasted sesame seeds.

2 Some prefer to slightly oil the *zaatar*. With oily hands, rub the spice blend between the palms.

Duqqa

This ancient blend of spices and nuts, recorded from the time of the pharaohs, was enjoyed by rulers and slaves alike. Duqqa was also buried in the pyramids to sustain the travellers on their 'journey across the river of time'.

The crunchy nuts and seeds, ground spices and mixed herbs are oven roasted for a dry spice blend that is usually eaten by first dipping pieces of bread into olive oil and then plunged in the bowl of duqqa.

A common folk version of duqqa uses 1 part salt or sumac, 1 part roasted coriander, 1 part roasted peanuts, 1/2 part roasted chickpeas and sometimes lentils and other dried and roasted pulses, 1/2 part dried mint and 1/2 part roasted sesame seeds.

Once the nuts are roasted, allow to cool before grinding. If the nuts are ground too quickly or too long, the slightly moist yet crumbly mixture will become oily. Duqqa can be eaten immediately, or stored for a short time in airtight containers.

Baharat

Almost any spice blend in the Arab world is called baharat, which literally means 'spices'. Each blend varies from family to family and region to region.

6 tbsp black peppercorns, ground
3 tbsp coriander seeds, ground
3 tbsp cinnamon or cassia bark, ground
3 tbsp cloves, ground
4 tbsp cumin seeds, ground
2 tsp cardamom, ground
3 tbsp nutmeg, grated
6 tbsp paprika

To make *baharat*, simply mix the ingredients together and store in an airtight container.

GENERAL GLOSSARY

A
ADAS - (see lentils)
AHMAR - Red
AJEEN - Dough
ALLSPICE - See Spice Glossary
ALMOND (*Prunus dulcis, amygdalus*) *Loz* - Kernel of a fruit of the peach and apricot family. The fruit of the almond is leathery and dark green, although enjoyed by children. The kernel is covered with a thin skin which is easily removed by pouring boiling water over the nuts and rinsing in cold water. Almonds are used in Arabic cooking for rice or *farika* stuffing in lamb or chicken and to top rice, *couscous* and sweet pastries.
ANCHOVY - Many species of the genus Engraulis are called anchovies. The tiny fish in the Middle East are typically spread out on the beach to dry.
APRICOT (*Prunus armeniaca*) *Qamar addine, Mishmish* - Grown in China almost 4,000 years ago, apricots were first cultivated somewhere along the Silk Road, between China and the Middle East. Today they are grown in fertile valleys of the Middle East and are usually dried or in the paste form, as fresh apricots travel badly. Reconstitute the dried or paste by soaking before use in a drink, compote or for cooking. *Allah*'s gift to the Arab sweet tooth is dried apricots stuffed with almonds or almond paste. As a savoury, apricots are occasionally added to a lamb stew.
ARNAB - Rabbit

ASAL - Honey
ASFAR - Yellow
AUBERGINE/Eggplant (*Solanum melongena*) *Badenjan* - range in colour from deep purple to white and in shape from round, oval or elongated. Small aubergines are preferred for stuffing. Remove the bitter juices by cutting and sprinkling with salt. Place in a colander with a heavy weight on top. Leave for 1 hour. Wash and pat dry. The flesh discolours when exposed to metal, therefore cut with a stainless steel knife and mash with a wooden spoon or fork. The spongy texture inclines the flesh to soak up oil when fried, unless first salted or battered. One of the most popular aubergine dishes of the Middle East is *Mutabbal*.

B
BADENJAN - (see aubergine/ eggplant)
BAHAR - Literally is a short word for 'spice', but sometimes refers to a spice blend of cloves, cinnamon and nutmeg. Allspice is a substitute.
BAHARAT - The above B*ahar* mixture of cloves, cinnamon, and nutmeg plus coriander, cumin, paprika, pepper and cardamom.
BAHAR HILU - Allspice
BAID - Egg
BAKLAWA - Layered filo pastries filled with ground nuts.
BAMIA - (see okra /ladies' finger)
BANDOURA - Tomatoes
BAQDOUNIS - Parsley
BARBERRY (*Berberis vulgaris*) - Shrub with elongated bright red berries.
BARLEY (*Hordeum vulgare*) - The first grain to be cultivated and used to make bread, even before wheat. It was made into unleavened barley cakes. Pearl barley, which has the husk removed is still used today.
BASAL - (see onions)
BASTIRMA - Spicy dried beef like pastrami.
BATATA - Potato
BEET/BEETROOT (*Beta vulgaris*) *Shamandar* - a deep red root, used for thousands of years .
BISMILLAH. - 'In the name of God' should be expressed at the beginning of most actions, especially before meal time.
BLANCHING - A slight simmer in hot water until the vegetable changes colours, or pouring hot water over nuts to remove the skins.
BROAD BEANS/SHELL/WINDSOR OR FAVA BEANS (*Vicia faba*) *Foul* - One of the first plants to be cultivated by man, the original hardy bean cultivated since the Stone Age.
BURGUL - Wheat that has been cracked by boiling, drying and grinding. Burgul is a staple of the Middle East, especially in Lebanon and Syria, and is used for stuffings, fillings, bindings, salads, and as a substitute for rice. See farika.

C
CAPSICUM/Bell pepper/Sweet pepper (*Capsicum annuum*) *Filfil hilu* - The green capsicum turns red or yellow when ripened. When dried

forms the spice, paprika.

CASHEW (*Anacardium occidentale*) *Cazo* The nut grows at the end of the fruit. The nut is used in the Middle East to adorn rice dishes.

CAVIAR - Commonly eaten in the Levant due to the proximity of the Caspian Sea, one of its sources, caviar is the ripe eggs of various species of sturgeon - a primitive fish which is rather shark-like in appearance. Beluga caviar, known to be the best quality, comes from an enormous fish which can live to be 100 years old and may weigh over 1000 kg (2200 lb). Also readily available in the countries near Iran, where beluga caviar is produced.

CHEESE *Jibnah* - In the Middle East, usually made primarily from goat's and sheep's milk into a soft fresh white cheese.

CHICKPEAS/Garbanzo (*Cier arietinum*) *Hummos* - These beige/tan peas provide a staple food of the Middle East when added to stews, pureed for a dip called *hummos* or layered with bread or other ingredients for *fatta hummos* or *musabaha*. Sometimes eaten fresh, chickpeas are also dried as a pulse.

CLARIFIED BUTTER *Samn* - Made from cow's, sheep's, or goat's milk. The advantage of *samn* over butter is the resilience to higher temperatures, thus rendering a different taste.

COFFEE (*Coffea arabica*) *Qahwah* - Originated in Ethiopia where it grows wild. The word coffee comes from the Arabic word *qahwah* where it was cultivated around 575 AD and was extensively grown in southern Arabia in the fifteenth century. Mocha coffee originated from the port of Mocha in Yemen.

COLOSTRUM/BEESTINGS - The milk from a newly-calved cow which is cooked in some parts of the Arab world to make a custard.

COURGETTE - (see squash)

CORNFLOUR/CORNSTARCH *Tahin thura* - A fine white flour of corn.

COUSCOUS - A cereal processed from semolina into tiny pellets by grinding the durum wheat and rolling in fine semolina flour. Also a North African dish of the same name (and known as *maghrebiya* by the Lebanese and *maftoul* by Palestinians).

COUSCOUSIER or COUSCAS - A steaming pot for *couscous*.

CRACKED WHEAT - (See *burgul* or *jaresh*)

CRIMPING - Cutting transverse slits in the sides of fish to allow penetration of marinade and spices, and to hasten cooking.

CUSA (*Cucurbit apepo*) Courgettes/ Zucchini/Italian squash/Marrow - The small long and light green variety is used in the Arab world to stuff and in stews. See also squash.

CUCUMBER (*Cucumis sativus*) *Khiyar* - One of the oldest cultivated vegetables, cucumbers have been grown for more than 4,000 years.

CUTTLEFISH - cephalopods, from the same family of squid and octopus. Cuttlefish have a stiffening 'bone', a familiar white porous object which is washed up on beaches and used to provide a grit for caged birds.

D

DATE (*Pheonix*) *Tamer* - Of Arab origin, today hundreds of varieties of the date are produced for export or domestic use. Iraq, formally a part of Mesopotamia, is one of the major exporters. Fresh, the date has a fruit-like texture. While drying the natural sugar forms a preservative and adds flavour. The shape of dates changes when dried and are pressed into slabs which are sold dry, semi-dry, and soft. The date is eaten raw or cooked in various stews and pastries.

DAMASSA - cooking pot for pulses

with a narrow neck and bell shaped bottom.

DAJAJ - Chicken

DHOWS - Wooden sailing ships, similar in design to Viking ships, used in the Arabian Gulf and Indian Ocean to ferry cargo from country to country. Originally they were built without nails or pegs, but by tying the reeds or wood with rope. Today, motorized vessels are replacing the traditional sails.

DIBS - A syrup made in the Arab world by boiling down fruit including dates, raisins, carob beans or sweet grapes with a little water until a thick solution forms.

DIBS RUMAN - Grenadine or syrup made from pomegranate.

DOLMA - Greek or Turkish for stuffed vine leaves, *waraq ainab*.

DUQQA - A spice/nut/herb mixture used as a dry dip.

E-F

EGGPLANT - (see aubergine)

EID - A religious holiday of feasting in the Arab World to commemorate the passing of Ramadan, the month of fasting, and the pilgrimage to Mecca.

FALAFEL - Chickpea and bean croquette

FARIKA - Unripened cracked wheat used as a replacement for rice, especially in stuffing. The grains must be cleaned of stones and roughage and washed before use.

FETTA - Goat's or sheep's cheese known to be of Greek or Turkish origin.

FIGS (*Ficus carica*) *Teen* - exported in large quantities out of the northern part of the Middle East, figs are usually eaten fresh or dried. Dried figs are soaked and used in compotes with other dried fruit.

FILFIL (*Capsicum frutescens*) Chilli pepper

FILFIL ABAID - White pepper

FILFIL AHMAR - Red chilli pepper

FILFIL ASWAD - Black pepper

FILFIL HILU - Literally translated means 'sweet pepper' referring to the capsicum pepper/bell pepper (see capsicum).

FILO - Sheets of pastry dough, thinner than paper.

FOUL MEDAMES (*Lathyrus sativus*)- Small round brown beans, a variety of the flat larger fava or broad bean also called foul medames in English.

FRY -

DEEP-FRY - to immerse in hot oil until golden.

SAUTE - to fry slowly in a little oil until lightly browned.

SHALLOW-FRY - to cook in hot oil until one side is golden (the food is usually turned to brown the other side).

STIR-FRY - to fry quickly with a little oil, stirring to prevent the food from burning.

G-H

GARLIC (*Allium sativum*) - A member of the same genus as leeks and onions, garlic is probably a native to Central Asia. Dozens of varieties abound, differing in bulb size, pungency and skin colour.

GRAPES (*Vitis*) - Raisins, sultanas and currents are dried grapes from various species of the same genus. Grape or other vine leaves are used to prepare *waraq ainab*.

GRENADINE *Dibs ruman* - A syrup made from juiced pomegranate and sugar.

HAIL - Cardamom

HALAL - Meat slaughtered in the Islamic manner.

HALAWA - Sweet

HALAWA BIL TAHINA - A sweet or dessert made from sesame seed paste.

HALEEB - Milk

HALOUM - White salty cheese

HARICOT (*Phaseolus vulgaris*) *Fassoulia* - A large white bean, the smaller pearl haricot is also known as the Boston bean, navy bean and pea bean.

HILBEH - Fenugreek

HILU - Sweet

HONEY *Asal* - The world's oldest sweetener traditionally used in baking bread. Today, mainly used in the Middle East to drizzle over pastries or breakfast breads.

HUMMOS - (see chickpeas/garbanzo beans)

J-K

JALLAB - A sweet purple drink made from berries with added pine nuts.

JAMEED - Dried yoghurt balls

JARESH - A finer cracked wheat than *burgul* used as a filler with a nutty taste.

JIBNAH - Cheese

JIRJEAR Watercress - A leafy plant only eaten raw in salads or on its own.

KANAFA - Shredded dough for making *kanafa*, the pastry.

KATAIF - Yeast pancakes filled with nuts, cheese or cream.

KEBAB - Meat cooked on a skewer whether cubed or minced.

KHOUBZ - Arabic bread

KIBBAH - A mixture of ground meat, *burgul* and spices, which can be stuffed or layered and baked, fried or eaten raw.

KISK - Milk, yoghurt and *burgul* fermented and cooked to a porridge-like consistency.

KISHTA/GAMMER - Clotted cream made traditionally from buffalo, cow, goat, sheep or camel milk.

KOFTA - Spiced minced meat usually cooked on a skewer.

KORAN - The holy book of the Moslem religion.

KUDAR - Green and also means vegetables

KURKUM - Turmeric

KUZBARA - Coriander

L-M

LABAN - Yoghurt, but also the name of a drink.

LEBNAH - Drained thick yoghurt.

LADIES' FINGER - (see okra)

LENTILS (*Lens culinaris*) *Adas* - flat rounded pulse. Originally from the Middle East, the red, yellow and brown variety are commonly used in Arabic cooking.

LETTUCE (*Lactuca crispa*) *Khas* - In the Arab countries with warmer climates, Cos or Romaine type of lettuce is the most common in the Middle East. The large elongated leaves, can be tough and special care should be taken before adding to delicate salads.

LIME (*Citrus aurantifolia*) *loomi* - A small, sour, citrus fruit much in common with the lemon, except that in the Middle East when it is dried and used as a spice. The acidic powder is delicious when sprinkled, for example, over rice.

LIQUORICE (*Glycyrrhiza glabra*) *Sous* - A root of a plant grown in the Middle East provides a bitter-sweet flavouring. Mainly used today for the Arabic sweet drink, *sous*.

LOZ - (see almonds)

LOCUST (*Nomadacris septemfasciata*) *Jirad* - The red or carmine locust is the one most commonly eaten in Arabia.

MAASEL - Date syrup

MAHSHI - Stuffed

MAI WARD - Rose water, which is used in cooking sweets and as a perfume.

MAI ZAHRA - Orange blossom water.

MAJLIS - Meeting place

MAKLI - Fried

MANAKISH - Flat bread topped with a variety of ingredients, including *zaatar* or cheese.

MANSAF - Festive jointed lamb, of Bedouin origin, to be served over rice for a special occasion. The word also means 'large tray'.

MEZZA - A great variety of mixed hors d'oeuvres often including dips, salads, savoury pastries, pickles, stuffed vegetables, cheeses and bread. Also an individual dish to go on the hors d'oeuvres table.

MISTIKA *Mastic* - an edible resin from an evergreen shrub used to enhance flavours and also as a chewing gum. It belong to the genus 'Pistacia', along with the pistachio nut.

MUHALLABIYA - Sweet creamy pudding

MUHAMMAR - Roasted

MUMBAR - Sausage, literally meaning the casing.

N-O

NAANA- Mint

NIYAH - Raw

NUTS - The most commonly used nuts in the Arab world are the almond, pistachio and pine nut. Nuts are used in savoury foods to enhance meat or rice and in sweet pastries for fillings and toppings. To easily remove the thin inner skin from the almond and pistachio, pour boiling water over the nuts and rinse in cold water.

OIL - In the Middle East oil is commonly from sesame seeds, *tahina* for dips or dressing and olives or *samn* (clarified butter) for cooking (see olive oil and *qawwrama*).

OKRA/Ladies' Finger (*Hibiscus esculentus*) *Bamia* - Cultivated around 575 AD, okra is the rocket-shaped pod of an annual plant of the cotton family.

OLIVE (*Olea europaea*) *Zeit* - Black olives are ripened green olives. Eaten pickled on the *mezza* or as a condiment, olives are not usually cooked in the Arab world except in the form of oil. Native olive trees of the Mediterranean are very long lived and perhaps span a thousand years.

OLIVE OIL *Zeit Zaytun* - Good olive oil, virgin oil, is pressed cold from fresh ripe fruit and is clear green and odourless. Yellow oil, pure olive oil, comes from secondary pressings of the pulp and lower grade olives under heat. The word 'oil' comes from the same root word as 'olive'. For oils, olives must be ripe. In the primitive method, the olives are crushed in a trough under a huge rolling stone like a millstone, and the liquid is squeezed out. This is purified by floating it on water. The modern method is to squeeze the pulp under hydraulic presses and separate the pulp with a centrifuge. Oil made by pressing without any other treatment is called virgin oil. Acidity, in fact, is the criterion by which oils are judged. Because light affects oils adversely, the best - short of visiting the farm - is purchased in cans and not in clear glass bottles. Keep bottles in the refrigerator to avoid rancid olive oil. In Middle Eastern tradition, always keep a little on the table to dress vegetables, salads or top-up dips.

ONION (*Allium cepa*) *Basal* - Certainly the most commonly used flavouring vegetable in the world and cultivated for so long that its wild ancestors are unknown. Varieties abound, differing in flavour, size, flesh, colour and longevity. In Arabic cooking, onions are usually sautéed to two stages: until tender or until dark and caramel coloured. The dark fried version is cut in a wing style, diagonally across the grain. Onions which are cut or chopped and allowed to stand emit a particular odour which is tolerated as part of the local colour of the kebab stalls in Eastern bazaars.

OREGANO- see wild marjoram

P-Q

PASTA - Noodles, the generic term for hundreds of shapes of this flour and water or flour and egg mixture.

PAPRIKA - Rich orange-red powder made of sweet pepper that is said to have been taken to Hungary by the Turks. Although these peppers are pointed in shape, they do not have the pungency of chillies. The core and seeds of the peppers are usually removed before drying. Paprika, like most ground spices, does not keep well and the dirty brown colour probably shows that the flavouring is stale.

PINE NUT (*Pinus pinea*) *Snober* - The seeds of the stone pine are commonly used in stuffings, *kibbah*, *musakhan* and to top various *mezza* dishes and rice. Lebanese and Palestinians sometimes pound the nuts to use as a thickener for sauces, costs being the deterrent. Although the seeds of pine trees are in general edible, many are too small to be of value, and others have a strong taste of turpentine which cannot be sufficiently reduced by roasting. The stone pine is the umbrella-shaped tree of Italian landscape paintings. It grows wild in coastal districts from Portugal to the Black Sea, and has been planted on the North African coast. The large, shiny cones of the stone pine are gathered between November and March and are stored until the summer, when they are spread out in the hot sun to open. The nuts can be then shaken out of the cones. The kernels keep well in cool, dry places or in a jar in the refrigerator. Gently fry or roast the nuts over low heat, as the tender kernels burn easily.

PISTACHIO (*Pistacia vera*) *Fustoq* - The fruit of a tree native to the Middle East. To easily remove the thin skin and keep the bright green colour, pour boiling water over the nuts and rinse in cold water. Pistachios are commonly used in stuffings, sweets and to top rice. The tree can withstand very poor conditions and will grow on dry, rocky hillsides as long as hot summers abound. The nuts look like clusters of small olives. The paper-like skin adhering to the nut can be red-brown to creamy. The inner flesh may be an intense green or sometimes paler, according to variety. Once gathered the nuts are spread out to dry in the shade for a week or more until the shell opens slightly to expose the kernel. Once dried, pistachios keep well.

PITTA - Similar to Arabic pocket bread

POMEGRANATE (*Punica granatum*) The succulent red seeds of the ancient pomegranate fruit are used raw, in cooking, or as a garnish. The juice is extracted for a drink or made into a syrup called grenadine. Pomegranate syrup is commonly used to give a sweet and sour balance. To juice the fruit, place a handful of seeds in muslin cloth and squeeze the juice into a bowl or place seeds into a sieve and press out the juice. Freeze in ice-cube trays, then pack cubes in plastic bags to be stored in the freezer. The cubes can be thawed for any recipes that call for the juice or used frozen to drop into drinks. The seeds also freeze well if required for a garnish.

PULSES - Pulses are ripe, dried, edible seeds of legumes, peas, beans, grams, and lentils.

QAHWAH - (see coffee)

QALIB - a small wooden mould carved with deep engravings to make impressions on the dough when making *maamoul*.

QAMAR ADDINE - Dried apricot paste used for a drink or in cooking.

QATER - Honey or sugar syrup to pour over pastries.

QAWWRAMA -Mutton preserved in its own fat, historically used in Lebanese cooking. The lean meat is cut in pieces, pressed to remove much of the liquid (it would not keep with too much water in it) and finally fried in mutton fat. It is simply seasoned with salt and pepper. Meat and fat are both packed into earthenware crocks and are sealed with clay. The jars of *qawwrama* keep all winter. Qawwrama is used in lamb stews, for stuffing vegetables, for frying with eggs and for many other purposes.

QUINCE (*Cydonia vulgaris*) - Related to the pear and apple, the fruit is made into a thick paste for a confection and cooked with lamb and chicken as a stew in Persia and North Africa, especially Morocco.

R

RAISINS (*Vitis vinifera*) *Zabib* - Dried grapes also known as sultanas and currants are major exports of the Middle East. Sultanas are very sweet and are used when not requiring the tartness of currants and acidity of raisins. Traditionally, raisins are from sun-dried muscatel grape varieties.

RAS - Head, in Arabic cooking usually referring to the lamb's head, which is reserved for special guests.

RAMADAN - the month of fasting from dawn to dusk, usually celebrated with big evening meals and plenty of sweets.

RICE (*Oryza sativa*) *Roz* - Over 7,000 varieties exist and are divided into long-, medium- and short-grain, plus the ground rice or rice flour. Long grain is used when cooking rice for a main course. Short grain is used in stuffing vegetables and vine leaves. Rice flour or ground rice is used to bind in stuffing meat for *koubba*.

RUMAN - Pomegranate

ROSE-WATER *Mai ward* - Of culinary importance in the Middle East where it appears as a flavouring in many sweet dishes as well as drinks. Rose petals are made into an extremely sweet and fragrant jam.

S

SALEQ - A leafy vegetable similar to sorrel. Some types of spinach may be substituted.

SAMAK - Fish

SAMBUSA - Savoury filled pastries

SAMN - Clarified butter also known as 'ghee' is made by simmering butter for a half hour. The water will evaporate, and the salts and sediments will settle. Strain and store unrefrigerated.

SAUTE - To fry gently in a pan with a little oil until slightly tender. The word comes from the French 'sauter' (to jump).

SAYADIYA - Fish with rice

SEARING - Sealing the surface of meat at the start of cooking by briefly exposing it to very strong heat.

SEMOLINA *Sameed* - A particle of a durum wheat grain, which is an essential element in *couscous* and some Arabic pastries. Semolina is originally large particles of endosperm which are sifted out in the milling of cereals. Once known as durum wheat, semolina may now mean any very coarse flour (i.e. rice semolina, maize semolina) It differs from flour, which is much finer, in that when cooked the texture is more like a porridge than a paste.

SESAME SEEDS (*Sesamum indicum*) *Simsim* - A historically valuable spice, used raw or roasted to garnish sweets, bread and in *zaatar*. Also used to make the oily paste, *tahina*. Sesame seeds are small, usually white and of a flat pear-shape, but can be cream to brown, red or black. The seeds contain about 50 per cent oil and often adorn sweet cakes and biscuits in the Middle East.

SHANKALIS - Thickened yoghurt

rolled in *zaatar* to make a cheese ball.

SHARBAT - Sherbet, usually a sweet drink made from fresh or dried fruit or flavourings.

SHAWARMA - Large amount of thinly sliced lamb or chicken cooked on a vertical skewer.

SHEIKH - Title of respect for civil or religious leaders.

SHORBAT - Soup

SHY - Tea

SIMMER - To cook gently over low heat, not boiling. Cooking just below boiling point, with the liquid just trembling.

SIMSIM - (see sesame seeds)

SNOBER - (see pine nuts)

SORREL (*Rumex*) - Several species are delicious additions to salads.

SOUK - Market

SOUS - (see liquorice)

SPRING ONION/GREEN ONION (*Allium cepa*) *Basal Kudar* - used in salads or stews. In the Arab world, whole green onions are found on the salad tray to nibble during the meal.

SQUASH/COURGETTES - (see *cusa*)

SWEET PEPPER - see capsicum.

T

TAGINE - A name for a conical shaped earthenware pot and for the stew by the same name in North Africa.

TAHINA - An oily paste made from ground sesame seeds, which have usually first been roasted for a strong nutty taste. Mixed with lemon juice and water to make a sauce for cooked foods. A staple in most of the countries around the eastern end of the Mediterranean, sesame seeds are difficult to grind or pound at home to the required oily state, but *tahina* is generally available anywhere where there are Greek or Lebanese shops. When lemon juice is added, *tahina* first goes to a sticky, crumbly paste. Continue to stir in drops of

lemon juice (or water if it gets too sour) and it gradually turns to a beautiful smooth cream. Used to make *hummos bil tahina* and *mutabbal* (*Baba ghannouj*) and a sauce for fish.

TAMARIND (*Tamarindus indica*) *Tamer Hindi* - Literally meaning date of India in Arabic, the tart fruit pod of a tree grown in Africa and India. Soak before separating the seed from the pulp and juice. The pulp around the seed is used, primarily in the Middle East to make refreshing drinks. It has a fruity sour taste, because it contains a lot of tartaric acid. Tamarind sold in shops is a brown sticky mass of pods, containing fibre and a number of seeds. To prepare, pour a small amount of boiling water on a knob of tamarind, then squeeze until a purée is formed. Fibre and seeds must be sieved out. Tamarind purée is mildly laxative. Sweetened tamarind syrup can also be bought and is used as a base for fruit drinks.

TAMER - (see date)

TEA (*Thea sinensis*) *Shy* - Black tea rather than the green is sipped sweet and strong in the Middle East. Often the tea has added herbs of mint, cardamom or saffron. Tea, the leaf of a tree, left alone will grow 7.5 m (25 ft) high, but it is pruned to form a low bush for ease of gathering. The leaves look something like bay leaves, and the flowers are beautiful, white and sweet smelling. For black tea the leaves are wilted, bruised by rolling and allowed to ferment in contact with air, so that oxidization occurs (like a browning apple) before drying. Leaves are still picked by hand. The green teas, sometimes called 'gunpowder', are popular in North Africa, especially in Morocco, where the tea is frequently flavoured with mint.

TEEN - (see fig)

TOUM - (see garlic)

U-Z

UJJAH - A flat egg and meat/vegetable/herb/spice cake somewhat like an omelette.

VINE LEAVES *Waraq ainab* - The leaves of grape vines are used to roll up a stuffing. The principal use of vine leaves is for stuffing to make the Levantine speciality known as '*mahshi*'. There are many stuffings; meat, rice, vegetables and pine nuts, flavoured with mint and parsley and served hot and cold. The young leaves are used. Before being stuffed the older leaves must have the stems removed and all leaves should be blanched for a few minutes in boiling water until they are pliable. Canned and salted leaves need to be gently rinsed in warm water to remove the salt before use.

WARAQ AINAB - Grape leaves

WHEAT (*Triticum spp*) *Qamah* - A cereal grass most probably cultivated first in Mesopotamia which has two main varieties - bread wheat and hard wheat. Bread wheat is used for preparing a number of varieties of bread and hard durum wheat is used to make semolina, *couscous* and pasta. In cooking, one should distinguish between hard-strong bread making wheat or soft wheat which is good for biscuits, cakes and pastries. Also see grains and pulses introduction.

WILD MARJORAM/OREGANO (*Origanum vulgare*) *Zaatar* - (see marjoram)

YAKHNI - Stew

YEAST - People used yeast for thousands of years without knowing it was composed of a mass of living organisms. Yeasts are single-celled, microscopic fungi which multiply. Bought fresh, yeast is a compressed tan, clay-like substance, or as dried active yeast granules. For baking, fresh yeast is replaced by half of its weight of dried yeast.

ZAATAR - Slightly oily yet dry and a crumbly blend of roasted sesame seeds, wild marjoram, thyme and sumac.

ZAHRA - The blossom or flower.

ZAYTUN - (see olives)

ZEIT - (see oil)

CONVERSION CHARTS

WEIGHTS

Ounces	g/ml (approx)	
1	30	
2	50	
3	75	
4	100	
5	150	
6	175	
7	200	
8	225	0.5 lb
9	250	
10	275	
11	300	
12	350	
13	375	
14	400	
15	425	
16	500	1 lb
20	575	
24	675	1.5 lb
32	1 kg	2 lb

Imperial pint = 20 fluid oz

American pint = 16 fluid oz

LENGTHS

Inches	cm (approx)
0.25 ($^1/_4$)	0.6
0.5 ($^1/_2$)	1.25
0.75 ($^3/_4$)	1.90
1.0	2.50
1.5 ($1^1/_2$)	3.80
36.0 (1 yard)	100.00

TEMPERATURES

°F	°C (approx)		Gas mark
200	90	Very Cool	$^1/_8$
225	100	Very Cool	$^1/_4$
250	120	Cool	$^1/_2$
275	135	Cool	1
300	150	Moderate	2
325	160	Moderate	3
350	175	Moderate	4
375	190	Moderately hot	5
400	200	Moderately hot	6
425	220	Hot	7
450	230	Hot	8
475	245	Very Hot	9
500	260	Very Hot	10

Ounces to One Cup - Dry measures (approximately)

Note: 8 fl oz is a cup

2 oz	breadcrumbs
3 oz	coconut, shredded
	dates
4 oz	plain (all purpose flour) shredded cheese
	whole almonds, pistachios and walnuts
	powdered icing sugar
5 oz	fine *burgul* or *couscous*
6 oz	raisins
	whole pine nuts
	dried apricots ·
	dried beans-lentils
	fassoulia
	broad beans
7 oz	coarse *burgul*
	foul
	chickpeas
8 oz	granulated sugar
	butter
	chopped nuts
	cottage cheese
9 oz	basmati rice
12 oz	honey

English-UK/American

Bicarbonate/baking soda

Plain/all-purpose flour

Sultanas/white raisins or golden seedless raisins

Aubergine/eggplant

Capsicum/sweet/green/bell pepper

Courgette/Zucchini squash

Spring/green onion

Pulse/bean

Cornflour/cornstarch

Chickpea/garbanzo

Broad bean/fava

Icing sugar/confectioner's sugar

Lady's finger/okra

Prawn/shrimp

Tomato purée/tomato sauce

Tomato sauce/ketchup

Chips/French fries

Crisps/potato chips

Biscuit/cookie

Saucepan/pot

NOTES ON QUANTITIES

1   All recipes are for four Arab serving sizes unless otherwise stated.

2   Since most Arabs cook by taste, adding a pinch, a handful and an Arabic coffee cupful, the translation to standard measures is approximate. The exact measures are determined by individual taste. The aim of this book is to preserve the traditional Arabic recipes.

3   All vegetables used are medium size unless otherwise stated.

4   Pints have purposely been converted to fluid ounces where the exact quantity is required since the American pint is 16 fl. oz. and the Imperial pint is 20 fl. oz.

5   Rice and beans are intentionally converted to cups as they should be cooked by volume and not by weight.

NOTES ON COOKING

1   Cooking times are an average calculation of the recipe testing. Times vary according to the ingredients, oven and cooker used.

2   Always pre-heat the oven to the specified temperature.

3   All recipes for deep-frying are in hot oil or *samn* (clarified butter). Shallow frying and sautéing can be done in any oil. It should be noted that butter and olive oil cannot successfully be heated to high temperatures.

MENU PLANNER

TYPICAL LEBANESE MEAL
Chickpea dip/*Hummos*
Aubergine dip/*Baba ghannouj/Mutabbal*
Chopped herb salad/*Tabouleh*
Stuffed meatballs/*Kibbah makliya*
Raw Kibbah/*Kibbah niyah*
Grilled meats/Kebab and *kofta*

TYPICAL EGYPTIAN MEAL
Green leaf soup/*Melokhiya*
Brown beans/*Foul medames*
Fried bean croquettes/*Falafel*
Dried fish/*Fesiekh*
Grilled pigeons
Semolina cake/*Basbousa*

TYPICAL PALESTIANIAN/JORDANIAN MEAL
Lamb stew/*Mansaf*
Yoghurt sauce
Mixed salad/*Fattoush*
Nut rice
Pickled olives
Fruit compote/*Ramadaniya*

TYPICAL IRAQI MEAL
Koubba soup/*Koubba hammouth*
Lamb with dill rice/*Timman bagella*
Yoghurt
Mixed pickles

MOROCCAN MEAL
Fish soup
Couscous
Hot chilli sauce/*Harissa*
Sweet *couscous*

GULF STATES MEAL
Lamb cooked in rice/*Machbous*
Wheat/*Hariss*
Dates and yoghurt
Vegetables in a tray

YEMENI MEAL
Hilbeh
Salonat Samak

TYPICAL ARAB WEDDING OF ABOUT 200
2 stuffed lambs/*qouzi*
2 lambs with rice/*machbous*
20 kg mixed grill
60 kg *mezza*
25 kg fresh fruit
20 kg dates
50 kg sweet pastries
tea
coffee

INDEX